African Americans
and the
Public
Agenda

*To the memory of A. Wade Smith and
other Black sociologists who have dared to do
the possible in the face of formidable obstacles.*

Cedric Herring
Editor

African Americans
*and the
Public
Agenda*

*The Paradoxes
of Public Policy*

SAGE Publications
International Educational and Professional Publisher
Thousand Oaks   London   New Delhi

For information address:

SAGE Publications, Inc.
2455 Teller Road
Thousand Oaks, California 91320
E-mail: order@sagepub.com

SAGE Publications Ltd.
6 Bonhill Street
London EC2A 4PU
United Kingdom

SAGE Publications India Pvt. Ltd.
M-32 Market
Greater Kailash I
New Delhi 110048 India

E
185.86
A3348
1997

Printed in the United States of America

Library of Congress Cataloging-in-Publication Data

Main entry under title:

African Americans and the public agenda: The paradoxes of public
  policy / editor, Cedric Herring.
    p. cm.
  Includes bibliographical references and index.
  ISBN 0-7619-0473-5 (acid-free paper).—ISBN 0-7619-0474-3 (pbk.:
acid-free paper)
  1. Afro-Americans—Government policy. I. Herring, Cedric.
E185.86.A3348 1997   96-25340
323.1'196073-dc20

Acquiring Editor:	Peter Labella
Editorial Assistant:	Francis Borghi
Production Editor:	Astrid Virding
Production Assistant:	Karen Wiley
Typesetter/Designer:	Danielle Dillahunt
Indexer:	Cristina Haley
Cover Designer:	Candice Harman

CONTENTS

PREFACE

Historians will record the very late twentieth century as being one of significant national change and turmoil. Our metropolitan areas increasingly reflect this transformation as the division between cities and suburbs grows—the former increasingly identified with minorities, the latter associated largely with whites. Cities have become darker in their racial and ethnic makeup, and revenue from federal sources have sharply declined, making municipal authorities struggle with depleted budgets to maintain an adequate quality of life. The concentrations of ghetto joblessness and poverty has grown, creating problems that have had disturbing effects, not only on the ghettos themselves, but on the entire cities and their surroundings. Crime and other problems now spill over into other parts of the city, creating fears that accelerate the out-migration from the city to the suburbs.

If one is concerned about the state of American race relations, the timing of these incidents could not have been worse. Why? Because they are occuring during a period of perceived hard economic times—a period when economic frustrations make Americans more receptive to demagogic messages.

This economic climate has only recently emerged. In the immediate post-war decades all income groups experienced economic advancement, including the poor. A rising tide did indeed lift all boats.

In fact, the lowest quintile in family income experienced the highest annual income growth rates, "which meant that the poor were becoming less poor in both relative and absolute terms" (Bronfenbrenner, Ceci, McClelland, and Wethington 1996:14). However, this pattern began to change in the early 1970s. Growth slowed and the distribution of inflation adjusted income started to reflect greater inequality. Whereas average income gains from 1973 to 1992 continued for the higher quintiles, but at a rate of growth considerably slower than in the previous two decades, the two lowest quintiles actually experienced annual declines in income during this period.

This trend of increasing inequality has been accompanied by a growing sense among an increasing number of Americans that their long-term economic prospects are bleaker. They would furthermore not be reassured to learn that the United States has had the most rapid growth of wage inequality in the Western world. In the 1950s and 1960s the average earnings of college graduates was only about 20 percent higher than that of high school graduates. By 1979, it had increased to 49 percent, and then rapidly grew to 83 percent by 1992. "When the American economy rebounded from a recession in the early 1990s, roughly 2 million new jobs were created per year, but a large percentage of these offered wages below $8 an hour (or about $16, 000 a year), with few of any health benefits and not much opportunity for advancement" (Bronfenbrenner et al. 1996:117).

In sum, since the late 1970s, real wages have fallen in the United States. Wage disparities between those with college degrees and those without have widened considerably. Working-class Americans feel economically pinched and barely able to maintain current standards of living, even on two incomes. Many are insecure about keeping their jobs and fear they will never be able to afford to send their children to college. Many believe that for all their hard work, their children's lives will be worse than theirs. One can see this pessimism, for example, in a 1995 Harris poll conducted for *Business Week*. The poll revealed that only half of all parents expected their children to have a better life than theirs; nearly seven out of ten believed that the American dream has been more difficult to achieve during the past ten years; and three quarters felt that the dream will be even harder to achieve during the next ten years (*Business Week* 1995:80).

In short, despite the recent economic recovery and low rates of unemployment, most families struggle with the problems of declining real wages, increasing job displacement, and job insecurity in the highly integrated and highly technological global economy. It is important to emphasize that during periods of high levels of economic anxiety the frustrations of citizens need to be channeled in positive or constructive directions. In the past several years, and especially since the Congressional elections of 1994, the opposite has frequently been true. In a time of heightened economic insecurities, the poisonous political rhetoric (featuring the demonization of minorities, immigrants, and welfare mothers, and the open attacks on affirmative action programs) of certain highly visible political spokespersons has increased racial antagonism and channeled frustrations along paths that divide the racial groups. During periods of economic anxiety, citizens tend to be more receptive to simplistic demagogic messages that shift attention away from the real and often complex causes of their frustrations. Instead of focusing on the economic and political forces that have disrupted the economic lives of citizens, these divisive messages encourage them to turn on each other—race against race.

Many of these messages associate problems in the inner-city (poverty, joblessness, welfare receipt, crime, family break-ups) with individual shortcomings. The very simplicity of "blame the victim" arguments resonate with many citizens. They not only reinforce the widespread view of the dominant American belief system that joblessness, poverty, and the receipt of welfare reflect individual inadequacies, but they also discourage public policy initiatives to address social inequality.

Indeed, in the last several years there has been an open retreat from the use of public policy to fight problems of social and racial inequality. It is important for social scientists to help reverse this trend. Now, more than ever, social scientists working on issues that reflect the public agenda should ensure that their research and scholarship is not uncoupled from concerns of social and public policy. Thoughtful and systematic arguments about social problems, their causes, and how to address them have been overshadowed in recent years by simplistic views that highlight personal responsibility and that tend to ignore the social inequalities of the broader society.

Yet there is resistance to the practical application or utility of social science. The orthodox view holds that it is not the business of the social scientist to point out what ought to be done to address a social wrong. This orthodox view has been challenged in many quarters, mainly on the grounds that it removes the social scientists from active participation in the public arena. In other words, it reduces the likelihood that their research and theories will be used to understand how and why a given social problem should be addressed.

Fortunately, the orthodox view is not reflected in this volume and is unlikely to be supported by any of the authors. As members of a minority group who have directly or indirectly experienced racial injustice, it is not surprising that black social scientists are concerned about the practical application of their work.

The chapters in this volume reveal that African-American social scientists can play an important role in recasting the terms of the racial public policy debate. They can also draw attention to important problems that have been ignored or down played by policymakers. As I read the individual chapters, I was reminded of a view expressed by Carol Weiss of Harvard University. She recently argued that because of a narrow vision in the social sciences approach to public policy, we often overlook the fact that the public discourse on a range of social problems has changed because of thought-provoking ideas from the social sciences. "Sociological ideas, more than discrete pieces of data, have influenced the way that policy actors think about issues and the types of measures they have been willing to consider," states Weiss (1993:28). The social sciences "bring fresh perspectives into the policy arena, new understandings of cause and effect; they challenge assumptions that have been taken for granted and give credibility to options that were viewed as beyond the pale. They provide enlightenment" (1993:28).

As the readers will see, Weiss' ideas are exemplified in the various chapters of this volume. New issues concerning the dynamics of race are raised and many contemporary views and assumptions are challenged. Given the current period in which so much of the racial discourse is shaped by negative rhetoric and simplistic messages, the publication of this collection of thoughtful essays could not be more timely.

References

Weiss, Carol H. 1993. "The Interaction of the Sociological Agenda and Public Policy." In *Sociology and the Public Agenda*, ed. William Julius Wilson. Newbury Park, CA: Sage.
Bronfenbrenner, Urie, Stephen Ceci, Peter McClelland, and Elaine Wethington. 1996. *The State of Americans: This Generation and the Next*. New York: The Free Press.
Business Week. March 13, 1995.

ACKNOWLEDGMENTS

This volume is a "Presidential Collection" of invited and refereed policy-oriented chapters selected primarily from the 25th Annual Conference of the Association of Black Sociologists. That 1995 conference was titled "African Americans, Societal Issues, and the Paradoxes of Public Policy." As the 1995 President of the Association of Black Sociologists, I had the honor of presiding over that timely gathering. I also took the opportunity presented by that occasion to call on some of the leading scholars, analysts, and activists involved in the debates about the merits and demerits of various race-relevant public policies. This particular book would not have been possible without my having had the privilege and good fortune of serving the Association of Black Sociologists.

Over the years, several members of the Association of Black Sociologists have been actively involved in helping find solutions to the problems that confront our communities. Still, I personally have felt that there is much more that the association could offer to a larger audience. I believe that the association has been poised to speak to the policy issues of the day because so many of its members have been seriously examining what has gone right and what has gone wrong with the design and implementation of public policy in areas such as education, health care, social welfare, criminal justice, employment, affirmative action, housing, economic development, race relations, political empowerment, and so on. This volume, although not a publication of the Association of Black Sociologists, presents the ideas and thoughts of many of its leading members. It is my expectation that this work will shed light on many of these contentious issues confronting American society.

In putting together this book, I have amassed a number of debts. First, as I mentioned above, this book would not have been possible without those members of the Association of Black Sociologists who entrusted me to serve them over the years. I particularly want to thank those who allowed me to review their work for inclusion in this volume. I also want to thank Dr. Yvonne Scruggs and Reverend Jesse Jackson, two nonmembers of the Association of Black Sociologists who graciously consented to having their contributions included in this volume. I also thank the Great Cities Institute of the University of Illinois at Chicago, which provided me with a fellowship and time to devote to editing the book. I also acknowledge the assistance of Charles Bright, Barbara Johnson, and Vernita Lewis. Without their assistance, this book would not be nearly as timely and would have taken much longer to complete.

PART

I

INTRODUCTION

AFRICAN AMERICANS, THE PUBLIC AGENDA, AND THE PARADOXES OF PUBLIC POLICY

A Focus on the Controversies Surrounding Affirmative Action

CEDRIC HERRING

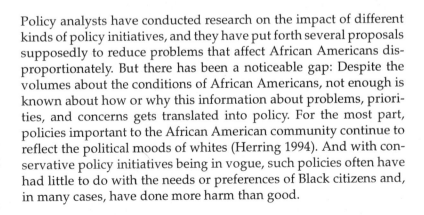

Policy analysts have conducted research on the impact of different kinds of policy initiatives, and they have put forth several proposals supposedly to reduce problems that affect African Americans disproportionately. But there has been a noticeable gap: Despite the volumes about the conditions of African Americans, not enough is known about how or why this information about problems, priorities, and concerns gets translated into policy. For the most part, policies important to the African American community continue to reflect the political moods of whites (Herring 1994). And with conservative policy initiatives being in vogue, such policies often have had little to do with the needs or preferences of Black citizens and, in many cases, have done more harm than good.

Possible examples include (1) "workfare" initiatives that require welfare recipients to work to receive state aid but may actually increase rates of poverty; (2) supposedly declining levels of racial prejudice from whites but greater white resistance to programs that would reduce racial inequality; (3) school integration strategies that lead to white flight and inner-city schools with higher concentrations of African Americans and lower public resolve to fund schools adequately; (4) drug laws that criminalize the activities of many jobless inner-city residents, lead to high rates of incarceration, and, consequently, to greater employment problems for these citizens; (5) affirmative action programs that supposedly neglect the "truly disadvantaged," unfairly stigmatize qualified African Americans and, at the same time, fuel charges of "reverse discrimination"; (6) job training programs that reduce the earnings and employment prospects of Black men who participate in them; and (7) welfare and family support programs that supposedly provide incentives for families to disband.

Given these seemingly paradoxical outcomes, the connection between policy initiatives, needs, and preferences is not well understood. This volume is aimed at shedding light on these apparent paradoxes. It is a "Presidential Collection" of invited and refereed policy-oriented chapters selected primarily from the 1995 Annual Conference of the Association of Black Sociologists titled "African Americans, Societal Issues, and the Paradoxes of Public Policy." Several of its contributions come from some of the leading senior scholars and research analysts involved in the debates about the merits and demerits of various race-relevant public policies. The volume also contains some fresh, new perspectives from more junior scholars who bring innovative approaches to the debates about which direction policy should be directed. All selected works, however, contribute to our understanding of public policy with implications for racial inequality by providing either new theoretical insights, fresh policy perspectives, or original empirical evidence concerning some of the most pressing policy issues confronting this nation as it enters the 21st century.

This introductory chapter serves two functions. First, it provides a substantive focus on many of the controversies surrounding affirmative action and equal opportunity policy. I take the liberty of incorporating some autobiographical materials and placing them in the context of current debates about the pros and cons of affirmative action. But as a social scientist and policy analyst, I also realize that it is not sufficient to use personal reflections and anecdotes to inform policy. Therefore, I provide an empirical assessment of many of the claims about the effects of affirmative action and other policies aimed at providing greater opportunity to disadvantaged groups.

The second assignment of this opening chapter is to fulfill the more traditional task of providing a preview of the contributions that comprise this volume. That section of this opening provides a synopsis of the wide range of policy initiatives of particular interest to members of the African American community that are included in this book. But first, I turn to a concrete policy where there is much contention, especially along racial lines: affirmative action.

Has Affirmative Action Ever Been Needed in This "Land of Opportunity"?

Recently, on a visit to my home town in rural Texas, I noticed something that struck me as being different. The railroad tracks that I had become so accustomed to as a child were gone. For me, these tracks had always been symbolic of racial segregation and class division, because that is clearly what these tracks demarcated during my childhood. Could it be that this town, so American in so many ways, had changed fundamentally? Could it be that many of the issues that had once divided Blacks and whites, rich and poor, were no longer relevant? Could it be that those "angry white men," who say that racial discrimination has been done away with and even become "reverse discrimination," were right after all? After pondering these questions for about 3 seconds, I came back to my senses and realized that this was still a part of America. Although many symbols in America have changed, certain realities persist.

Nevertheless, there are several people who are ready and willing to claim that America has solved its race problem. Ironically, many of those who claim that race is no longer a problem in the United States are among those who saw no problems with race relations prior to the modern civil rights movement when Jim Crow laws mandated that whites and African Americans were to be segregated in virtually every aspect of life, when Black Americans were relegated to the lowest paying and dirtiest jobs, when Blacks were systematically disenfranchised in the political institutions of this nation, and when lynchings and other forms of terrorism against Black citizens were all too common. These are many of the same people who now say they want America to return to being a color-blind society where people are judged by the content of their character rather than the color of their skins. Not surprisingly, these people are also among the many detractors of affirmative action who make several claims about the inefficacy of this controversial policy for creating racial equality. Below, I will review, critique, and empirically assess many of the claims about affirmative action.

Setting the Record Straight on the Effects of Affirmative Action

What would you guess would be the response of the typical American to a public policy that substantially increases the incomes of those from impoverished backgrounds, helps shatter the glass ceiling that women and people of color experience, prevents corporations from engaging in socially undesirable and illegal behavior, adds to the productivity of America's workforce, and costs the average tax payer virtually nothing? In the case of affirmative action, there is mounting opposition, despite the fact that such initiatives have what most Americans would consider desirable effects. My, how things have changed.

Affirmative action consists of activities specifically to identify, recruit, promote, and/or retain qualified women and members of disadvantaged minority groups in order to overcome the results of past discrimination and to deter employers from engaging in discriminatory practices in the present (Herring and Collins 1995). Such policies have come under siege for supposedly being unnecessary, unfair, and ineffective in reducing levels of inequality for targeted groups (e.g., Ornati and Pisano 1972; Berry 1976; Cole 1981; Wilson 1987; Loury 1991). Some opponents have also challenged affirmative action because it purportedly does little for those who are among the "truly disadvantaged" (e.g., Wilson 1987) at the same time that it unfairly stigmatizes qualified minority candidates who must endure the perception that they were selected or promoted only to fill quotas (Loury 1991; Carter 1991). Some have derided affirmative action policies as "reverse discrimination" (e.g., Glazer 1975; Sher 1975; Cole 1981), and still others claim that affirmative action is a drag on the resources of employers and the economy. But these claims have little basis in fact.

Now, in my hometown, when I was growing up, I would guess that most whites thought there was no need for affirmative action of any kind. This is despite the fact that virtually every African American lived at or below the poverty level. Virtually no Blacks were employed in the public sector in any capacity. After the schools were desegregated, virtually no Blacks even taught in the public high school. There were no Black doctors, lawyers, or elected representatives. Virtually no Blacks held professional positions of responsibility, especially if they were to be in the public arena. Quite clearly, these patterns of racial inequality were due to blatant racial discrimination.

Many opponents of affirmative action today say it is unnecessary because discrimination is a thing of the past and does not hamper the opportunities of women and people of color in the present. But research by the Fair Employment Council of Greater Washington, the Legal Assistance Foundation of Chicago, the Urban Institute, and the University of Colorado provide clear and convincing evidence of job discrimination in Chicago, Denver, San Diego, and Washington (Fix and Struyk 1993). In these studies, Black, Latino, and white job seekers with exactly matched educational credentials (e.g., degrees, schools attended, fields of study, and GPAs) and labor market-relevant characteristics were sent to apply for the same positions. Blacks and Latinos were treated significantly worse than were identically matched whites more than 20% of the time. It is clear that discrimination does still exist in the labor market, and that it adversely affects minority job seekers in more than one job application in five.

In the old days, Black Americans were told that we were held back because we were not qualified or did not have as much education as whites. But in the area of educational attainment, African Americans have steadily increased their levels of educational attainment, from an average of 5.8 years of education in 1940 to an average of 12.4 years in 1990. Accordingly, the educational attainment gap between Blacks and whites had dwindled to less than half a year by 1990 (Morris and Herring 1996).

Yet the impressive gains in education have not cashed in to the kinds of rewards that one usually associates with educational credentials. For example, in 1948, the personal incomes of Black males were 54% of those of white males; in 1990, Black males had personal incomes that were only 60% of those of white males (Herring 1995;

Thomas, Herring, and Horton 1996). The bulk of these earnings differences persist even after one takes educational attainment into consideration, as the earnings gaps occur for each educational attainment level. Even Black males with college degrees earned only 70 cents to every dollar that their white counterparts received. This translated into a disparity of more than $13,000 per year. There were parallel but even larger differences that existed between Black women and white men. Perhaps even more disturbing is the fact that these earnings disparities become larger over the life course (Thomas, Herring, and Horton 1994). Still, claims about discrimination being a thing of the past survive.

Other opponents of affirmative action use some of the same kinds of numbers I just presented to say that affirmative action is ineffective in enhancing the positions of women and people of color. The facts just do not support this notion. EEO-1 reports show that affirmative action has played a major role in improving the economic position of minorities and women (Leonard 1984b, 1985, 1990). Firms that promise to employ more minorities and women do actually employ more in subsequent years (Leonard 1985), but these goals are not being fulfilled with the rigidity of quotas. Minority and female employment have increased much faster at contractor establishments that have affirmative action commitments than in establishments with no such commitments. And as Figure 1.1 shows, according to data from the 1990 General Social Survey, employment by affirmative action firms is associated with higher average incomes for Blacks, Latinos, and women, because the incomes of racial minorities who work for affirmative action employers are more than $5300 higher and the incomes of women employed by affirmative action firms are more than $6000 higher than those who work for nonaffirmative action firms. Figure 1.2 shows that this is in addition to the fact that racial minorities who work for affirmative action firms have higher occupational statuses and are more likely to hold professional, managerial, or technical jobs. So, it is clear that affirmative action has been quite effective in enhancing the positions of women and people of color.

Still, there is the commonly held view that affirmative action helps the wrong women and people of color because it does little for those who are "truly disadvantaged," who lack the resources and skills to compete effectively in the labor market. Contrary to this view, however, is the fact that those from impoverished backgrounds working for affirmative action employers earn about $6100 per year

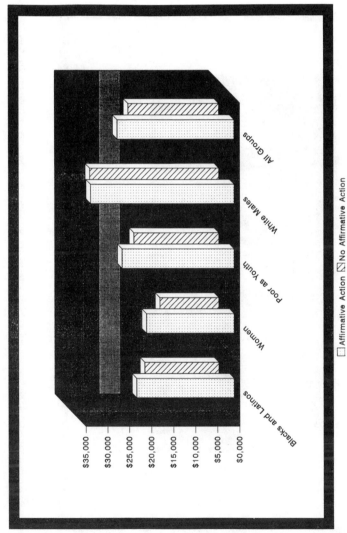

Figure 1.1. Mean incomes of selected groups by the presence of affirmative action programs.

☐ Affirmative Action ☒ No Affirmative Action

9

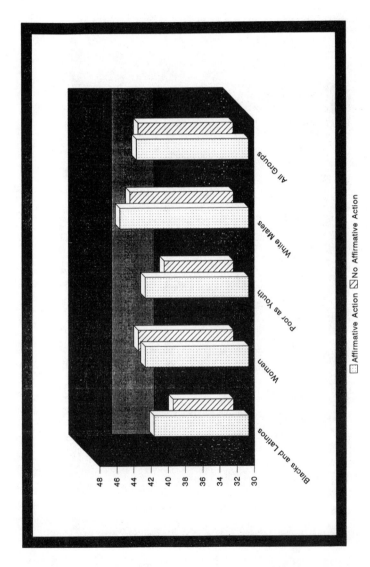

Figure 1.2. Mean occupational statuses of selected groups by the presence of affirmative action programs.

10

more than people from impoverished backgrounds not currently employed by affirmative action firms.

Some people oppose affirmative action because they think it stigmatizes minorities and women. They think it leads to the belief that women and people of color are less qualified, less intelligent, or less hard working than white males. These are some of the concerns that even some Black people have raised when they find out that my first faculty position was as an affirmative action hire at a place that was historically all-male, all-white, and quasi-military and hired Blacks and women only when ordered to do so by the courts. But again, data from the GSS are instructive. Figures 1.3 and 1.4 show that the reality is that when affirmative action brings whites into greater contact with people of color, it enables whites to see that people of color are intelligent and hard working. Indeed, it is white men who work where there are no provisions for affirmative action who are the least favorable in their impressions of Blacks' and Latinos' levels of intelligence and work effort.

Many people say that affirmative action is "reverse discrimination" because they believe white males suffer economically. But the incomes of white males who work for affirmative action firms are higher than those of white males who do not work for affirmative action companies. Moreover, the incomes of women and racial minorities under affirmative action do not eclipse those of white males (neither those working for affirmative action firms nor those employed by other companies).

Finally, there are those who like to argue that affirmative action is a drag on employers and the economy. But the reality is that affirmative action has decreased discrimination and has had the net benefit for employers of leading to more effective and efficient use of pools of talent that were previously excluded from the labor market. As less discriminatory practices have allowed women and people of color to be reallocated to jobs more suitable to their skills, they have become more productive relative to white males (Leonard 1984c).

So, the reality is that affirmative action programs in the workplace are associated with higher incomes, better jobs, and more coworker acceptance for those whom they were intended to help. Indeed, they are correlated with higher incomes for racial minorities, women, and people from low-income backgrounds without appearing to do significant harm to the economic well-being of white males who work in such settings. The analysis presented here, admittedly, does not provide definitive evidence in support of or in opposition to

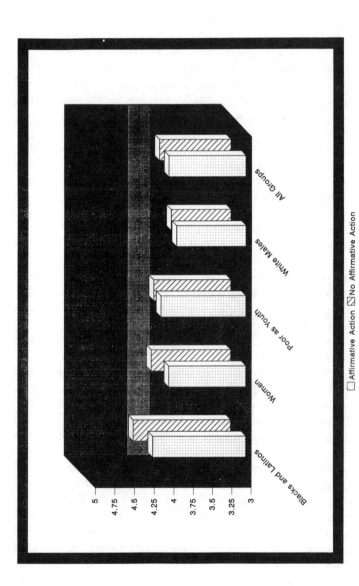

Figure 1.3. Selected groups' assessments of Blacks' levels of intelligence by the presence of affirmative action programs (1 = *unintelligent*, 7 = *intelligent*).

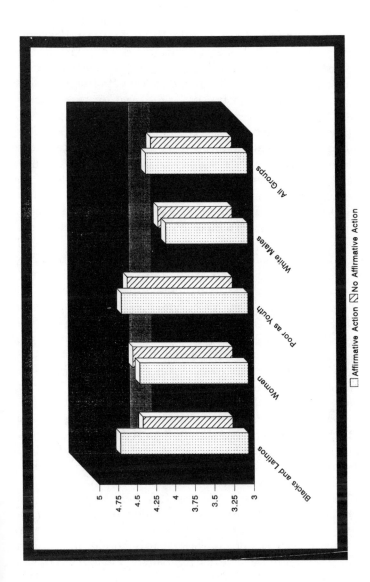

Figure 1.4. Selected groups' assessments of Blacks' work habits by the presence of affirmative action programs (1 = *lazy*, 7 = *hard working*).

13

affirmative action. But these results hold up even in a multivariate framework.

But we also should be clear that facts alone are not enough. Most white Americans, for example, are well aware that African Americans have been victims of discrimination. Yet few are willing to acknowledge the need for affirmative action or other initiatives to provide greater opportunity and equity. This is despite its desirable effects and several additional arguments that could be invoked to justify its existence: (1) the need for compensatory justice for the victims of discrimination; (2) the need to truly equalize opportunity so that genuine merit can be demonstrated; (3) the need for proportional representation so that African Americans' collective needs, interests, and sensitivities can be better served; and (4) the need to monitor and guard against current and future discriminatory behavior. From the less lofty perspective of "enlightened self-interest," better representation of Blacks can also enhance marketing savvy vis-à-vis African American consumers, help to pacify challenges to the policy decisions of predominantly white male governments or agencies, and, in general, help to keep a lid on a volatile bubbling cauldron.

Unfortunately for proponents of affirmative action, the current debate about the merits and demerits of affirmative action is taking place in a context involving two apparent complications that have made the case for affirmative action more difficult to promote: (1) periodic economic stagnation that provides real threats to the very existence of good jobs, and (2) new antiminority sentiments that couch prejudice in terms of abstract ideological symbols and symbolic behaviors. Indeed, the Reagan and Bush administrations actively promoted antiaffirmative action policies and fostered misleading information about such policies (Wilson, Lewis, and Herring 1991). Moreover, as a public policy and strategy for social change, affirmative action faces many peculiar dilemmas: to bring about a "color-blind" and gender-equal society, it must be color and gender conscious; to deliver equality of opportunity, it calls for greater efforts to educate, recruit, train, employ, and promote only some citizens; to determine whether progress is being made, it must measure present-day employment practices against some standard of what has occurred in the past and what might be achieved in the future; and to monitor the progress of women and people of color, it must subject itself to allegations that it is nothing more than "quotas" that promote "reverse discrimination" and the selection of people who are less qualified than their white male counterparts.

Proponents of affirmative action are confronted with a tricky political process that revolves around the obstacles and dilemmas mentioned. As Hochschild (1989) points out, there are

> four rules of thumb [that] can help to shape [a] tricky political process. First, do not expect people to do more than they can—that road leads simply to frustration and rejection of the whole enterprise. Second, do not easily allow people to do much less than they can— that road vitiates the basic principle and demoralizes the full contributors. Third, give people direct, even self-interested, incentives to take action—few people will participate for long in a program that asks them to sacrifice themselves or their resources to an unknown other. Fourth, give people reasons beyond direct incentives for taking action—Americans have a long history of acting to help others if they believe that their actions will be efficacious, are morally right, and are not evidence of being a sucker. (p. 29)

In other words, selling affirmative action will require (1) demonstrating to white males that it does not cost them much, (2) convincing America that it can and should do much better by women and people of color, (3) showing employers that it is in their best interests to pursue equal opportunity policies, and (4) establishing for the nation that affirmative action is a policy that will strengthen rather than weaken its international competitiveness and general welfare. But proponents of affirmative action will also need to pressure public leaders into helping disadvantaged groups realize equal opportunity. If these public leaders are sincere in their concerns about assisting minorities to realize equal access, they will need to understand that having the facts about the positive effects of affirmative action is not enough. They will need to be shown that the cost of abandoning equal opportunity, equity, and other positions that coincide with the needs of African Americans is as high, if not higher, than what it will take to appease angry white men.

Preview of Other Issues
Examined in This Volume

There are several other issues on the public agenda where the connection between policy initiatives and African Americans' needs and preferences is not well understood. This point is illustrated, for example, by the current debate about welfare reform and workfare initiatives that require welfare recipients to work to receive state aid but may actually increase rates of poverty. The basic idea of workfare is to make employment or job training mandatory for those able-bodied adults who receive welfare benefits and who do not have preschool-aged children. Proponents of such proposals often argue that workfare initiatives motivate good work habits and attitudinal predispositions in welfare recipients by requiring that they either work or be enrolled in job training programs to receive state aid.

But the effects of job training programs on the incomes and employment prospects of those who have participated in such programs are still questionable. It is plausible that some job training programs have had perverse, unanticipated effects on the incomes and employment prospects of their enrollees. Because eligibility restrictions and low expected returns to enrollment in such programs have radically transformed the types of people who have enrolled in job training programs, some employers have argued that such programs attract only the most disadvantaged would-be workers with the fewest skills (Levitan and Gallo 1992). It is possible, then, that in the minds of many employers, enrollment in job training programs has become synonymous with "untrainable" workers who are not productive even after successful completion of their job training. In other words, such workers potentially become stigmatized because they enroll in job training programs. Although job training programs may do much to enhance the "hard" skills of their enrollees, these gains may be offset by the tainting that occurs as a result of being marked as an inferior worker in need of remedial assistance.

It is likely that such stigmatization interacts with race and ethnicity to reinforce stereotypes that employers hold about workers' skill levels (Kirschenman 1992). In particular, Kirschenman and Neckerman (1991) suggest that race interacts with markers of class and space to screen out inner-city Black applicants whom employers suspect possess the pathological traits stereotypically associated with inner-city residents. To the degree that enrollment in a job training program acts as such a marker, especially in light of more restrictive eligibility requirements that identify one as a member of the "underclass," it is possible that among inner-city job applicants, the positive effects of job training are offset by employers' greater inclination to see them as inferior, less productive workers.

In some of my research on the effects of various job training programs on the earnings and prospects of employment for residents of Chicago's inner city, I found that those who had participated in various job training programs earned $150 less per month than their counterparts who had not participated such programs. Although this might not seem like a large amount for most American workers, it is quite substantial for this low-income population, which had mean earnings of just $683/month. African Americans who received training earned $178/month less than those who had not participated in training.

The detrimental effects of many training programs on the probability of being employed were also evident. Training reduced the probability of being employed. For example, for married African American men with children, training reduced the probability of being employed by about 15%. In proportional terms, training hurt unmarried, childless, African American men the most. It reduced their probability of being employed by 27%.

Other policy issues with seemingly paradoxical effects that warrant further investigation include (1) challenges to the leadership and representation in the African American community; (2) African American disadvantages in health that often reflect erroneous assumptions about the causes and consequences of racial differences in behavior; (3) limitations on Black upward mobility in corporate America because of job structures that were created to help corporations respond to pressures for civil rights and affirmative action; (4) changes in the ideological and rhetorical climate that make it even easier to scapegoat people of color and the poor for their disadvantaged positions; (5) school desegregation strategies that appear to lead to white flight, inner-city schools with higher concentrations of African Americans, and lower public resolve to adequately fund schools; (6) family support and welfare programs that supposedly undermine family stability; and (7) drug laws that make illegitimate the activities of many unemployed, inner-city inhabitants, lead to elevated rates of imprisonment, and consequently lead to greater labor market woes.

In Chapter 2, Yvonne Scruggs examines some of the cross-cutting issues affecting the changing role of government vis-à-vis the African American community. She argues that the more prominent Blacks have become, the greater have been the efforts to displace our leadership and influence. She examines America's swing to the right and the implications of that swing for maintaining African American gains in such areas as elected representation, jobs, income, and educational attainment. She calls for harnessing the strengths of the Black community and of its young leadership at state and local levels.

In Chapter 3, Michael I.J. Bennett, Doug Gills, and I make the observation that Black political empowerment has been correlated with such outcomes as improvements in health, reductions in levels of political alienation, and greater access to jobs in the government sector for African Americans. We also note, however, that high concentrations of African Americans (which often make political empowerment possible) have corresponded to high concentrations of poverty rather than power. Along with these concentrations of poverty is the loss of civic and commercial services to the segregated neighborhood, in the forms of falling retail demand, increasing residential abandonment, business disinvestment, deindustrialization, and massive job loss. We carry out an empirical analysis that leads us to conclude that when African American population concentration is combined with Black political empowerment, it is meaningful and does advance greater equality between Blacks and others.

Chapters 4 and 5 examine the intersection of race, gender, class, and health status. Rae Banks and Assata Zerai examine the impact of the policy agenda on the relationship between maternal drug abuse and infant mortality. They provide a critical assessment of the existing research on the birth outcomes of pregnant drug abusers, their children, and their families. After doing so, they propose an alternative framework that incorporates socioeconomic variables, macroeconomic and politico-social factors that shape health care policy, practices, and maternal behavior. They suggest that these variables interact to affect infant and child mortality.

Although Katrina Bell McDonald also examines maternal health, her focus is on middle-class Black women and how the assumptions of the "poverty paradigm" do little to help our understanding of the psychosocial conditions of Black mothers in America. She argues that there is a range of tangible and intangible costs of social class oppression for Black mothers that has been hidden from mainstream social researchers. She calls for health policy that is part of a broader social policy agenda to eradicate all forms of oppression against Black women.

In Chapter 6, "Race Up the Corporate Ladder," Sharon Collins examines the intersection of race and class that has allowed some African Americans to experience the American Dream. This chapter challenges the thesis that changes in the employment patterns of educated African American males in the corporate world are largely responses to market conditions. Collins offers an alternative argument that change is strongly mediated by political factors. She presents evidence for the existence of a political model of change in the creation of specialized jobs for African American executives—what she calls racialized jobs—the limits on opportunities for mobility beyond them, and the recent downgrading of those jobs in a changed political climate. Collins makes clear that the paradox is that the same political pressures that created opportunities to gain professional positions for these African American managers during the height of the modern civil rights movement have created stumbling blocks to their chances for assimilation as major players in the corporate environment.

Chapters 7 and 8 examine race relations and racial separation in educational settings. Gail Thomas provides an analysis of race relations and campus climate for minority students on college campuses. In doing so, she reviews the existing research on campus race relations and racial conflict at colleges and universities and presents findings from site visits within states that operated previously under legally sanctioned racial segregation. She provides a profile of racial demographics of students on predominantly white and predominantly Black campuses. She provides an explanation of the impact of changing demographics on these institutions and American society. She concludes the chapter with recommendations for improving campus race relations and diversity in public higher education.

In Chapter 8, "Afrocentric Education," Kerry Rockquemore explores the social organization of Black male academies. She reviews the relationship between student attendance at an academy and academic achievement, which is theorized through the students' exposure to various organizational mechanisms. These include role modeling, the implementation of an Afrocentric curriculum, and the maintenance of an immersion environment. She suggests that these variables have indirect effects on academic achievement through increased locus of control and self-esteem. She argues that because some grade levels of the Black male academies have shown California Achievement Test (CAT) scores ranking in the top fifth percentile of their respective states, these new institutions provide possibilities for progressive educational policy and for a radical structural change in public education for African American students.

Chapters 9, 10, and 11 discuss changes in the ideological and racial climate that make it easier for those with power to blame people of color and the poor for their disadvantaged positions. Steven Rosenthal unleashes a critique of both conservative opponents and liberal defenders of affirmative action. He provides a historical overview of affirmative action as a concept, and he points out its limitations as a tool for bringing about genuine equality within the context of capitalism. He also debunks the arguments of those from the Right who would chop affirmative action "down to a stump." Although there are no easy solutions, Rosenthal calls for building a mass multiracial, antiracist movement not only to oppose further attempts to destroy affirmative action, but also to contest cuts in other social programs.

In Chapter 10, Charles Jarmon argues that effective social reform for the poor has not developed because the government has been ambivalent in promoting their economic well being. He demonstrates that dominant religious and ideological interpretations, which have evolved over time, continue to be principle sources for defining, justifying, and legitimating the low social standing of the poor in American society. He also suggests that such negative definitions have become institutionalized with distinctive cultural and social meanings, which are infused in the mind of the American public—that is, in what Americans believe about the poor. He argues that scholars and activists must take the lead in debunking myths and paving the way for a more favorable climate for the kinds of decisions that will reduce levels of inequality and deprivation experienced by the poor.

In Chapter 11, Juan Battle and Michael Bennett address the dual legacy of the Moynihan report. They point out that whereas many policymakers fixate on the theory that the Black "underclass" are the victims of their own decimated family structures and failed morals, few of them have chosen to take seriously those portions of the report that emphasize the impact of macroeconomic forces on African American families—those portions that helped to spur on the War on Poverty. Battle and Bennett suggest that the renewed interest in welfare reform and the problem of "illegitimacy" has given a "Black face" to welfare that has made it easier for conservatives to convince mostly white voters that it is better to blame African American families than to go to the socioeconomic roots of poverty. They argue that the public policy options best suited to serve the needs of impoverished African American families are to bypass race-based solutions and to push for more universal sociopolitical programs.

Chapters 12, 13, and 14 generally assess differential treatment and representation of African Americans in the criminal justice system. In "Race, Representation, and the Drug Policy Agenda," Rae Banks delves into some of the paradoxes associated with American drug policy: whereas America's failed drug policy successfully reproduces African American oppression, African Americans are among the nation's staunchest defenders of strict drug enforcement and strong advocates of drug treatment. But, in practice, seeking protection in enforcement and relief in treatment both reproduce structures of domination. Banks proposes an alternative framework for understanding race and drug policy that is grounded in the conceptual cross-currents of agenda-setting research and the discursive analysis of racism. She identifies techniques that go beyond stereotypes, misrepresentations, and signifiers that can be used to shape policy that now selectively targets African Americans.

In Chapter 13, Verna Keith and Garry Rolison provide an analysis of race, gender, and the timing of justice. They examine the factors associated with early arrest and incarceration among African American female inmates in state correctional institutions. They allude to biases in the criminal justice system that punish African American women more harshly, especially for drug-related offenses. Indeed, they suggest that the drug war is also a "war on African American women" in which Black women have become casualties of war earlier and more often.

Chapter 14, by Darnell F. Hawkins, presents some additional dilemmas and paradoxes associated with public policies affecting crime and punishment. He examines several concerns for which the public policy implications and the nature of the social goals thought to be derived from racial comparisons are much less straightforward and much more contestable. He provides an analysis of three domains within the study of crime and justice in which there are documented racial inequities: (1) racial differences in the imposition of the death penalty, (2) laws and sentencing guidelines that provide different levels of punishment for "crack" cocaine versus powdered cocaine, and (3) race-of-victim effects in media coverage of homicides. Hawkins seeks to move the discussion of racial inequality beyond the public policy objectives inherent in a purely legalistic approach. Rather, his analysis starts with the premise that racial equality in both treatment and outcome is a valued American ideal that does not readily lend itself to a purely statistical approach. He argues that such a mechanical approach to equality may produce outcomes that are substantively unjust for those very groups to which American civil rights law refers as "protected classes." It may also produce social problems for the larger society as significant as those targeted for "correction." Even more sobering is his conclusion that limited and bounded strides toward equal treatment and outcome in a society characterized by deeply rooted and widespread racial, ethnic, and class inequality inevitably will produce policy paradoxes.

The final chapter, by Reverend Jesse Jackson, is a call for more even-handedness with respect to policies that currently disadvantage African Americans. It is also a call to action. In his chapter, Reverend Jackson provides an overview of the political landscape as it exists in the wake of the Republicans' Contract With America. He outlines options available to progressives who want to help advance the causes of special importance to African Americans. In doing so, Reverend Jackson presents a critique of the policies of so-called "New Democrats" as well as those of the right wing. This provocative essay points out many of the built-in contradictions of the "Jail-Industrial Complex." It shows why economic policies provide less security for those at the bottom of the income pyramid. Reverend Jackson's chapter also examines the nation's retrenchment on affirmative action policies. It looks at the nation's retreat from meaningful voting rights measures. This chapter also points out how and why drug policies are destructive to families and communities, and it discusses other issues that those who are trying to undermine a progressive agenda might use to drive a wedge between potential partners in coalitions.

These are the seemingly paradoxical policy issues currently on the public agenda of special relevance to African Americans that this book discusses. And I believe that these are precisely some of the kinds of issues in which social science researchers should be engaging policymakers and the general public so that we can affect the direction of policy by helping to set the record straight on some of these issues. But again, we also should be clear that facts alone are not enough in resolving these issues that are on the public agenda.

References

Berry, Margaret C. 1976. "Affirmative Action?" *Journal of the National Association for Women Deans, Administrators, and Counselors* 39:1-60.

Carter, Stephen L. 1991. *Reflections of an Affirmative Action Baby.* New York: Basic Books.

Cole, Craig W. 1981. "Affirmative Action: Change It or Lose It." *EEO Today* 8:262-71.

Fix, Michael and Raymond J. Struyk. 1993. *Clear and Convincing Evidence: Measurement of Discrimination in America.* Washington, DC: Urban Institute Press.

Glazer, Nathan. 1975. *Affirmative Discrimination: Ethnic Inequality and Public Policy.* New York: Basic Books.

Herring, Cedric. 1994. "Who Represents the People? African Americans and Public Policy During the Reagan-Bush Years." In *African Americans and the New Policy Consensus: Retreat of the Liberal State?* ed. M. Lashley and N. Jackson, 77-97. New York: Greenwood.

———. 1995. "African Americans and Disadvantage in the U.S. Labor Market." *African American Research Perspectives* 2:55-61.

Herring, Cedric and Sharon Collins. 1995. "Retreat From Equal Opportunity? The Case of Affirmative Action." In *The Bubbling Cauldron,* ed. M. P. Smith and J. Feagin, 163-81. Minneapolis: University of Minnesota Press.

Hochschild, Jennifer L. 1989. "The Politics of the Estranged Poor." Paper presented at the annual meeting of the American Political Science Association, Atlanta, GA.

Kirschenman, Joleen. 1992. "Low-Wage Labor Markets in a Restructured Economy: Skill Requirements and Black Men." Paper presented at the Race, Ethnicity, and Urban Poverty Workshop sponsored by the University of Chicago and Northwestern University.

Kirschenman, Joleen and Kathryn M. Neckerman. 1991. "'We'd Love to Hire Them, But . . . ': The Meaning of Race for Employers." In *The Urban Underclass,* ed. C. Jencks and P. Peterson, 203-32. Washington, DC: Brookings Institution.

Leonard, Jonathan S. 1984a. "Antidiscrimination or Reverse Discrimination: The Impact of Changing Demographics, Title VII, and Affirmative Action on Productivity." *Journal of Human Resources* 19:145-73.

———. 1984b. "The Impact of Affirmative Action on Employment." *Journal of Labor Economics* 2:439-63.

———. 1985. "What Promises are Worth: The Impact of Affirmative Action Goals." *Journal of Human Resources* 20:3-20.

———. 1990. "The Impact of Affirmative Action Regulation and Equal Employment Law on Black Employment." *Journal of Economic Perspectives* 4:47-63.

Levitan, Sar A. and Frank Gallo. 1992. *Spending to Save: Expanding Employment Opportunities.* Washington, DC: George Washington University, Center for Social Policy Studies.

Loury, Glenn C. 1991. "Affirmative Action as a Remedy for Statistical Discrimination." Paper presented at a colloquium at the University of Illinois at Chicago.

Morris, Aldon and Cedric Herring. 1996. "The Civil Rights Movement: A Social and Political Watershed." In *Immigration, Race, and Ethnicity,* ed. S. Pedraza and R. Rumbaut, 206-23. Belmont, CA: Wadsworth.

Ornati, Oscar A. and Anthony Pisano. 1972. "Affirmative Action: Why It Isn't Working." *Personnel Administration* (September):50-2.

Sher, George. 1975. "Justifying Reverse Discrimination in Employment." *Philosophy and Public Affairs* 4:1159-70.

Thomas, Melvin, Cedric Herring, and Hayward Derrick Horton. 1994. "Discrimination Over the Life Course: A Synthetic Cohort Analysis of Earnings Differences Between Black and White Males, 1940-1990." *Social Problems* 41:608-28.

———. 1996. "Racial and Gender Differences in Returns to Education" In *Race and Ethnicity in America: Meeting the Challenge in the 21st Century,* ed. G. Thomas, 239-52. New York: Taylor and Francis.

Wilson, Cynthia A., James H. Lewis, and Cedric Herring. 1991. *The 1991 Civil Rights Act: Restoring Basic Protections.* Chicago: Urban League.

Wilson, William Julius. 1987. *The Truly Disadvantaged: The Inner City, the Underclass, and Public Policy.* Chicago: University of Chicago Press.

PART

Challenges to Leadership and Representation in the African American Community

CROSS-CUTTING BLACK ISSUES EFFECTED BY THE CHANGING ROLE OF GOVERNMENT

Yvonne Scruggs

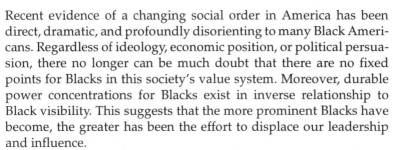

Recent evidence of a changing social order in America has been direct, dramatic, and profoundly disorienting to many Black Americans. Regardless of ideology, economic position, or political persuasion, there no longer can be much doubt that there are no fixed points for Blacks in this society's value system. Moreover, durable power concentrations for Blacks exist in inverse relationship to Black visibility. This suggests that the more prominent Blacks have become, the greater has been the effort to displace our leadership and influence.

Black elected officials have grown in number from a national total of about 700 in 1965—no more than 6 of whom were members of Congress—to a basic national total in 1994 of 8015—40 of whom are members of the House and one of whom is a senator (Joint Center for Political and Economic Studies 1993). Just under 3000—or roughly one third—of these Black elected officials are women. These numbers apply only to offices at the level of School Board and above. Not included in this 8000-plus number is a vast infrastructure of poll workers, precinct and district committee people, ward leaders, organized party Central Committee members, and convention delegates—most of whom are elected and, in majority Black districts, most of whom are Black.

This vast political resource is composed of a disproportionate number of African American women who still remain greatly underrepresented among the ranks of elected officials who are mayors and higher. In numbers as well as in gender, this is a rich, untapped source of Black political muscle.

It may seem paranoid to conclude that the growing power of Black elected officials provided the impetus for the electoral revolution in 1994. But paranoia is relative. Just because you're paranoid does not mean that they're not out to get you. In fact, there is now considerable evidence that as far back as the mid-1960s, the push by extreme conservative and radical reactionary forces got under way to reclaim political hegemony from the liberals—right after the successful battles for the Civil Rights Act of 1964 and the Voting Rights Act of 1965 (Williams 1994).

It is not a complex equation, this clash of seismic power shifts to the right of the political spectrum with national and local Black political ascendancy. I believe today, as I have been taught to believe by irrefutable evidence, that Black Americans in general, are positioned at the very bottom of most non-Blacks' rank-ordered lists of minority groups.

Take the example of a classic paradigm of choices between which A or B would be preferred by a potential employer. With A being a white person and B being a Black person, national polls show that Blacks as well as others believe that most whites would choose A—the white option—and some Blacks also would choose A. In his classic study of certain Black children's preference for white dolls, Dr. Kenneth Clark demonstrated the inevitability of this latter choice of Blacks affected by prejudice (Clark 1963). We all remember this too well, I am sure.

But more unsettling today, as was clearly reflected in the choices of a majority of the 1500 multiethnic respondents in a national 1992 Joint Center scientific survey, is the model that has many more options. For example, where the choices are A through E, with A equaling white, B equaling Black, C equaling Hispanic, D equaling Asian, and E equaling anything other than Black, B is still the least desirable choice (Arrow 1951). A significant majority of non-Blacks who were surveyed agreed on this issue. And most Blacks surveyed also felt that they would be at the very bottom of almost any preference list (Joint Center for Political and Economic Studies 1992).

Blacks, from among the groups already named, also were thought to be the least "compassionate and generous to the poor and disadvantaged," and the least "devout" (National Conference 1994). Blacks are not most of the American public's favorite flavor of the month or of this era. I wonder what our Black slave ancestors, who powered the preindustrial-revolution agricultural engine, would think about that?

Why do I relate these horror headlines? I believe that our first reality check is to understand the danger in placating the jailers, pandering to the persecutors, and thinking that patient silence will extract the civility to which African Americans are due.

There will come a day, I hope, when the actual history of Black industry, community compassion, and spiritual depth will be widely known and recognized. But in the meantime, we, and those who are our supporters, must speak out, reject bigotry, challenge distortion, and repeat the truth until it is understood like a liturgy by our own community as well as by others who pretend to be, or actually are, misinformed.

We cannot beat our oppressors by joining them. I remember, in fact, a popular slogan: "I'd rather fight than switch." That is a lesson that I sometimes feel is lost on some of our friends in the Clinton administration as well. As the classic Joint Center essay from the Committee on Racial Justice asserts—more relevantly now even than in 1987, when it first was written: Black initiative and governmental responsibility are a matched pair. Black initiative has its place—and so does governmental responsibility. They are not interchangeable; they are complementary. One cannot exist effectively without the other (Committee on Policy for Racial Justice 1987).

And contrary to a particular conventional wisdom, which would have us believe that Spencer Tracy is a good role model for a present-day Boy's Town "adventure," Black initiative has existed for centuries. Government, on the other hand, has not always been responsible—certainly not so far as the African American community is concerned. And that assessment applies in the 1990s—almost as fully as it applied before 1965.

As the authors of *Black Initiative and Governmental Responsibility* emphasize:

The Black community always has been an agent for its own advancement. Action by government in addressing social and economic
needs has been important, but it has been both recent and modest.
Blacks made the transition from a largely impoverished mass of
former slaves to a strong, vibrant community largely through individual effort and through the work of civil rights, cultural, fraternal,
religious, social, professional, and service organizations in the Black
community. . . . Indeed, without our own vigorous, creative, and
persistent efforts, many of our needs would not have been met at all.
    In spite of this proud history, Blacks are often skeptical of assess-
ments of Black community responsibility as compared with government's proper role—and no wonder. The history of Black people is
the history of countless unsuccessful efforts to get government to
allow Blacks the ordinary privileges of citizenship that were routinely
a matter of right for whites. That history has been characterized by a
societal racial obsession replete with the most negative stereotypic
attitudes that blamed Blacks for problems that arose directly from
oppressive and unequal treatment by the majority. As a result, Blacks
have a valiant history of protest and demands for equity from which
we shall not retreat. But as so often in the past, Black people and their
leadership, armed with confidence from long years of struggle and
angry at recent years of retreat, are also calling on the internal
strengths of the community. (Committee on Policy for Racial Justice
1987:6-7)

There also are other data that should be mentioned in this context.
Black Americans, especially those living in urban metropolitan centers, are being challenged by increasingly diverse competitors for
jobs, space, and attention. In the census decade between 1980 and
1990, more than 40% of the population growth in the United States
resulted from immigration; more than 75% of those immigrants were
either Asian or Hispanic/Latino; and more than 95% of those immigrants of color settled in and around the largest metropolitan areas.
    These are the same metropolitan areas in which three out of four
Black Americans already live. The same is true of 60% of Native
Americans. Native Americans, however, are largely concentrated in
the West and Southwest. In the 10 largest cities, in fact, the most
recent wave of immigration changed the 1990 population from a loss
to a respectable net population gain of 4% to 5%. The number of new
immigrants exceeded the gross number of urban disinvestors who

outmigrated to suburbia by as much as 10% in several cities (Barker 1993; Business Week 1992).

Demographics also continue to reflect the subordinate social and economic positions of many Blacks in the United States. Black median family income continues to be about one half that of whites, while the Black poverty rate quadruples that of whites. *The Wall Street Journal* glamorizes the progress of Black women within major white firms. This report exaggerates Black women's progress by comparing their situation to Black men's positions. Therefore, it underemphasizes significantly just how small both groups are in actual numbers. Black women constitute a mere 4% of those employed in all white-collar jobs in the private sector; Black men constitute 3% (Gaiter 1994). The Bureau of the Census reports that in 1993, Black women's median earnings were 89% of those of white women (Leonard 1990). Perhaps even more alarming is the fact that a college degree translates into less than half as much in terms of personal earnings for a Black woman ($19,384) as it does for a white man ($39,487) (Thomas, Herring, and Horton 1996).

Frank Parker, legal expert and specialist in civil rights law, has written recently:

> In the labor market, Blacks who, with nearly 23 million persons of working age, constitute the largest minority group, are disproportionately employed in lower-paying laborer and service jobs and remain substantially under-represented in (managerial through skilled craft) positions. Despite recent gains, minorities continue to hold disproportionately fewer jobs than whites and have higher unemployment rates.
>
> Hispanics comprise one of this country's fastest growing minority groups . . . and their labor force has doubled over the past decade. While they tend to be better off than Blacks in some categories, they still lag behind whites in almost every socioeconomic indicator. (Parker forthcoming)

Black families' median income was almost the same in 1993—$21,550—as it was in 1969—$22,000. And given the quantum increase of white median family income—which rose from $35,920 in 1969 to $39,310 in 1993—Black family income as a percentage of white family income, dramatically fell during that same period from 61 percent in 1969 to 55 percent in 1993.

Many scholars will refine, expand upon, and augment these grim indicators of Blacks' position within society at this time and in the face of challenges that would ignore and discount these very statistical realities.

Educational attainment, housing access and quality, health care availability, child care opportunities, and entrepreneurial avenues all exist at suboptimal levels throughout the Black community. Those who would sugarcoat this are cynical or mendacious or both. One of the first rules for the social scientist is to have all of the facts. No scenario for remedies, no strategies for defense nor countermandation are of any consequence if not grounded in reality.

My intention is not to dwell on the "woe is me" scenario, nor is it desirable to catalogue in great detail the number of ways that Black Americans have been victimized. Any people would be considered victimized if they, like African Americans, were to have been deprived of their language and culture, transplanted and subjugated for centuries, and, moreover, continued to be enslaved for 89 years after the rest of the nation was freed from the yoke of servitude. Although this country declared itself independent in 1776, Blacks did not even begin to be declared free until 89 years later, in 1865.

Any people who, just as recently as 1965—100 years after their so-called emancipation, and just 30 years ago—finally became full, voting, constitutionally protected citizens—should be seen as victims. I know that white America knows and understands that simple logic. I know this, even as reactionary Americans today try to push forward several surrogates for the real basic issue of racism. They attempt to convince themselves, others, and Blacks that the debate is about taxes, preferences, quotas and set-asides, reverse discrimination, "bizarre-shaped voting districts," perverted instances of affirmative action run amok, or any of these sundry, diverting distractions.

Tom and Mary Edsall have bluntly written this truth in their book titled *Chain Reaction: The Impact of Race, Rights, and Taxes on American Politics.* They have said that whenever the official subject is presidential politics, taxes, welfare, crime, rights, or values, the real subject is race (Edsall and Edsall 1991).

So, victimization is not the point. The point that I am making is that in spite of the forces that have gathered to push Blacks back into the subservient victim's role that we thought we had finally overcome regardless of the fundamental unfairness of the obstacles to be faced and the prevailing conditions to be corrected, there must be focused, laser-targeted thrusts along multiple fronts simultaneously to build a juggernaut offensive for recovery. I believe that there are strategies that are worthy of consideration that do undertake this daunting task. There are also examples of the application of these strategies in communities and localities across the country.

I wish to describe briefly one such national event where the cross-cutting issues for the Black community informed the discussions and strategy building for several high-profile and high-priority issues. The Seventh National Policy Institute (NPI VII), which occurred in January 1996 in Washington, was cosponsored by the seven national caucus organizations of Black Elected Officials and convened and coordinated by the Joint Center for Political and Economic Studies. The theme of NPI VII was "The Changing Role of Government." In addition to the cross-cutting issue of Black initiative and governmental responsibility, other obvious cross-cutting issues were job development and economic participation; equal opportunities, affirmative action, and legal remedies; voter participation affecting the political process today; harnessing the strengths of the Black community and of its young leadership at state and local levels; fitting it all together into an effective strategy; and shaping the message through communication. The conference also addressed a number of timely topics in the context of these cross-cutting issues, including acceptable welfare reform; HIV-AIDS; the changing role of public education; keeping cities alive and affecting the agenda for Habitat II: The City Summit; school-to-work and worker retraining; and minority business development, among other issues.

Finally, the NPI VII sessions were enriched by concurrent clearinghouse sessions, as well as panel presentations by people from across the country who are conducting programs that really work.

My colleagues have accused me recently of great zeal in considering the options and the consequences in this most critical time. I certainly feel that we have been challenged to a Holy War. Many of the programs to address human needs and powers to protect the rights of citizens, administered by the federal government over the past 60 years, are now being "devolved" and transferred to the states as part of the GOP's "Contract With America." Americans in general, and Black Americans in particular, have no idea whether this massive shift of power to states will work or how it will be implemented. We will need to monitor the new conservatism in making public policy, paying special attention to what is in the best interest of African Americans and examining how African Americans can assert their influence in the new political landscape.

Many questions remain as to who is going to benefit and who is going to suffer as a result of the shift in resources and authority to the states. In many respects, the shift recalls a history in which the poor, Blacks, and other politically and economically marginal groups were neglected before the Great Depression, when state governments could not or would not meet their special needs. There has never been a more important time for African American leaders to communicate America's problems and possible remedies to them.

References

Arrow, Kenneth J. 1951. *Social Choice and Individual Values.* 2d ed. New York: Wiley.

Barker, Lucius. 1993. "Limits of Political Strategy: A Systemic View of the African American Experience." *Presidential Address presented before the American Political Science Association in Washington, DC.*

Business Week. 1992. "The Immigrants: How They're Helping the U.S. Economy." *Business Week* Jul. 13:114-22.

Clark, Kenneth B. 1963. *Prejudice and Your Child.* 2d ed. Boston: Beacon Press.

Committee on Policy for Racial Justice. 1987. *A Policy Framework for Racial Justice: Black Initiative and Governmental Responsibility.* Washington, DC: Joint Center for Political and Economic Studies.

Edsall, T. B. and M. D. Edsall. 1991. *Chain Reaction: The Impact of Race, Rights and Taxes on American Politics.* New York: Norton.

Gaiter, Dorothy J. 1994. "The Gender Divide: Black Women's Gains in Corporate America Outstrip Black Men's." *Wall Street Journal* (March 8):A1-A4.

Joint Center for Political and Economic Studies. 1992. HBO/Joint Center Poll, September.
————. 1993. *Black Elected Officials: A National Roster.* 21st ed. Washington, DC: University Press of America.

Leonard, Jonathan S. 1990. "The Impact of Affirmative Action Regulation and Equal Employment Law on Black Employment." *Journal of Economic Perspectives* 4:47-63.

National Conference. 1994. *Taking America's Pulse: A Summary Report of the National Conference Survey on Inter-Group Relations.* New York: National Conference.

Parker, Frank R. Forthcoming. *For the Common Good: The Case for Affirmative Action.* Washington, DC: Joint Center for Political and Economic Studies.

Thomas, Melvin, Cedric Herring, and Hayward Derrick Horton. 1996. "Racial and Gender Differences in Returns to Education" In *Race and Ethnicity in America: Meeting the Challenge in the 21st Century,* ed. G. Thomas, 239-52. New York: Taylor and Francis.

Williams, Linda Faye. 1994. *Address delivered before the Congressional Black Caucus Foundation, Washington, DC.*

POLITICAL CONSOLIDATION OR AMERICAN APARTHEID?

Some Political and Economic Consequences of Black Empowerment

MICHAEL I.J. BENNETT
CEDRIC HERRING
DOUGLAS GILLS

For decades, urbanologists and demographers have noted the flight of whites from America's central cities to the surrounding suburbs. As a consequence, America's cities have become more heavily concentrated with Blacks and other people of color. In observing these demographic patterns, some analysts also have asserted that departing whites were also taking with them the cities' industrial base, high-wage jobs, and the tax base that made it possible to provide quality education and necessary municipal services (e.g., Massey and Denton 1993). Others, however, point out that as African Americans have become greater proportions of the residents in central cities, Blacks have been better able to empower themselves by electing African Americans to city councils, to school boards, and as mayors of major cities (e.g., Bobo and Gilliam 1990).

35

During the 1970s and 1980s, Black political empowerment was correlated with such outcomes as reductions in Black neonatal mortality rates (LaVeist 1992), lower rates and levels of Black political alienation (Bobo and Gilliam 1990), and increases in minority employment in administrative, professional, and protective jobs in cities (Dye and Renick 1981; and Eisinger 1982). Still, there are questions about whether population concentrations of African Americans provide political consolidation and empowerment or whether patterns of racial concentration and segregation might better be thought of as apartheid. In this chapter, we examine this issue by investigating the relationship between Black population concentration in America's cities and racial differences in such outcomes as earnings, the capacity to elect an African American mayor, the probability of living below the poverty threshold, and the likelihood of holding a professional position. In particular, we use data from the U.S. Census Bureau's Public Use Microdata Samples and information about areas where African Americans held key political offices to examine the relationships among racial composition of communities, race of mayors, earnings, poverty statuses, and types of employment.

We focus on the following questions in this chapter: (1) Are higher proportions of Black residents within communities systematically related to higher probabilities of having African American mayoral incumbents? (2) Net of other factors, do higher proportions of Black residents and greater levels of Black empowerment within communities systematically lead to lower probabilities of living in poverty for African Americans? (3) Does having Black mayors or greater concentrations of African Americans lead to higher earnings for African Americans? and (4) Net of other factors, to what extent do Black political empowerment and population concentration affect Blacks' prospects for employment as professionals?

We examine these questions in the context of two explanations of the consequences of Black population concentration: (1) the Black political empowerment thesis and (2) the American apartheid formulation.

The Black Empowerment Model

In their "Black empowerment model," Bobo and Gilliam (1990) argue that in areas where Blacks control the political apparatus, such empowerment enhances Black participation because of its instrumentality. This instrumentality, in turn, affects the cost-benefit calculations that Blacks carry out in determining whether it is worthwhile to participate in politics. In other words, Black empowerment should influence African Americans' political participation because people's sociopolitical environments affect their cost-benefit calculations. For example, the degree to which policymakers are responsive to different kinds of citizens depends on legal factors, electoral conditions, organizational arrangements, mobilization efforts by political parties, and cues from other political figures.

Bobo and Gilliam hypothesize that "where blacks hold more positions of authority, wield political power, and have done so for longer periods of time, greater numbers of blacks should see value in sociopolitical involvement" (Bobo and Gilliam 1990:379). A postulate of this would be that where Blacks hold more positions of authority, wield political power, and have done so for longer periods of time, greater numbers of Blacks should see value in sociopolitical involvement because they stand to gain greater access to opportunities in employment and other realms.

With more than 30 million African Americans, more than one third of whom are concentrated in 20 cities, the Black population in America constitutes a potential force of formidable dimensions in American political affairs. In those locales where African American policymakers are backed by a concerned and responsive African American electorate, they can approach the negotiating table with plans and proposals that are aimed at improving and sustaining the Black community. Thus, proponents of the Black empowerment perspective suggest that it is through political strength that African Americans can begin to influence the operation of the market and maneuver their way out of poverty and disadvantage by gaining access to more and better jobs. Moreover, the provision of services geared toward the needs of the African American population also should serve to ameliorate the conditions that engender poverty and its consequences.

There are, however, reasons for questioning whether the election of African Americans to highly visible political posts translates into socioeconomic gains for the Black community. Keech (1968), for example, suggests a "threshold model" of Black empowerment. He claims that there is a direct relationship between the size of the Black electorate and Black socioeconomic gains until a threshold point of white fear and resistance occurs. When Blacks as a percentage of the electorate approach 30% through the point where they constitute a clear majority of the voting age population (at more than 50% of the electorate), whites' fears and opposition will be greatest. When Blacks become more than 50% of the voting age population, the Black majority is able to overcome any white resistance; thus, socio-economic and political gains for Blacks will occur again after that threshold has been reached.

Similarly, Lineberry (1978) suggests that minority representation in city government may not have any significant impact on the substantive choices of municipal government because city budgets are composed of "uncontrollable" items over which neither Black nor white officials have much command. Minority officeholders find the same problems and fiscal constraints confronting them as their white male predecessors did. Thus, greater Black representation will do little to change substantive issues or to change the distribution of resources in a community.

If nothing else, however, the African American community can exert pressure on government officials and negotiate over access to (better) jobs in the public sector. Thus, it seems reasonable to reach a conclusion similar to that suggested by Eisinger (1986) that "local civil service, with its more abundant jobs, swifter rate of job growth, and greater sensitivity to local political conditions than the federal system, has functioned as a true mobility channel" (p. 170). Thus, it is expected that the larger the size of the minority population in a community, the better the access to high-status and high-paying positions.

Expectations regarding the relationship of African American population size and access to opportunities seem, at first glance, to contradict findings reported in a series of studies within the ecological tradition. These studies have demonstrated repeatedly that an increase in the relative size of the minority population (i.e., Blacks) in local labor markets is likely to increase minority groups' socio-economic (mostly occupational) disadvantages (e.g., Tienda and Lii 1987; Semyonov, Hoyt, and Scott 1984).

This literature offers two explanations of the positive association between minority population size and socioeconomic subordination. The first contends that increases in minority size generate greater threats and fear from competition. Consequently, hostility, antagonism, and motivation to discriminate grow as the proportion of the minority in the labor market rises (Blalock 1967; Allport 1954). A second, alternative view suggests that increases in the size of the minority population expands the supply of cheap labor as a target for economic exploitation. Because occupational labor markets are organized across racial lines, the availability of subordinate minority workers increases the potential pool of workers for the less desirable low-status jobs. Consequently, race-linked socio-economic inequality is likely to increase with increases in the proportion of the population that is minority (e.g., Glenn 1962; Semyonov et al. 1984).

However, research in the ecological tradition does not consider reactions, strategies, and the ability of the minority population to resist discrimination. Several researchers have suggested that when the minority population is large enough and reaches a critical mass, it can mobilize resources and develop independent labor markets, or it can exert pressure (political or otherwise) for reallocation of resources. Indeed, when the minority population is large enough and highly concentrated in a labor market, it can attain occupational positions even against the will of majority group members (Semyonov 1988; Lieberson 1980). In this regard, Lieberson (1980) has persuasively argued that "if the black population is large enough there will be support for black doctors, black clergy, and so on, even if they remain totally unacceptable by others" (p. 297). This idea is also consistent with the enclave thesis (e.g., Portes and Jensen 1989; Zhou and Logan 1989; Wilson and Portes 1980) and with other studies on sheltered economies (Semyonov 1988). So, greater African American employment in professional positions and lower rates of poverty in cities with African American leaders would be fully consistent with the Black empowerment model.

Racial Segregation and American Apartheid

Black empowerment is not necessarily synonymous with Black population growth and concentration. Rather, it has more to do with the ability of African Americans to elect and select those who will represent them in political decision making. This requires relatively high levels of organization among those in the African American community. Moreover, the election of Black politicians has not automatically empowered the African American community, nor has it necessarily translated into social and economic equality.

Indeed, some critics of Black empowerment strategies that rely on high levels of racial segregation suggest that ghettos remain concentrations of poverty, not power. Massey and Denton (1993), for example, suggest that segregation is not empowering. They describe several deleterious effects of segregation. Among the most powerful is the loss of civic and commercial services to the segregated neighborhood in the forms of falling retail demand, increasing residential abandonment, business disinvestment, deindustrialization, and massive job loss. Furthermore, such "segregation also concentrates conditions such as drug use, joblessness, welfare dependency, teenage childbearing, and unwed parenthood, producing a social context where these conditions are not only common but the norm" (p. 13). In short, it concentrates self-destructive behavior in ways that are likely to offset any empowering effects of Black neighborhoods.

Massey and Denton agree that segregation offers the appearance of political power in virtually all-Black districts because such districts provide super majorities and effectively guarantee that African Americans can elect their own to office. They argue that although "the existence of solid black electoral districts . . . [does] create the potential for bloc voting along racial lines" (pp. 155-56), it does not translate into the delivery of city services nor even patronage jobs. Rather, racial segregation and isolation translate into the loss of opportunity to participate in effective coalition building with other groups and the subsequent loss of city services. Consequently, many of these African American officials find it challenging to establish legislative coalitions with their non-Black colleagues. Even worse, these representatives from hypersegregated districts have little incentive to dilute their political base by exhorting any changes that would reduce levels of segregation. Thus, racial segregation makes it easier for white leaders to disregard and disinvest in African American communities.

Marable (1985, 1986) also suggests that racial segregation can lead to the political marginalization and insignificance of African Americans. He describes the mere concept of a "Black politician" as being essentially absurd. He reasons that the political system in America was designed to exclude the representation of Blacks. So, he argues, Black politicians are often locked into a world of meaningless symbols that reinforce the ability of the white ruling class to rule. He argues that Black politicians serve only as a necessary buffer between the capitalist state—where the real power resides—and the Black majority in certain urban and isolated rural jurisdictions.

Because Black politicians are so dependent on the decisions of others with real power, they do not have the ability to define the political agenda, they have only limited horizons, and they are limited in their ability to deliver goods, services, and jobs to their constituents. Thus, according to Marable, there is little reason to expect that having African American political incumbents will produce much in the way of real improvements for the Black community.

So, according to proponents of the American apartheid formulation, racial segregation of African Americans should lead to worse rather than better socioeconomic conditions for African Americans. Racial segregation by itself will ensure that African Americans will be exposed to social and economic conditions that are far harsher than what would exist were they more thoroughly integrated into American society because all-Black neighborhoods go beyond the threshold of stability into disinvestment, abandonment, and commercial decline. Thus, proponents of the American apartheid perspective suggest that high concentrations of African Americans will have detrimental consequences on the quality of life for African Americans, net of other factors.

Below, these competing expectations of the Black empowerment model and the American apartheid perspective about the relationship among Black population concentration, political empowerment, earnings, poverty status, and African Americans' access to professional employment are examined. First, however, we present a basic overview of the data and the variables used in the analysis.

Method

Data

The *Census of Population and Housing, 1990: Public Use Microdata Sample 1-Percent Sample* (1-Percent PUMS) was derived from responses to the 1990 Census long-form questionnaire. It is a 1-percent stratified sample of people and housing units enumerated in the 1990 Census. The long-form questionnaire was administered to approximately 15.9 percent of households counted by the Census Bureau. The data set used in this analysis was prepared by the Inter-University Consortium for Political and Social Research. It comprises 1 percent of the cases in the 1-Percent PUMS. As 1 percent of the 1-Percent PUMS, the file constitutes a 1-in-10,000 sample. It contains all housing and population variables in the original 1-Percent PUMS. We also used data from the Black Elected Officials National Roster and incorporated them into the PUMS data set.

Operationalizations

Variables used in this analysis include personal earnings, poverty status, professional status, race of respondent, race of respondent's mayor, and racial composition of one's census tract.

Results

To what extent is the racial composition of one's city correlated with having an African American mayor? Figure 3.1 presents an answer to this question by illustrating the probabilities of having Black mayoral incumbents for cities with different percentages of African Americans. This chart shows some support for the threshold caveat of the Black empowerment model, because it was respondents who lived in locales where African Americans made up between 30 percent and 50 percent of the residents who were the least likely to have had African American mayoral incumbents (6.2 percent). In contrast, more than 45 percent of those who lived in predominantly Black areas had African American mayors. Even those who lived in census tracts where less than 30 percent of the population was African American were slightly more likely to have had African American mayors (6.9 percent) than were those living where Blacks exceeded 30 percent but not 50 percent of the population.

Although Figure 3.1 provides basic information about the relationship between racial composition of communities and the probability of having a Black mayoral incumbent, it does not indicate whether these associations are related to other patterns or outcomes. Figure 3.2 presents mean earnings by race of mayor and racial composition of community for Blacks and non-Blacks. This chart shows that for any given racial composition, both Blacks and non-Blacks earned more on average when the mayor was African American. Blacks had their lowest average earnings, however, when they were the majority of the population but the mayor was not African American. Furthermore, for both Blacks and non-Blacks, the highest average earnings occurred when the mayor was African American and the majority of the population was African American.

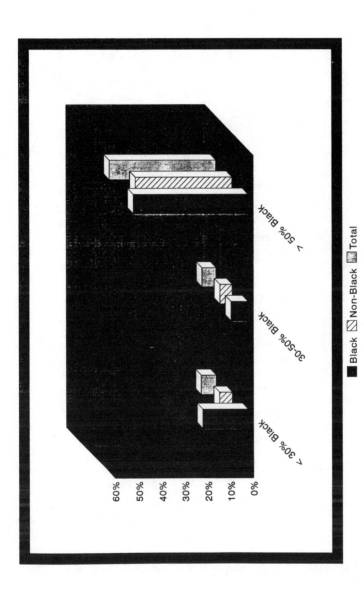

Figure 3.1. Percentage living in a municipality with a Black mayor by race and percentage Black residents in community, 1990.

43

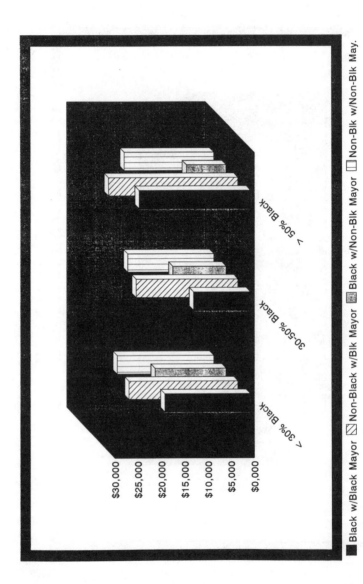

Figure 3.2. Average personal earnings by race, race of mayor, and percentage Black residents in community, 1990.

■ Black w/Black Mayor ▨ Non-Black w/Blk Mayor ▦ Black w/Non-Blk Mayor ☐ Non-Blk w/Non-Blk May.

When the mayor was African American and the percentage of Black residents was less than 30 percent, non-Blacks earned $23,410 on average and Blacks earned $18,372. When the mayor was Black and the percentage of Black residents was between 30 percent and 50 percent, non-Blacks averaged earnings of $21,828 and Blacks averaged $12,240. And when there was an African American mayor and Blacks constituted more than half of the population, non-Blacks earned an average of $27,901 and African Americans earned an average of $23,816. This suggests that Black political empowerment corresponded to higher earnings for African Americans without reducing the earnings of non-Blacks (and possibly even increasing non-Black earnings). Racial concentration of Blacks, however, generally showed a U-shaped relationship to average earnings for both Blacks and non-Blacks. These patterns generally provide support for the threshold version of the Black empowerment model.

Figure 3.3 presents the percentage of the population below the poverty threshold by race of mayor and racial composition of census tract for Blacks and non-Blacks. This chart shows that among Blacks, the poverty rate generally increased as the proportion of the population that was Black increased. This general pattern was somewhat different, however, when Blacks lived in cities with Black mayors. Communities with Black mayors and with more than 50 percent Black residents had poverty rates of 10.7 percent compared with poverty rates of 42.1 percent for majority Black communities with non-Black mayors. Among non-Blacks, there was an inverted-U relationship between the proportion of the population that was Black and the poverty rate. This pattern held true regardless of whether or not the mayor was African American. Again, these patterns are not inconsistent with the threshold model of political empowerment.

Figure 3.4 presents the percentage of those employed with professional employment by race of mayor and racial composition of municipality for Blacks and non-Blacks. This chart shows that for any given racial composition, both Blacks and non-Blacks were more likely to be employed as professional workers when the mayor was African American. Blacks had the lowest probability of being professional workers when the mayor was not African American and when Blacks were more than 30 percent but less than 50 percent of the population. Furthermore, for both Blacks and non-Blacks, the highest percentage of professional workers occurred when the mayor was African American and the majority of the population was

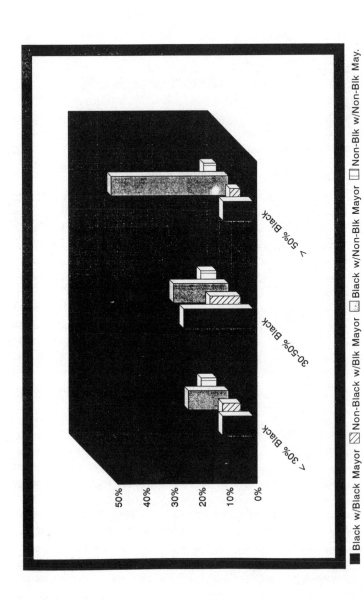

Figure 3.3. Percentage below poverty threshold by race, race of mayor, and percentage Black residents in community, 1990.

Black w/Black Mayor   Non-Black w/Blk Mayor   Black w/Non-Blk Mayor   Non-Blk w/Non-Blk May.

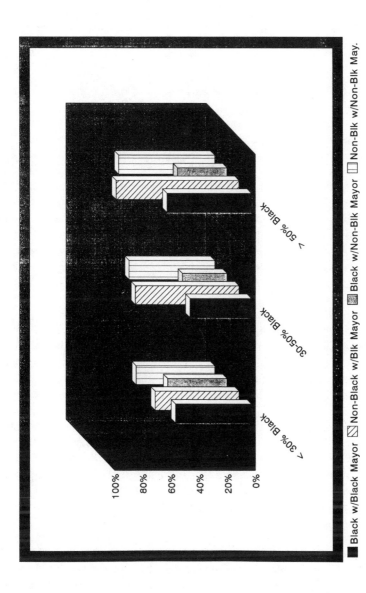

Figure 3.4. Percentage with professional status by race, race of mayor, and percentage Black residents in community, 1990.

■ Black w/Black Mayor ▨ Non-Black w/Blk Mayor ▨ Black w/Non-Blk Mayor ▢ Non-Blk w/Non-Blk May.

47

African American. This again suggests that Black political empowerment corresponded to higher professional status for African Americans without reducing the prospects for non-Blacks. Racial concentration of Blacks, however, generally showed a U-shaped relationship to percentage of Blacks employed as professional workers. These patterns generally provide support for the threshold version of the Black empowerment model.

Summary and Conclusions

In this chapter, we started out with the observation that Black political empowerment has been correlated with such outcomes as improvements in health, reductions in levels of political alienation, and greater access to jobs in the government sector for African Americans. We also noted, however, that high concentrations of African Americans (which often make political empowerment possible) have corresponded to high concentrations of poverty rather than power. Along with these concentrations of poverty is the loss of civic and commercial services to the segregated neighborhood, in the forms of falling retail demand, increasing residential abandonment, business disinvestment, deindustrialization, and massive job loss.

We then carried out an analysis of census and related data to examine the relationship between Black population concentrations and the likelihood of municipalities having African American mayors. We focused on the following questions in this chapter: (1) Are higher proportions of Black residents within communities systematically related to higher probabilities of having African American mayoral incumbents? (2) Net of other factors, do higher proportions of Black residents and greater levels of Black empowerment within communities systematically lead to lower probabilities of living in poverty for African Americans? (3) Does having Black mayors or greater concentrations of African Americans lead to higher earnings for African Americans? and (4) Net of other factors, to what extent do Black political empowerment and population concentration affect Blacks' prospects for employment as professionals?

We found that higher proportions of Black residents within communities do correspond to higher probabilities of having African American mayoral incumbents. Higher proportions of Black residents and greater levels of Black empowerment within communities also correlate with lower probabilities of living in poverty for African Americans. Having Black mayors in conjunction with greater concentrations of African Americans lead to higher earnings for African Americans. And greater levels of Black political empowerment and higher Black population concentrations are associated with greater chances of Blacks being employed in professional positions. There were some caveats, however: Although the results of our analysis supported the idea that municipalities with more than 50 percent Black residents are most likely to have African American incumbents as mayor, our analysis also indicated that towns that contain between 30 and 50 percent Black residents were least likely to have African American mayors.

These findings were consistent with the threshold model of the Black empowerment thesis, which argues that it is only when Blacks become more than 50 percent of the population that they will reap benefits from the existence of Black empowerment. Indeed, our results consistently supported the idea that socioeconomic gains for Blacks occurred after Blacks were the majority of the population and an African American held the position of mayor. This pattern held true with respect to personal earnings, poverty status, and professional status.

What are we to conclude from these results, and what do they tell us about Black political empowerment as a mechanism for advancing equality? Despite rising expectations on the part of African Americans and greater demands being placed on elected officials, Black empowerment by itself does not automatically enhance the socioeconomic positions of African Americans. But although control of city hall has not necessarily translated into social and economic equality for African Americans, at any given concentration of African Americans, those Blacks who live in cities with Black mayors tend to fare better than those who live in cities with non-Black mayors. In other words, when Black empowerment is coupled with African American population concentrations, Black political empowerment is meaningful and does advance greater equality between Blacks and others when a Black threshold has been met.

References

Allport, Gordon. 1954. *The Nature of Prejudice.* Cambridge, MA: Addison-Wesley.
Blalock, Hubert. 1967. *Toward a Theory of Minority Group Relations.* New York: Wiley.

Bobo, Lawrence and Franklin D. Gilliam, Jr. 1990. "Race, Sociopolitical Participation, and Black Empowerment." *American Political Science Review* 84:377-93.

Dye, Thomas R. and James Renick. 1981. "Political Power and City Jobs: Determinants of Minority Employment." *Social Science Quarterly* 62:475-86.

Chen, Lincoln. 1983. "Child Survival: Levels, Trends, and Determinants." In Bulatao, R., Rudolfo, Ronald Lee with Paula Hollerbach, John Bongaarts (eds.) *Determinants of Fertility in Developing Countries, Vol. I.* New York: Academic Press, pp. 199-232.

Eisinger, Peter K. 1982. "Black Employment in Municipal Jobs: The Impact of Black Political Power." *American Political Science Review* 76:380-92.

———. 1986. "Local Civil Service Employment and Black Socio-Economic Mobility." *Social Science Quarterly* 76:169-75.

Glenn, Norvall. 1962. The Negro Population in the American System of Social Stratification: An Analysis of Recent Trends. Ph.D. diss., University of Texas, Austin.

Keech, William R. 1968. *The Impact of Negro Voting.* New York: Random House.

LaVeist, Thomas A. 1992. "The Political Empowerment and Health Status of African-Americans: Mapping a New Territory." *American Journal of Sociology* 97:1080-95.

Lieberson, Stanley. 1980. *A Piece of the Pie.* Berkeley: University of California Press.

Lineberry, Robert L. 1978. "Reform, Representation and Policy." *Social Science Quarterly* 59:173-77.

Marable, Manning. 1985. *Black American Politics: From the Washington Marches to Jesse Jackson.* New York: Verso.

———. 1986. *How Capitalism Underdeveloped Black America: Problems in Race, Political Economy and Society.* Boston: South End Press.

Massey, Doug and Nancy Denton. 1993. *American Apartheid: Segregation and the Making of the Underclass.* Cambridge, MA: Harvard University Press.

Portes, Alejandro and Leif Jensen. 1989. "The Enclave and the Entrants: Patterns of Ethnic Enterprise in Miami Before and After Mariel." *American Sociological Review* 54:929-49.

Semyonov, Moshe, Danny R. Hoyt, and Richard Ira Scott. 1984. "Place, Race, and Differential Occupational Opportunities." *Demography* 21:259-70.

Semyonov, Moshe. 1988. "Bi-Ethnic Labor Markets, Mono-Ethnic Labor Markets, and Socioeconomic Inequality." *American Sociological Review* 53:256-66.

Tienda, Marta and D. T. Lii. 1987. "Minority Concentration and Earnings Inequality: Blacks, Hispanics and Asians Compared." *American Journal of Sociology* 93:141-65.

Wilson, Kenneth and Alejandro Portes. 1980. "Immigrant: An Analysis of the Labor Market Experience of Cubans in Miami." *American Journal of Sociology* 86:295-319.

Zhou, M. and John Logan. 1989. "Returns on Human Capital in Ethnic Enclaves: New York City Chinatown." *American Sociological Review* 54:809-20.

PART

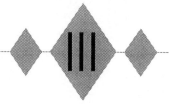

III

Racial Differences in Health

MATERNAL DRUG ABUSE AND INFANT HEALTH

A Proposal for a Multilevel Model

RAE BANKS
ASSATA ZERAI

One of the most riveting images of the 1980s was the spectacle of pregnant crack cocaine abusers and their drug-exposed newborns. The media did not create this phenomenon, but it did construct and manipulate its representation and contribute to the reified image of the pathogenic African American mother—an already politicized symbol at the center of the public discourse on race, rights, and the distribution of the nation's resources. Accompanying the "crack mother" image was a continuing narrative of the consequences of her addiction: dramatically increasing infant mortality rates, innocent children handicapped by long-term biological and neurological effects, and the ominous social threat of a "generation born at risk. A generation which may pose an even greater risk" (Reeves and Campbell 1994:214).

In the midst of a national hysteria, the politics of blame fostered the presumption, held by adversaries and advocates for these women alike, that the addicted mother's interests and those of her developing child were antagonistic (King 1991). This presumption, along with the distorted images, became the basis for imposing jail sentences on drug-abusing mothers to protect their unborn children. But the practice did not necessarily protect the drug-exposed fetus nor improve the life chances of drug-affected newborns. In fact, the threat of imprisonment proved an ineffectual deterrent to maternal drug abuse as well as an impediment to those seeking prenatal care (Hawk 1994; King 1991; Petrow 1991). Attempts to implement these sanctions led to legal challenges and overturned convictions in a significant number of these cases (Petrow 1991). But even though punitive sanctions for pregnant cocaine abusers proved to be ineffi- cient in practice, a distorted drug discourse and a public consensus that allowed the arrest of drug-abusing mothers still informs sim- plistic policy and research perspectives.

Today, maternal cocaine abuse is still taking its toll on an un- known number of infants and children. But the images projected in the rush to judgment of a decade ago proved far from the reality. Infant mortality rates are not as high, and permanent physical and neurological effects attributable to drug use are not as prevalent as originally projected (Cooper 1992; Dicker and Leighton 1994; Habel, Kaye, and Lee 1990). Dire predictions of drug-affected children as a social threat have not been borne out. But, in the interim, neither a comprehensive conceptual framework for understanding the prob- lem nor rational policy to ameliorate it has emerged. To date, there is still a great deal of ignorance about women, cocaine abuse, and drug-exposed children (Barton, Harrison, and Tse 1995; Hawk 1994; U.S. Department of Health and Human Services [DHHS] 1992).

There is some agreement among analysts that a confluence of social, economic, and biological factors affect drug-exposed new- borns and infants (Johnson and Rosen 1990) in myriad ways that have mostly social consequences (Burns et al. 1991; Habel et al. 1990; Johnson and Rosen 1990; Vega et al. 1993). But too much remains unknown. For example, estimates of the incidence and prevalence of maternal drug use remain problematic (Barton et al. 1995; Dicker and Leighton 1994; Hawk 1994); the effects of the common problem of polydrug use have been largely unexamined; the particular ef- fects of powdered cocaine versus crack cocaine abuse on birth outcomes are unknown; and the isolated effects of cocaine over and above factors such as poor nutrition and lack of prenatal care remain unidentified (Cooper 1992). As a result, there are too few interventionist strategies and inadequate treatment facilities to meet identified needs. Furthermore, existing research models do not address the as yet unidentified needs of pregnant drug abusers, their children, and their families.

Our objectives in this chapter are to (1) provide a critical analysis of the existing conceptual models and the findings of the research to date, and (2) propose an alternative multilevel, multirisk model. This alternative model is proposed as a theoretical framework with the potential to explain the interdependence of structural, environmental, and behavioral factors that shape maternal drug abuse and birth outcomes. Equally important, it also can lay the theoretical foundation for effective intervention.

Conservative Perceptions Influence Policy and Research on In-Utero Drug Exposure

In its broadest outlines, the context for examining drug abuse and birth outcomes is one of the pivotal issues of American life since the 1970s: the tensions between race, rights, and the distribution of public resources (Edsall and Edsall 1991). Within this framework, the status of African American women was politicized as early as 1976 with Ronald Reagan's repeated and distorted references to an alleged "welfare queen" as a centerpiece of his presidential campaign (*New York Times* 2/15/76; *Washington Post* 1/28/76:A2). Over time, a portrait of Black women as undisciplined, undeserving dependents siphoning off scarce public funds became a powerful subtext in a conservative, profamily agenda formulated as a "moral ideal and a political project" (Reeves and Campbell 1994:184). With Reagan at the helm, conservatives succeeded in forging a public discourse centering on values and morality, deservedness and entitlements, and group versus individual rights.

In this general climate, support for the health and well-being of poor Americans declined precipitously. Individual states began cutting Medicaid rolls as early as 1975. But between 1975 and 1984, the share of Medicaid services spent on families dropped from 39 percent to 27 percent. In 1981 alone, the Omnibus Budget Reconciliation Act dropped two million people from Medicaid rolls. Eligibility for the working poor was reduced from 40 percent to 25 percent by 1983 (General Accounting Office [GAO] 1990).

Resources for women and their children were seriously affected. Between 1977 and 1984, Maternal and Child Health Care Block Grants were reduced by one-third (Cooper 1992). As a result, federally mandated comprehensive health clinics, including well-baby, prenatal, and immunization clinics, were eliminated; Community and Migrant Health Centers were cut by one-third; and the National Health Service Corps' budget was reduced by 64 percent (between 1981 and 1991). The WIC program did not sustain budget cuts, but by 1989, it still served only one-half of those eligible (GAO 1990).

By 1984, rising infant mortality rates and increases in poor birth outcomes became the impetus for Congressional counteraction. Congress began to restore earlier cuts primarily by expanding Medicaid coverage. By 1989, one-half of Medicaid's increased revenues were for pregnant women and children. But positive effects were not as great as anticipated for two reasons. First, although access to health care for the poor increased slightly, the states' share of the burden of increasingly expensive coverage proved prohibitive. Starting from a low of $17 billion, by 1989, the states' share increased to $61 billion. Together, the states asked for and received a moratorium on expansion and an assessment of the trend. The resulting General Accounting Office (GAO) report made it clear that services to pregnant women and children were the least costly of the expanded services, but the states were unwilling to absorb any more of the burden (GAO 1990).

Second, Washington's incremental approach to a national health care problem encouraged competition between health maintenance organizations (HMOs) and Medicaid to the exclusion of other alternatives (Schlesinger and Kronebusch 1990). But there are built-in disincentives for physicians in HMOs to treat the stigmatized poor (Ginzburg 1994; Schlesinger and Kronebusch 1990). A comparison of the effects of Medicaid versus state programs on birth outcomes indicated that expanding Medicaid coverage increased access to prenatal care but not the quality of that care. Infants whose mothers were served by state programs that included outreach and case management had birthweights greater, on average, than those served through Medicaid. Medicaid also did nothing to reduce existing barriers to prenatal care. Minority women still had substantially less access to care, and the quality of the care they did receive was dependent on the generosity of Medicaid payments to physicians. In specific terms, imposing a 10 percent cut in provider pay translated to 165 grams less in the average birthweight of neonates born to Medicaid recipients (Schlesinger and Kronebusch 1990).

A report from the GAO in 1993 summarized the state of affairs; unlike all the other industrialized nations of the world, the U.S. sponsored virtually no well-baby care (cited in Keigher 1994). For impoverished African American women and children trapped in communities with diminishing resources, national and local disinvestment in health care for the poor places lives in jeopardy.

In the midst of this trend, the media sounded the alarm about increasing drug use among women. Initial media coverage featured white, upwardly mobile women who abused powdered cocaine (see *New York Times* 2/18/85). But by 1986, crack abuse among poor, pregnant African American women became a major focal point of a veritable onslaught of media coverage. In the ensuing frenzy, a narrowly focused and distorted picture of women and cocaine abuse emerged.

Although the media did call for more adequate prenatal care and drug treatment programs for "crack mothers," they gave insufficient attention to structural impediments to adequate care. Instead, the media blamed the women. Consequently, when research studies indicated that prenatal care lowers infant mortality rates for drug-exposed infants (Dugger 1991; Habel et al. 1990), crack mothers without prenatal care were presumed to be lazy and uninterested in their children. This kind of interpretation justified punitive sanctions on the grounds that the mothers' and fetuses' interests were antagonistic.

Arguably, the politics of blame justified the government's token efforts to increase drug treatment for pregnant women. In 1984, Congress "encouraged" states to use a 5 percent set-aside for expansion and innovation in drug treatment for women. But in 1990, less than 14 percent of the four million women in need of these programs were served. A GAO (1991) report revealed that the federal government supplied no guidelines for the content, evaluation, or reporting of these services.

Legal advocacy proved a more efficient method of expanding treatment. A class action suit in New York City on behalf of pregnant cocaine abusers is considered the impetus not only for expanding treatment in that city and five others across the country but also for meeting addicted women's special needs for prenatal and child care services (Chavkin 1990; Breitbart, Chavkin, and Wise 1994).

In summary, the demonization of poor, African American crack mothers inevitably led to punitive sanctions. Between 1990 and 1992, the number of women prosecuted tripled in spite of the fact that the incidence of drug-exposed newborns declined and despite evidence that the potential for prosecution actually prevents many women from seeking prenatal care (Hawk 1994; King 1991; Petrow 1991). To date, more states (24) choose to prosecute pregnant drug abusers than to provide treatment and/or coordination of services (14).

Traditional Models:
Maternal Behavior in a Vacuum

The research in the past has been driven by the theoretical premise articulated in the media that maternal behavior solely affects the pregnancy outcome. In this section, we analyze the content of past research on the maternal drug abuse-infant health relationship in order to suggest directions for future research. We divide the research into two categories. First, this section of the chapter discusses traditional models that posit maternal behavior as the main determinant of poor infant health outcomes resulting mainly from maternal drug abuse (see Figure 4.1). In the second category are newer, more progressive models that take into account multilevel factors in the relationship. We will summarize the results of each and suggest a more holistic model.

Results from studies that use nationally representative samples are only recently being published. Earlier estimates of the number of infants born per year who were exposed to drugs prenatally range from 100,000-739,000. However, from an analysis of the National Hospital Discharge Survey, Dicker and Leighton (1994) suggest that for the 1988-1990 period, "only 29,196 drug-using women or newborns [were] exposed to drugs. The best annual estimate of drug-affected newborns is 15,846" (p. 1436). The National Hospital Discharge Survey accounts for more than 99 percent of births in the United States. Between 1979 and 1989, this same survey reported a 284 percent increase (10.1 per 10,000 in the 1979 to 1981 period and 80.5 per 10,000 in 1989) and then a 13 percent decline in the number of drug-exposed infants between 1989 and 1990 (Dicker and Leighton 1994:1435). Accounting for underreporting, the most recent annual estimate (1988 to 1990) is 224 pregnant abusers and 124 drug-affected

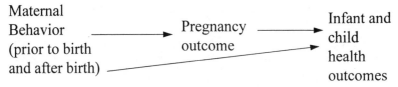

Figure 4.1. Traditional models: Maternal behavior in a vacuum.

newborns per 10,000 (Dicker and Leighton 1994:1437). Whereas one drug-affected newborn is too many, previously published overestimates have only contributed to perceptions of the "epidemic." Public consciousness of these more realistic assessments of the problem could lead to informative research and more focused policy initiatives.

The effects of maternal drug abuse on infant health occur in two distinct time periods. The first occurs while the fetus is developing. The final result of this short-term effect is the birth outcome, including perinatal morbidity and mortality. The second are delayed effects extending from the late neonatal period up to the first birthday. The incidence of short- and long-term health problems among the infants exposed to illicit substances in utero is unknown. The infant mortality rate encompasses deaths in the neonatal and postneonatal period. A study of in utero drug exposure in New York City demonstrates that the mortality rate among these infants is almost 2½ times higher than that of their nonexposed counterparts (Habel et al. 1990). But the specific disease vectors are still unidentified. This is complicated by the fact that the multirisk environment probably synergistically affects birth outcome and infant health. Drug exposure is seldom a direct cause of infant mortality and is more likely to be indirectly related.

Prenatal drug exposure probably compromises the in utero development of some fetuses. "Intrauterine growth retardation . . . may be seriously confounded by in utero exposure" to illicit drugs (Bandstra 1992:212). Negative consequences of in utero underdevelopment include stillbirth (Bandstra 1992; DHHS 1992; Vega et al. 1993), shortened gestational length, pregnancy complications, and neonatal morbidity, including neonatal abstinence syndrome.

Interuterine growth retardation is evident in low birthweight babies. Low birthweight (less than 2500 grams) infants are either small for gestational age or premature (less than 37 weeks gestation length). According to Bandstra (1992), "the most frequently described consequence of in utero cocaine exposure is low birth weight" (p. 215). And neonatal mortality rates among low birthweight and premature infants are higher than those for normal birthweight and full-term infants (Cramer 1987; Hummer 1993).

Neonatal abstinence syndrome is probably the most publicized effect of in utero drug exposure on infant health (DHHS 1992). The incidence of this condition, the amount of exposure to illicit substances, and the timing of such exposure that correlates with neonatal withdrawal are still not known.

Traditional models also posit various late neonatal and postneonatal infant health outcomes directly or indirectly resulting from the mother's prenatal drug abuse. Illicit drug and alcohol use are cited as possible causes of sudden infant death syndrome (SIDS), usually occurring in the late neonatal or postneonatal period (Gaines and Kandall 1992). In the media, the emotional issues and frustration surrounding SIDS lead the public to blame drug-addicted and drug-using mothers for the deaths of their infants. This makes it more difficult for these mothers to deal with the loss of their infants and to recover from their addiction (Gaines and Kandall 1992).

If infants are fortunate enough to survive, their behavior is often affected by in utero drug exposure. Some suffer from apnea or abnormal sleeping (Habel et al. 1990), conditions that are also associated with SIDS. Others might suffer from what has been termed "difficult baby syndrome" (Johnson and Rosen 1990). These infants are very irritable and difficult to calm down, and consequently are hard to parent.

Traditional models have identified some of the possible effects of drug use on maternal and infant health. It is important to keep in mind that fewer than half of drug-exposed infants show any adverse effects at birth (Chasnoff 1989; Dicker and Leighton 1994). Future research must take into account the various types of drugs that could be used: crack versus powdered cocaine, heroin, methadone, and polydrug use, as well as the timing and intensity of drug use. For instance, although the incidence of maternal drug use has declined, the number of mothers using drugs immediately prior to the delivery has increased (Dicker and Leighton 1994). A multilevel model that takes these variables into account will give us a better indication of the extent of the problem and ways to intervene.

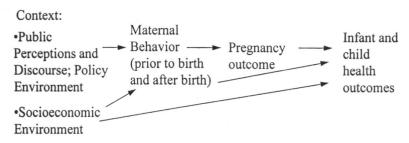

Figure 4.2. Progressive models: Drug use and maternal and child health in context.

Progressive Models: Pregnant Women's Illicit Drug Use in Context

Recent advances in research on the effects of drug abuse on infant health support the idea that it is necessary to examine both the social and biological determinants of infant health outcomes (Johnson and Rosen 1990). This allows the researcher to consider the interactions between a more complete set of factors surrounding the maternal drug use-infant health relationship. A multilevel approach that takes into account macrolevel environmental variables and microlevel behaviors is common (at least conceptually) in child health models (Mosley and Chen 1984).

The multilevel approach allows the researcher to observe micro- and macrolevel processes simultaneously, which has obvious benefits. Microlevel variables include the mother's behavior and infant health outcomes, and macrolevel variables include the policy environment and the socioeconomic environment (see Figure 4.2). However it is important to move beyond merely associating the individual and contextual variables to provide a theoretical explanation connecting the two (Tienda 1991).

In our conceptual formulation, we will attempt to explicate not only the main categories of macro- and microlevel variables that influence the mother-infant dyad but also the mechanisms linking independent and dependent variables. We delineate various determinants of health outcomes for the drug-exposed infant that are both more proximate to the resulting outcome and more distal to it. The proximate determinants tend to be biological and behavioral, and the distal determinants tend to be social structural and economic.

Maternal drug use takes place in a context that must be taken into account when examining the relationship between illicit drug use during pregnancy and maternal and child health outcomes. Johnson and Rosen (1990) posit that it is important to consider multiple risk factors.

> Initially, the research on maternal drug abuse during pregnancy focused on comparing drug-exposed and drug-free infants on a variety of neonatal and neuro-behavioral developmental measures. These analyses suggested some areas (e.g. neurological development) which appear to be particularly vulnerable to the negative impact of maternal drug abuse. However, the interpretation of these findings must be tempered by the fact that several important risk factors—poor prenatal nutrition, poor prenatal care, chaotic home conditions—were inextricably intertwined with maternal drug abuse in the population studied. Thus, rather than proving evidence of direct effects of specific drugs, the data reflect the impact of the mother's life-style, which exposes the fetus and developing child to multiple risk factors, including drugs. (pp. 281-82)

According to these analysts, multiple risk factors include maternal behaviors, such as prenatal care and nutrition, and the home conditions that the mother provides (as in Figure 4.1). But we argue that they also include the context: the socioeconomic status of the mother's community, the political climate, and the public discourse that shapes relevant policy. In turn, the context affects both the level of resources available and mothers' behaviors. These factors work in concert to affect infants' risk of birth complications and ill health early in life.

For Black America, the deleterious effects of structural change in the economy and federal disinvestment in urban areas and in health care have been well documented (Harrell and Peterson 1992). Socioenvironmental factors such as social isolation and stigma have been shown to influence drug use and recovery. Gender differences, however, exacerbate both isolation and stigma for women. In contemporary urban America, poor African American women are more socially isolated than are men (Fernandez and Harris 1992). They are more stigmatized for using drugs (Fullilove and Fullilove 1989), and they receive less familial and social service support for their recovery (Boyd and Mieczkowksi 1990). We propose a multilevel model that encompasses the relative contributions of both structural and socioenvironmental factors to maternal adaptive and maladaptive behaviors and infant health.

If a healthy and supportive environment is provided, there are cases in which infants are quite resilient (Johnson et al. 1988; Johnson and Rosen 1990). Further exploration into the factors that lead to this outcome is necessary. But it is clear that the factors are not just biological and behavioral. Maternal behavior takes place within a context, whether it is using illicit substances, getting adequate prenatal care, or providing a healthy environment for the newborn. This context is affected by social, political, and cultural factors that must be addressed to ensure the health of all children.

The needs of families with drug-exposed infants are stated clearly in the health and social welfare literature. They include low birthweight and drug-addicted baby care (Cooper 1992; Hawk 1994; LaFrance et al. 1994), drug rehabilitation for the mother (Hawk 1994), and social service support (Cooper 1992; Saunders 1992; Wilson 1991). An example of a program that has integrated the various types of care necessary for these mothers is the Des Moines, Iowa Project Together Program (Saunders 1992). The problem with this program and the potential for others like it is financial backing. The right wing leanings of the Congress today give a discouraging indication of things to come.

Many mothers are relying on extended family for support. The phenomenon of grandparents as caretakers is growing (Burton 1992; Minkler and Roe 1993). But grandparents caring for an adult child's offspring are often not eligible for the same social welfare support to care for their grandchildren as the child's parents (Minkler and Roe 1993). The problem, again, is structural.

The impact of the public policy debate on the social environment of the drug-affected infant/mother dyad is significant. When in utero drug exposure is viewed as a crime, child protective services agencies step in to threaten the mother's right to custody of her child. In the most extreme instances, mothers are arrested when illicit substances are found in the newborn's urine (DHHS 1992). If public policy takes a therapeutic and supportive stance toward the mother, services will be offered to ensure that the addicted mother gets the support she needs to recover from her addiction, and mothers using illicit substances during their pregnancies will be granted access to resources that will help them provide for a healthy environment.

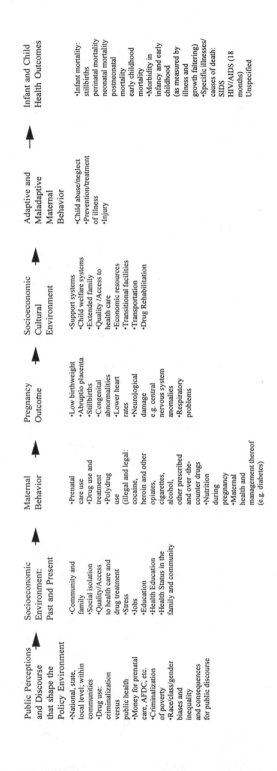

Public Perceptions and Discourse that shape the Policy Environment	Socioeconomic Environment: Past and Present	Maternal Behavior	Pregnancy Outcome	Socioeconomic Cultural Environment	Adaptive and Maladaptive Maternal Behavior	Infant and Child Health Outcomes
•National, state, local level; within communities •Drug use: criminalization versus public health •Money for prenatal care, AFDC, etc. •Criminalization of poverty •Race/class/gender biases and inequality and consequences for public discourse	•Community and family •Social isolation •Quality/Access to health care and drug treatment •Stress •Jobs •Education •Health Education •Health Status in the family and community	•Prenatal care use •Drug use and treatment •Polydrug use (illegal and legal: cocaine, heroin and other opiates, cigarettes, alcohol, other prescribed and over-the-counter drugs •Nutrition during pregnancy •Maternal health and management thereof (e.g. diabetes)	•Low birthweight •Abruptio placenta •Stillbirths •Congenital abnormalities •Lower heart rates •Neurological damage e.g. central nervous system anomalies •Respiratory problems	•Support systems •Child welfare systems •Extended family •Quality /Access to health care •Economic resources •Transitional facilities •Transportation •Drug Rehabilitation	•Child abuse/neglect •Prevention/treatment of illness •Injury	•Infant mortality: stillbirths perinatal mortality neonatal mortality postneonatal mortality early childhood mortality •Morbidity in infancy and early childhood (as measured by illness and growth faltering) •Specific illnesses/ causes of death: SIDS HIV/AIDS (18 months) Unspecified

Figure 4.3. The impact of the policy/political context on the relationship between drug abuse and infant mortality among African Americans: Theoretical model.

Conclusion

A holistic model of maternal drug abuse and infant mortality that accounts for multilevel influences offers many alternative research strategies. Simple multivariate analysis that estimates models for dependent variables such as maternal behavior, pregnancy outcomes, and long-term health outcomes would be very useful. This model has implications for policy. For example, an immediate intervention strategy is to use the main determinants of maternal behavior and poor pregnancy outcomes to set up a schedule of high-risk indicators of drug abuse during pregnancy. This risk approach could be used to promote prenatal care use and increase the chances of a normal birth weight.

Finally, ethnographic data collection based on human agency models would help us to understand some of the adaptive behaviors of mothers that lead to the phenomenon of resilient children. It would be useful to learn creative strategies that could be adapted for community health programs.

It is important to look at maternal behavior in context. Figure 4.3 offers a suggestion for how the variables in Figures 4.1 and 4.2 might work in concert to influence the health of a child that was exposed to illicit substances in utero. The policy environment and the socioeconomic environment influence the kinds of resources to which a woman has access, including drug abuse treatment and timely prenatal care. Social environments that are the most supportive increase the chances that children can recover from ill effects of drug exposure. America is a long way from a drug-free society. But in the interim, the evidence suggests that a multilevel, multirisk model can help us to ask the right questions and find more effective, humane answers to the problem of maternal substance abuse and infant health.

References

Bandstra, E. S. 1992. "Assessing Acute and Long-Term Physical Effects of in Utero Drug Exposure on the 1 Perinate, Infant, and Child." *NIDA Research Monograph Series* 117:212-27.

Barton, S. J., R. Harrigan, and A. Tse. 1995. "Perinatal Cocaine Exposure Implications for Practice, Policy Development, and Needs for Future Research." *Journal of Perinatology* 15(1):10-22.

Boyd, C. J. and T. Mieczkowski. 1990. "Drug Use, Health, Family and Social Support in 'Crack' Cocaine Users." *Addictive Behaviors* 15:481-85.

Breitbart, V., W. Chavkin, and P. H. Wise. 1994. "The Accessibility of Drug Treatment for Pregnant Women: A Survey of Programs in Five Cities." *American Journal of Public Health* 84(10):1658-61.

Burns, K., L. Chethik, W. J. Burns, and R. Clark. 1991. "Dyadic Disturbances in Cocaine-Abusing Mothers and Their Infants." *Clinical Psychology* 47:316-19.

Burton, L. M. 1992. "Black Grandparents Rearing Children of Drug Addicted Parents: Stressors, Outcomes, and Social Service Needs." *The Gerontologist* 32:744-51.

Chasnoff, I. J. 1989. "Cocaine, Pregnancy, and the Neonate." *Women and Health* 15(3):23-35.

Chavkin, W. 1990. "Drug Addiction and Pregnancy: Policy Crossroads." *American Journal of Public Health* 80:483-87.

Chen, Lincoln. 1983. "Child Survival: Levels, Trends, and Determinants." In *Determinants of Fertility in Developing Countries,* Vol. 1. eds. R. Bulatao, Ronald Lee Rudolfo with Paula Hollerbach and Joan Bongaarts, 199-232. New York: Academic Press.

Cooper, M. H. 1992. "Infant Mortality: Why is the U.S. Death Rate High Compared to Other Nations." *Congressional Researcher 2(28):643-63.*

Cramer, J. C. 1987. "Social Factors and Infant Mortality: Identifying High-Risk Groups and Proximate Causes." *Demography* 24:299-322.

Dicker, M. and E. A. Leighton. 1994. "Trends in the US Prevalence of Drug-Using Parturient Women and Drug Affected Newborns 1979 through 1990." *American Journal of Public Health* 84:1433-38.

Dugger, C. 1991. "Cocaine Use and Infant Mortality Decline Together in New York City." *New York Times* Apr. 20:A1.

Edsall, T. B. and M. D. Edsall. 1991. *Chain Reaction: The Impact of Race, Rights and Taxes on American Politics.* New York: Norton.

Fernandez, R. and D. Harris. 1992. "Social Isolation and the Underclass." In *Drugs, Crime, and Social Isolation: Barriers to Urban Opportunity,* ed. A. V. Harrell and G. E. Peterson. Washington, DC: The Urban Institute.

Fullilove, M. T. and R. E. Fullilove. 1989. "Intersecting Epidemics: Black Teen Crack Use and Sexually Transmitted Disease." *Journal of the Medical Women's Association* 44(5):146-53.

Gaines, J. and S. R. Kandall. 1992. "Counseling Issues Related to Maternal Substance Abuse and Subsequent Sudden Infant Death Syndrome in Offspring." *Clinical Social Work Journal* 20:169-77.

General Accounting Office. 1990. *Medicaid Expansions: Coverage Improves But State Fiscal Problems Jeopardize Continued Progress.* Report to the Chairman, Committee on Finance, U.S. Senate.

————. 1991. *ADMS Block Grant: Women's Set-Aside Does Not Assure Drug Treatment for Pregnant Women.* Report to the Chairman, Subcommittee on Health and the Environment, Committee on Energy and Commerce, U.S. House of Representatives.

Ginzburg, E. 1994. "Improving Health Care for the Poor: Lessons from the 1980s." *Journal of the American Medical Association* 271:464-67.

Habel, L., K. Kae, and J. Lee. 1990. "Trends in Reporting of Maternal Drug Abuse and Infant Mortality Among Drug-Exposed Infants in New York City." *Women and Health* 16(2):41-58.

Harrell, A. V. and G. E. Peterson. Eds. 1992. *Drugs, Crime, and Social Isolation: Barriers to Urban Opportunity.* Washington, DC: The Urban Institute.

Hawk, M. A. N. 1994. "How Social Policies Make Matters Worse: The Case of Maternal Substance Abuse." *Journal of Drug Issues* 24:517-26.

Hummer, Robert A. 1993. "Racial Differentials in Infant Mortality in the U.S.: An Examination of Social and Health Determinants." *Social Forces* 72(2):529-54.

Johnson, H. and T. S. Rosen. 1990. "Mother-Infant Interaction in a Multi-Risk Population." *American Journal of Orthopsychiatry* 60(2):281-88.

Johnson, H., M. B. Glassman, K. B. Fiks, and T. Rosen. 1988. "Resilient Children: Individual Differences in Developmental Outcome of Children Born to Drug Abusers." *Journal of Genetic Psychology* 151:523-39.

Keigher, S. M. 1994. "The Morning After Deficit Reduction: The Poverty of U.S. Maternal and Child Health Policy." *Health and Social Work* 19(19):143-47.

King, Patricia. 1991. "Helping Women Helping Children: Drug Policy and Future Generations." *Milbank Quarterly* 69:595-621.

La France, S., J. Mitchell, K. Damus, C. Driver, G. Roman, E. Graham, and L. Schwartz. 1994. "Community Based Services for Pregnant Substance-Using Women." *American Journal of Public Health* 84(10):1688-89.

Minkler, M. and K. Roe. 1993. *Grandmothers as Caregivers: Raising Children of the Crack Cocaine Epidemic.* Newbury Park, CA: Sage.

Mosley, W. Henry and Lincoln C. Chen. 1984. "An Analytic Framework for the Study of Child Survival in Developing Countries." *Population and Development Review,* Supplement to Volume 10.

Petrow, Julie. 1991. "Addicted Mothers, Drug-Exposed Babies: The Unprecedented Prosecution of Mothers Under Drug-Trafficking Statutes." *New York Law School Law Review* 36:573-607.

Reeves, J. and R. Campbell. 1994. *Cracked Coverage: Television News, the Anti-Cocaine Crusade, and the Reagan Legacy.* Durham, NC: Duke University Press.

Saunders, E. 1992. "Project Together: Serving Substance-Abusing Mothers and Their Children in Des Moines." *American Journal of Public Health* 82:1166-67.

Schlesinger, M. and K. Kronebusch. 1990. "The Failure of Prenatal Care Policy for the Poor." *Health Affairs* Winter:91-111.

Tienda, Marta. 1991. "Poor People and Poor Places: Deciphering Neighborhood Effects on Poverty Outcomes." In *Macro-Micro Linkages in Sociology,* ed. Joan Huber. Newbury Park, CA: Sage.

U.S. Department of Health and Human Services. 1992. *Maternal Drug Abuse and Drug Exposed Children: Understanding the Problem.* Washington, DC: U.S. Department of Health and Human Services.

Vega, W. A., B. Kolody, J. Hwang, and A. Noble. 1993. "Prevalence and Magnitude of Perinatal Substance Exposures in California." *New England Journal of Medicine* 329:850-54.

Wilson, B. L. 1991. "Treatment for Two." *Journal of the American Public Welfare Association* 49(4):30-36.

THE PSYCHOSOCIAL DIMENSION
OF BLACK MATERNAL HEALTH

An Intersection of Race,
Gender, and Class

KATRINA BELL MCDONALD

The maternal health care community has long been concerned with both the persistently high rates of infant mortality (deaths of children not yet one year old) among African American mothers and the infant mortality rate differential between Blacks and whites. The rate among Blacks remains more than twice as high as that among whites. African American mothers continue to suffer unequally from complications associated with pregnancy and childbirth despite technological advances in obstetrics, social programs to alleviate poverty, and public health projects to inform and educate expectant mothers "at risk." Thus, developing health policy that helps to minimize the complications of pregnancy and childbirth in order to yield more acceptable rates of infant mortality has been a major preoccupation.

African American mothers in the inner city who are young, unmarried, and socioeconomically disadvantaged have been especially targeted for maternal interventions because of their disproportionate representation among those most lacking in maternal resources, potentially putting them at a higher risk for experiencing adverse pregnancy outcomes. However, recent studies comparing Black and white pregnancy outcomes have shown that urban Black mothers considered socioeconomically at low risk for infant mortality are also more likely to experience the deaths of their babies relative to white mothers who are at low risk (Kleinman and Kessel 1987; Schoendorf et al. 1992). This revelation (among others) suggests that researchers have failed to adequately model the etiology of infant mortality for Black mothers, and that progress in this area has been seriously retarded by the lack of theoretical attention to causal factors beyond the traditional medical and sociodemographic risks (Kleinman and Kessel 1987).

Maternal activists in the African American community have joined with the interdisciplinary social research community to garner support for a broad public health initiative to better pinpoint the roots of this social problem by determining all of the specific pathways through which disadvantage materializes in the form of poor maternal health for Black mothers and death and illness for Black babies. Although the "poverty paradigm" perspective provides a framework with which to interpret the poor material plight of disadvantaged mothers and from which to design appropriate health policy, it does not encourage a critical analysis of the plight of middle-class Black women. Through a series of professional meetings and community forums led largely by the Centers for Disease Control's Division of Reproductive Health and the National Institutes for Child Health and Development over the past three or four years, consensus has grown over the lack of attention paid specifically to the underlying *psychosocial* condition of Black mothers in America—the impact of everyday struggles with racism, sexism, and class inequality on the quality of their maternal health—and to the biomedical translation of psychosocial stress to increased susceptibility to infant mortality. Few have taken on the task, that is, of conceptualizing pregnancy outcomes for Black women (rather than for poor women or all women in general) as directly or indirectly consequential to the unique historical and contemporary social environment within which they must cope physically and psychologically.

In this chapter, I provide an overview of the research on the psychosocial dimension of maternal health and focus on demonstrating the negative direct and indirect influences of racism, sexism, and class inequality on the emotional and physical health of Black mothers, disadvantaged and advantaged alike. These three forms of oppression are to be understood as contributing to a multidimensional psychosocial reality for Black mothers, each one shaping and reinforcing the other. Not all social theorists are in agreement about how much each of these forms of oppression contributes to poor psychosocial health (i.e., whether class inequality shapes racism or racism shapes class inequality); no attempt will be made to resolve these particular theoretical questions here. However, I have devoted a great deal of space to working out the nature of *classism* within the lives of Black women, relative to the space given to racism and sexism, to broaden the scope of our conceptualizing of social class as a hazard to psychosocial health.

In my discussion of class inequality, I describe a range of tangible and intangible costs of social class oppression for Black mothers; some costs are more hidden from mainstream social researchers than others. I contend that it is the more hidden psychosocial costs of classism for Black women that have been lacking from our theoretical models. Particularly lacking is attention to the psychosocial ramifications of the sociocultural detachment or isolation of urban Black women from their traditional maternal safety net of cross-class communal support, for underprivileged as well as for middle-class Black mothers. I offer this in contribution to the paradigmatic shift that is currently taking place within the interdisciplinary maternal health research and policy arena.

A recent issue of the *American Journal of Preventive Medicine* (supplement to Volume 9[6]) pulls together the work of many ardent social researchers and maternal activists who are unified in arguing that a good deal of the mystery surrounding this subject reflects "the absence of a more intellectually penetrating paradigm—grounded in historical analysis as well as in the contemporary life experiences of Black women" (James 1993:v). Many of their concerns and findings are incorporated throughout this section alongside my own, as they help satisfy the need for a culturally sensitive understanding of the context within which salient problems of Black maternal health are experienced and addressed.

Psychosocial Stress

According to Kaplan (1983), psychosocial stress is a socially derived, conditioned, and situated poor psychological state that arises from an individual's inability to positively affect those life circumstances, personal attributes, and personal behaviors that are devalued by various significant social groups and entities, and the inability to fully cope with being the object of devalued institutional and interpersonal responses. Although we are far from discovering exactly how the socioenvironmental-to-physiological stress process works to adversely affect Black pregnancy outcomes, psychosocial stress is clearly a necessary contributor to the etiology of poor maternal health.

Istvan (1986) explains that "despite such historical precedents for interest in the role of psychosocial factors in reproductive dysfunction, it has been claimed that this is the least well-understood area in psychosomatic research" (p. 331). McLean et al. (1993) provide the empirical basis for that proposition:

> Various research efforts have recently contributed cumulative support for the hypothesis that high levels of exposure to stressors and other psychological factors may put women at increased risk for adverse reproductive outcomes, particularly low birth weight and preterm delivery. (p. 39)

These stressors may venture directly to physiological effects that threaten the normal reproductive process ("hard" pathways) or indirectly through behavioral channels (e.g., smoking, substance abuse, or "soft" pathways). In either case, the relative poorer maternal health of Black mothers and, therefore, their poorer infant mortality rates may be a reflection of a higher exposure to psychosocial stress in their lives because of the historical and pervasive devaluation of Black mothers in American society, and to the forced internalization of that devaluation. (See discussion of "internalized oppression" in Yamato 1990.)

The "life stress" conceptual model for predicting pregnancy outcome has maintained a dominant role in research on maternal health across many disciplines. This approach seeks, in part, an understanding of the dimensions of concrete, life-changing events (versus daily, more chronic stressors) that have demonstrated associations with poor maternal health outcomes and the importance of the events' timing, frequency, desirability, and perceived threat to personal well-being (McLean et al. 1993; Levin and DeFrank 1988). Because the vast majority of the research conducted has focused on stressful events immediately surrounding the pregnancy (recent), we know very little about psychosocial stressors existing long before the pregnancy and the long-term effects of those stressors that expose and reexpose themselves to prospective mothers throughout the life course (remote). Furthermore, the dimensions of both recent and remote stressors have been so generalized (random stressors—e.g., family death, job loss, getting married) and assessed more quantitatively than qualitatively that they offer little, if any, understanding of stressors unique to Black mothers—or of the unique impact of common stressors—that may be exacerbated by the other factors known to be so vital to health outcomes.

The stressful life experiences of Black mothers, and of every other social group, are rooted in their sociostructural contexts and arise substantially from the historical and contemporary conditions of their lives:

> The social context of stressful experiences is not limited to the realm of stressful live events, but also includes the ongoing and difficult conditions of daily life that are now usually termed chronic stressors. . . . Systemic stressors are tied to social locations and/or social group experiences, and thus are directly relevant to understanding the ties between the social conditions of life and psychiatric disorders. . . . [a] broad array of stressful experiences must be measured." (Turner, Wheaton, and Lloyd 1995:105, 119, 120)

Thus, as a step toward developing a new research agenda, this alternative "systemic" (versus random) approach is being promoted as a more promising avenue to a better understanding of how Black maternal physical and emotional health is influenced negatively by stressful social divisions based on race, gender, and social class (Krieger et al. 1993).

The current intense political agenda to dismantle "affirmative action" rests largely on the conservatives' belief that the associations between social oppression and poor social, health, educational, and economic outcomes are generally unsubstantiated; these effects of social oppression are ultimately dismissed as trite. Therefore, as we move toward developing this new health research and policy agenda, we must encourage an intellectual sensitivity to the nonmaterial nuances of social oppression in the everyday lives of Black women: The processes by which the oppression of Black mothers materializes in the form of psychosocial stress and poor maternal health must be detailed clearly. The recent work of Krieger et al. is particularly promising to that end. Because their comprehensive definitions of racism, sexism, and class inequality were derived from an extensive review of sociological, feminist, and Black intellectual thought, I have chosen to employ their definitions here.

Disaggregating the Psychosocial Dimension

Gendered Racism

In recognizing the poorly explained yet significant contribution of race to the differences in rates of infant mortality, Krieger et al. discuss various forms of racism to help break the conceptual deadlock. By shifting focus away from observations of proxy measures for racism that generally manage to capture only the material effects of institutionalized racial discrimination,[1] and by redirecting focus to the nonmaterial manifestations of racism expressed intentionally by individuals and institutions in people's lives, we open up the possibility for a better understanding of why the pregnancy outcomes of women who are Black are so strikingly different from those who are white. After an extensive study of the research done over the years that tried to build a definition that would fully capture the experience of racism, Krieger and her colleagues (1993) finally arrived at this conceptualization:

We define "racism" as an oppressive system of racial relations, justified by ideology, in which one racial group benefits from dominating another and defines itself and others through this domination. Racism involves harmful and degrading beliefs and actions expressed and implemented by both institutions and individuals, as linked to their membership in racially defined groups. . . . Ranging from blatantly overt to insidiously subtle, the phenomena of racism typically include multiple forms of segregation (e.g., political, occupational, residential), as well as demeaning and often daily insults. Members of the oppressed group are routinely marginalized and patronized by members of the oppressor group. They are suspected of cheating and thievery, suffer rude service at public accommodations and restaurants, encounter hate stares and racial epithets from strangers on the street, and are treated unfairly by law enforcement and other government officials. They face a pervasive threat of violence, ranging from

the extremes of hate crimes to the more general fear for one's safety
and that of friends and family, particularly those who must live in
impoverished areas plagued by drug-related and other violence.
(pp. 85-86)

Krieger and her colleagues argue that the move toward a more
frank inclusion of the historical, persistent significance of the "color
line" in health research is likely to result in new attempts to develop
measures that represent more validly the disadvantage of race.
Specifically, they explain that past research has well-documented
reports of institutionalized racial discrimination in health-related
areas. These reports reveal that it is more likely that Black women
will be treated "less aggressively" by health professionals than will
white women, and that Black women perceive the quality of the care
they receive as "inferior" to that of whites. Another health-related
institutionalized form of racism is "environmental," whereby, for
example, hazardous materials are placed disproportionately within
close proximity to African American communities by corporations
and public waste disposal agencies.

This body of research, however, fails to address how any of these
bear psychosocially on the health of those affected. Furthermore, the
influence of intentional forms of racism as a potential psychosocial
risk factor for Black mothers has not been rigorously tested. [Re-
search on hypertension has been most explicit in connecting a minority individual's exposure to social stress with bodily dysfunction
(Krieger et al. 1993).] Every day, the Black mother must face the
reality that she is perceived by the larger society as a representative
of the "lesser race," whether or not she personally has exhibited any
"undesirable" traits or behaviors. Simply by being Black, she is
forced into an emotional battle to prove herself worthy on a daily
basis, whether or not anyone ever directly says or does anything
negative to her.

The Black mother is also burdened emotionally during pregnancy
and thereafter with how to protect her Black child from those same
racist social forces that threaten her own psychosocial and physical
health. I am reminded frequently of one particular day in my own
life when, while out walking, I came to a grinding halt as it suddenly
dawned on me that the obstetrician had said, "You're having a boy!
Congratulations!" The sense of fear that came over me was overwhelming. I thought, how could I have possibly been crazy enough
to bring a Black boy into this world only to have him die violently

before he reaches his manhood? Black mothers are challenged to overcome such feelings of powerlessness every day and to invest heavily in the protection of their Black children, whom they realize are at risk for numerous negative social outcomes, such as poor infant health, poverty, substance abuse, and violent crime (Collins 1991). Of vital importance is the child's racial socialization, which must be made rich with self- and race-affirming messages to help the child cope with his or her status as an African American in a white-dominated world. The pressure to succeed as a Black mother presents yet another health-threatening psychosocial stressor in her life.

Racialized Sexism

Krieger et al. (1993) further explain that close examination of and theoretical attention to Black mothers' exposure to sexism—the oppressive system of gender relations justified by men—is as necessary as that to racism. Because the mother is the central person in the study of infant mortality, sex or gender issues regarding Black women generally are taken for granted; therefore, researchers have been equally neglectful of the role of everyday sexism in the personal experiences of psychosocial stress.

In reviewing the many facets of sexism, Krieger et al. (1993) explicate as follows:

> Like racism, sexism involves harmful and degrading beliefs and actions expressed and implemented in both overt and subtle forms by institutions and by individuals, as linked to their membership in gender-defined groups. . . . As expressed in daily life, [sexist] beliefs and practices both justify and result in vast inequalities between men's and women's living conditions and opportunities . . . women are routinely treated as sex objects and face the daily harassment of street remarks, the fear of rape, and for some, the threat of memories of sexual abuse and domestic violence. Moreover, for Black women, these and other everyday expressions of sexism, both within and outside the Black community, are filtered through presumptions about racial and gender characteristics. (pp. 89-90)

Institutionalized gender discrimination against Black women has received far more research attention than other forms of sexism. Black women's subordinate positions within the economy and other major societal institutions (i.e., their gender segregation), including medical and public health institutions, has received the greatest attention. As a result, the psychosocial impact of both institutional and noninstitutional forms of sexism against Black women is poorly understood. Being a Black woman presupposes that one fulfill certain social roles that may be personally undesirable, difficult, largely unattainable, and/or denigrating. This is itself a chronically stressful factor in the etiology of Black women's psychosocial health. That these roles are generally viewed as "lesser" roles in comparison to those of men and white women further exacerbates the psychosocial struggle throughout one's life for more personally meaningful roles to play.

In addition, battling the controlling images of Black women that pervade the society makes it all the more difficult to maintain positive self-identities. The historical characterization of them as uncommonly "strong" sets them up for fierce self-competition in living up to that expectation (Collins 1991); each day that they find themselves fighting to cope with life's circumstances adds to their risk for negative health effects. The emotional self-battering and the physical and emotional battering of Black women by others fueled by these controlling images is a generally unrecognized health problem in their lives before, during, and after pregnancy (Weitz 1994). The psychosocial struggles with sexism that Black women experience every day are a potentially harmful force on the normal physiological functioning of the woman's body, setting her up for poor maternal health.

Black Women's Experience of Class Inequality

It is unfortunate that the extreme lack of consensus over how best to conceive and measure "social class" and the ideological denial of America as a class-based society (see Navarro 1993) have led to little direct study of the effects of social class on the health of Black women. As a direct result of this neglect to address and/or disentangle the mystery of social class, the significance of class inequality in the lives of Black women and its consequences for psychosocial health is virtually nonexistent.

Social class is a theoretical concept (imperfectly captured empirically) used to indicate the social location of a group composed of people who share similar economic, educational, and occupational experiences, and to determine that group's relative access to material resources, influence, and information (Dutton and Levine 1989). Social class status has demonstrated a strong effect on illness and health, yet we know very little about why.

Conventionally, "Blackness" and "womanness" taken together have been equated with being socioeconomically poor, which, in effect, groups all Black women in a subordinate social "class" or "classes." The logic underlying this is that Black women, who as a whole are particularly vulnerable socioeconomically, are swept into poverty by benign (nonracist, nonsexist) political and economic decisions of government and business. Thus, the social class status of Black mothers typically is taken for granted as something that is an important part of the Black/white infant mortality puzzle, but it is included simplistically as a control variable in models of reproductive outcome.

Alternatively, a radical, frank identification of the malignant impact of *classism* on reproductive outcome is crucial to the progress of future research in this area. By classism, I mean the meritocratic ideology that justifies the structural divisions of social groups and the class stereotypes that tend to ensue. There is sufficient cause from both scholarship and everyday Black life to implicate classism as a conscious tool of the oppressing group that has potentially injurious ramifications for Black maternal health (Essed 1991; Navarro 1993).

On this point, I found the work of Krieger et al. (1993) somewhat unsatisfying. James (1993) hailed them for their descriptions of how racism and sexism have historically interacted with "social class oppression to create and maintain the current 'structure of domination' " (p. v), yet I found a far less provocative discussion by them of the nature of class oppression in everyday life than they had done with the other two forms of oppression:

> [Social class shapes] who has and who lacks the basic material necessities of life (adequate food, clothing, shelter, sanitation, and health care), who is exposed to—and spared from—a variety of occupational and environmental hazards, and who has and who lacks control over the essential content of daily life (at work, at home, and in the neighborhood). Also pertinent is the relationship between social class and the different types of behaviors and ways of living that are promoted or denigrated by one's peers and the society at large. (Krieger et al. 1993:93)

Implicit within this definition are both institutional and noninstitutional forms of classism, although what is glaringly absent is how the principles of the dominant, classist, meritocratic view of American society guide how material and social resources are doled out.

Meritocratic ideology posits that American society relies on individuals to rationally sort themselves into the various hierarchical class strata via society's educational and occupational institutions (Davis and Moore 1945). People are materially and socially rewarded according to how successful they are in accessing these institutions and accumulating their human capital. Success, in turn, affords one a bounty of social benefits; included among them are protection from certain health-threatening environments, the availability and affordability of health care, and an assurance that one's character will be highly regarded by the ruling class and society at large (Sennett and Cobb 1973).

Thus, one interpretation of Black women's disproportionate representation in the lower class strata is that, as a whole, they have made poor choices that have led to their occupying those lower strata; either they have recognized their lack of personal ability to access and adequately use relevant social institutions to attain a higher status, or they lack the desire to work as hard as is required to do so. Ultimately then, Black women, supposedly lacking the character of a social competitor, have "chosen" to place themselves at a higher risk for a number of materially, health-, and socially related problems and have "given up" their opportunities for greater social prestige and power.

The foregoing discussions of racism and sexism demonstrate, on the contrary, that oppressive ideologies like classism have preceded Black women's "choices" and have limited in varying degrees their material aspirations, their productive potential, and their power: "Being oppressed means the *absence of choices*" (hooks 1984:5). This conscious depression of Black women's class attainment and mobility has resulted, in part, in Black women disproportionately occupying the lower social class strata, where they are likely to be embedded within a stressful environment with job conditions that are likely to cause ill health; neighborhoods that are chemically polluted and housing that is inadequate and unsafe; diets that provide little nutrition; regular exercise that is virtually nonexistent; fear abounding over which friend, neighbor, or relative will die next; health- and life-endangering behaviors that are encouraged; and access to both preventive and therapeutic health care that is severely limited (Weitz 1994).

The tangible costs of these effects of classism on many Black women's lives traditionally have been acknowledged in Black maternal outcome models, which is why the variable "social class" is almost always included; but relatively little notice has been given to how classist social processes devalue Black women and how this might pose a direct, intangible psychosocial risk to their health. Living the life of a low social status person creates its own unique forms of psychosocial stress for a large segment of the Black population of mothers. In addition to what is directly related to their material condition, a portion of their stress is related to, for example, their everyday personal encounters with capitalist-motivated institutional decision making in the health care system (Navarro 1993). The poor delivery of health services for uninsured or government-assisted Black mothers and preconceived notions about their "low-class" health values are just two ways in which Black women are institutionally denigrated on a daily basis, bearing directly on the quality of their maternal health care and on the psychosocial stress in their lives.

At yet another level of stress on reproductive outcome, Adler et al. (1993) suggest that "one's relative position in the SES hierarchy, apart from the material implications of one's position, may affect risk of disease" (p. 20). They argue that a distinctive "behavioral repertoire" is developed and promoted by members of the lower class in response to their consciousness of their vulnerability to the actions of the dominant class. Although this "behavioral repertoire" is intended to protect members of the lower class from classism, the process of developing and maintaining that "repertoire" may prove to be a major source of psychosocial stress and, thus, a potentially health-threatening mechanism. This suggests that the ongoing process of learning to adapt one's ways of living to survive as a member of the devalued lower class may be another form of psychosocial stress venturing directly to physiological effects that threaten the quality of one's health, and that the effects of this process of learning to adapt are separate from the effects of the behavior itself. It is plausible, therefore, that because African American mothers are disproportionately represented in the lower class strata, many are very likely to be forced into this life-adapting process and to be susceptible to psychologically driven physiological injury by classism in this way.

The potential awareness of one's relative position in the social hierarchy to adversely affect one's psychosocial health may also apply to the more privileged members of an oppressed group, such as middle-class African Americans, though to a lesser degree than for their lower-class counterparts. In direct response to the deepening social class schism in the Black community over the past two decades, for example, middle-class African Americans also have had to adapt their ways of living to accommodate their increasing social distance from the masses of Black people. This process of adapting to Black middle-classness sometimes involves using classist logic to justify one's higher social position (internalized classism). For instance, whereas many middle-class African Americans largely attribute their higher social class status to having been fortunate enough to receive the emotional, educational, and material resources necessary to reach their potential in spite of the social odds against them, some have been seduced into believing that their middle-classness is solely a reflection of their having made better educational and occupational choices. It is my contention that, for some middle-class Blacks, their consciousness of this internalizing of classism operating within the Black community is a hidden source of psychosocial stress for them.

The internalization of classism among Black women is a highly sensitive issue (airing of "dirty laundry") in the Black community, yet negative reactions by middle-class women to their observations of and interactions with women from the lower class are evident in the everyday lives of Black people. These reactions seem to stem from a sense of distaste for lower-class attitudes and behaviors, which middle-class women believe reflect a lack of personal initiative or pride as Black women—a pride that they believe is essential to the social and personal progress of African American women. Tensions arise over things as superficial as what members of the lower class choose to wear, drive, read, or watch on television, to things more substantial like the poor choices they believe lower-class women make in prioritizing their values (e.g., caring more about illegitimate acquisition of material goods than about how that activity creates an unsafe environment for their children).

Although it is clear that internalized classism within the Black women's community—among women who traditionally have maintained a strong gender/ethnic solidarity for maternal support across social class strata—potentially contributes to the poor maternal health of lower-class mothers, its potential cost to middle-class

Black mothers is much more hidden; it can be a particularly painful source of psychosocial stress for Black women throughout the social class spectrum. As Collins (1991) has explained,

> Sometimes the pain most deeply felt is the pain that Black women inflict on one another. . . . By claiming that they are not like the rest, some African American women reject connections to other Black women . . . [and try] to muffle the negative status attached to [their] Blackness by emphasizing [their] allegedly superior class position. (pp. 81, 84)

Several observations of classism among African American women were made during a recent study of the California-based "Birthing Project," where middle-class Black women volunteer to recreate maternal support to disadvantaged young mothers (McDonald 1995). The project seeks to secure the healthy future of young mothers and their children by evoking a sense of traditional gender/ ethnic solidarity in crossing class lines. Through intensive interviews with 19 of these volunteer women, it was revealed that, contrary to their ideal model of "activist mothering," they possess something of a middle-class "wisdom" about the lower classes that protects them in the face of discomforting social differences (also see Lykes 1983). That wisdom is evident from the class-conscious language that the volunteers use in assessing the young mothers' quality of life: she's bound for a brighter future than most of the others because she comes from a "traditional family"; her problem is that she is the product of a teen mother herself, and she was probably "exposed to things" to which she should not have been exposed; she's just caught up in the "cycle" of poverty (McDonald 1995:180).

The testimonies of the volunteers help to illustrate the complex ways in which contemporary Black middle-class women struggle to maintain their commitment to racial/gender uplift in the midst of a deepening class schism in the Black community. The intimate nature of their voluntarism serves to accentuate the consciousness of class, and this accentuation, at least for some, becomes a serious, frustrating hindrance to the provision of maternal care for those they feel obligated to support, and a potential threat to the psychosocial health of both parties.

The concepts of classism and internalized classism may be useful to our understanding of why social class mobility for Black women does not provide protection from adverse pregnancy outcomes as is predicted by the long-standing "poverty paradigm." Middle-class Black women suffer the burden of having to learn to adapt to their lives being so socially distant and detached from that of lower-class Black women with whom they traditionally have shared many meaningful community connections. Thus, like those who are socially disadvantaged, middle-class Black mothers are also likely to be injured psychologically by classism in this way and to be placed at risk by this injury for poor pregnancy outcomes. These class-related stressors are not related simply to middle-class Black women's attempt to live a "middle-class lifestyle" or their attempt to deflect race and gender insults from those they thought were respectful of them as members of the middle class; they are also related to the women's struggle to manage the historical ideal of a "classless" gender/ethnic identity and to maintain solidarity with other Black women.

Summary

Maternal health policy at all levels of administration must be informed by the complexity of psychosocial forces that affect the health of Black mothers. Improvements in the collection of data and the employment of methodologies that specifically address the everyday, nonmaterial, lived experiences of race, gender, and class inequality, oppression, and internalized oppression would greatly increase our understanding of the association of social disadvantage and psychosocial stress with the maternal health of all Black women across social class strata.

My analysis of the role of classism in the lives of Black women may help broaden our understanding of social class as a subjective aspect of life experience observed among African American women, and of how the consciousness of social class differences among the Black women produces ill effects for the disadvantaged and the privileged alike. Few social scientists have taken on the task of conceptualizing poor social outcomes for Black women as directly consequential to the unique historical and contemporary social environment within which they must cope psychologically. Thus, little notice has been given to how classist social processes of various kinds might pose a direct psychosocial threat to all Black mothers.

This perspective of social class, although not denying the severity and uniqueness of the problems faced by disadvantaged Black women, acknowledges that middle-class Black women are not immune from injuries of social class inequality. The undermining of gender/ethnic solidarity among urban Black women by the socio-structural transformation of the Black urban community may have serious implications for the maintenance of good physical and psychosocial health among women from all social class backgrounds. Health policy, then, must be developed in concert with a larger social policy agenda to eradicate all forms of oppression against Black women.

Note

1. By "institutionalized" discrimination, I am referring to the decisions and routinized practices of social institutions that effectually segregate people in some way along socially constructed lines (e.g., race, gender, class) or result in a disproportionate burden being placed on one group of people. Social institutions usually justify these results by calling them unintentional effects of (nonracist/nonsexist/nonclassist) institutional policy.

References

Adler, Nancy E., Thomas Boyce, Margaret A. Chesney, Sheldon Cohen, Susan Folkman, Robert L. Kahn, and S. Leonard Syme. 1994. "Socioeconomic Status and Health: The Challenge of the Gradient." *American Psychologist* 49(1):15-24.

Collins, Patricia Hill. 1991. *Black Feminist Thought: Knowledge, Consciousness, and the Politics of Empowerment.* New York: Routledge.

Davis, Kingsley and Wilbert E. Moore. 1945. "Some Principles of Stratification." *American Sociological Review* 10:242-49.

Dutton, D. B. and S. Levine. 1989. "Overview, Methodological Critique, and Reformulation." In *Pathways to Health,* ed. John P. Bunker et al., 29-69. Menlo Park, CA: The Henry J. Kaiser Family Foundation.

Essed, Philomena. 1991. *Understanding Everyday Racism: An Interdisciplinary Theory.* Newbury Park, CA: Sage.

hooks, bell. 1984. *Feminist Theory from Margin to Center.* Boston: South End Press.

Istvan, Joseph. 1986. "Stress, Anxiety, and Birth Outcomes: A Critical Review of the Evidence." *Psychological Bulletin* 100:331-48.

James, Sherman A. 1993. "Foreword: Racial Differences in Preterm Delivery." In *Racial Differences in Preterm Delivery: Developing a New Research Paradigm,* ed. D. Rowley and H. Tosteson. Supplement to *American Journal of Preventive Medicine* 9:v-vi.

Kaplan, Howard B. 1983. "Psychological Distress in Sociological Context: Toward a General Theory of Psychosocial Stress." In *Psychosocial Stress: Trends in Theory and Research,* ed. Howard B. Kaplan, 195-264. New York: Academic Press, Inc.

Kleinman, Joel C. and Samuel S. Kessel. 1987. "Racial Differences in Low Birth Weight: Trend and Risk Factors." *New England Journal of Medicine* 317:749-53.

Krieger, Nancy et al. 1993. "Racism, Sexism, and Social Class: Implications for Studies of Health, Disease, and Well-Being." In *Racial Differences in Preterm Delivery: Developing a New Research Paradigm* ed. D. Rowley and H. Tosteson. Supplement to *American Journal of Preventive Medicine* 9:82-122.

Levin, Jeffrey S. and Richard S. DeFrank. 1988. "Maternal Stress and Pregnancy Outcomes: A Review of the Psychosocial Literature." *Journal of Psychosomatic Obstetrics and Gynecology* 9:3-16.

Lykes, M. Britton. 1983. "Discrimination and Coping in the Lives of Black Women: Analyses of Oral History Data." *Journal of Social Issues* 39(3):79-100.

McDonald, Katrina Bell. 1995. Sister-Friends: Re-Creating Maternal Support in the African American Community. Ph.D. diss., University of California, Davis.

McLean, Diane E., Kendra Hatfield-Timajchy, Phyllis A. Wingo, and R. Louise Floyd. 1993. "Psychosocial Measurement: Implications for the Study of Preterm Delivery in Black Women." In *Racial Differences in Preterm Delivery: Developing a New Research Paradigm.* Supplement to *American Journal of Preventive Medicine* 9:39-81.

Navarro, Vincente. 1993. *Dangerous to Your Health: Capitalism in Health Care.* New York: Monthly Review Press.

Schoendorf, Kenneth C., Carol J.R. Hogue, Joel C. Kleinman, and Diane Rowley. 1992. "Mortality among Infants of Black as Compared with white College-Educated Parents." *New England Journal of Medicine* 326(23):1522-26.

Sennett, Robert and Jonathan Cobb. 1973. *The Hidden Injuries of Class.* New York: Knopf.

Turner, R. Jay, Blair Wheaton, and Donald A. Lloyd. 1995. "The Epidemiology of Social Stress." *American Sociological Review* 60(1):104-125.

Weitz, Rose. 1994. "Sex, Class, Race: Health and Illness in the United States." *Race, Sex, & Class* 2(1):127-43.

Yamato, Gloria. 1990. "Something about the Subject Makes It Hard to Name." In *Making Faces Making Soul=Haciendo Caras: Creative and Critical Perspectives by Feminists of Color,* ed. G. Anzaldua, 20-24. San Francisco: Aunt Lute Foundation Books.

PART

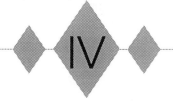

IV

Racial Inequality and Social Policy

RACE UP THE CORPORATE LADDER

The Dilemmas and Contradictions of First-Wave Black Executives

SHARON M. COLLINS

During the 1960s and 1970s in the business world, a new elite of African Americans emerged as professionals and managers in major white corporations. Previous to these decades, employment discrimination in the South restricted Blacks primarily to field jobs in agriculture and to subservient positions, such as maids and cooks in private households (Newman et al. 1978). Even in the North, Blacks were cast as inferior workers and excluded from lucrative industries and establishments and from jobs that white workers found attractive (Newman et al. 1978). Employers' response to modern civil rights legislation, however—in particular, regulatory policies associated with the passage of the Civil Rights Act of 1964—increased dramatically the demand for skilled and college-educated Blacks in labor markets that had once almost universally excluded them.

In this chapter, we look at some of the dilemmas confronting the initial cohort of African American managers who entered professional and managerial jobs in white private industry. Presented here are cases from a panel study of 76 Black executives in major Chicago companies. More than one-half of these executives integrated the professional and managerial job structure of a white corporation during the 1960s and 1970s. I interviewed these managers in 1986 and again in 1992.

We will see that political mandates created opportunities for Black managers during the 1960s and 1970s, but also put behind-the-scenes elements in play that created stumbling blocks in their careers. The majority of people I interviewed (51 of 76) moved into and stayed in, or moved through, a "racialized" set of administrative roles, such as affirmative action and urban affairs functions, created by a company to address the problem of Black constituents. Only a much smaller fraction of careers were entirely in "mainstream" corporate functions that lacked racial implications. Put a different way, Black corporate managers filled race-relevant roles designed to alleviate political pressures associated with a specific period in history. I identified three dilemmas associated with filling such jobs in corporations. These dilemmas create the context to explore a series of career trade-offs and contradictions that confronted this nascent business elite.

Mobility Traps versus Fast Tracks

Racialized jobs represented both mobility traps that sidetracked Black managers out of the corporate job mainstream and, simultaneously, fast tracks on which the first wave of talented Blacks could get ahead in corporations. Thus, the first dilemma associated with emergent opportunities in affirmative action and urban affairs jobs simply was whether or not to take the position. Fifty percent of African Americans recruited into racialized jobs received higher salaries and more prestigious job titles than their Black job counterparts during that period. But what appeared to be good avenues for upward mobility led to exclusion from conventional routes up the corporate ladder and premature career stagnation. Such was the pattern in the career of the frustrated manager.

The Frustrated Manager

In the late 1960s, this 46-year-old man was the second Black ever hired by a major Chicago steel company for a professional/managerial job. Prior to holding this job—which was to administer a federally funded manpower training program run in-house for disadvantaged (i.e., Black) youth—this executive was a social worker employed by the city of Chicago. It was, in fact, through his work with inner-city youth and gang members that company representatives identified him as a potential candidate for the administrative position. This man recalled that during the initial interview, the personnel manager noted that his active ties to Chicago's inner-city youth had positive implications for program development and were a key reason the company was interested in hiring him.

The offer to run the steel company's manpower training program could dramatically alter this man's occupational status. From inner-city social worker, a job where Blacks were already well represented, he would become a manager in the white private sector, where Blacks were historically excluded. On the other hand, his initial response signals his wariness that jobs offered to Blacks during that period could be mobility traps in white corporations. He said: "I told [the personnel manager] that I don't want a nigger job and I don't want to be dead ended."

The frustrated manager defined a "nigger job" as one of "those [corporate] positions pre-identified for Blacks only." He said:

> Those jobs have high-ranking titles and are highly visible but do not have any power in a company. Those jobs are not with the mainstream of [a] company [so they] would [not] turn into any kind of career with the company. [In contrast,] real jobs [were positions by which] good performers could rise [in a company].

In other words, people in "real jobs," but not "nigger jobs," performed valued corporate functions and thereby were able to move up the corporate ladder over time.

Ultimately, he accepted the job because he did not perceive it to be a dead-end position. To the contrary, he perceived it as a springboard that allowed him to develop new work experiences. He believed the job to be valid preparation for a career in personnel management, and he wanted to become a director of personnel. He said, "This was a way to get there [and] that was agreed upon in that interview with [the personnel manager]."

Because the company explicitly recruited him for his networks in the Black community, it is doubtful the personnel director of the steel company in this case seriously viewed the manpower training job as a route to a personnel director's job. Much less doubtful is that management hired this man because they needed a Black person. The company was based in a riot-torn community, and the manpower training program was part of an effort to improve the company's poor record of employment and training of African Americans. At the time, according to this African American executive, the company employed only one other Black professional. Apparently, no one else on board was willing, or capable, in the company's judgment, to fill the function of manpower director.

After two years of running the manpower training program for minorities "very successfully," he was promoted to a newly created community relations job. Two-and-a-half years later, he was promoted in both title and salary to a second, newly created job as a community relations director. In this role, the executive was in charge of the expanding community relations department.

Although the company promoted the frustrated manager and increased his salary because he was serving a function, promotion should not be confused with moving into mainstream personnel areas. When I asked what this last job meant in light of his original career goals, this man admitted he was aware, even then, that his future in the company might be limited. He said:

> You have a little stepladder . . . a logical progression [of personnel functions] you have to go through if you are to ever become a personnel director. I wasn't doing any of that. As far as I could see, the company wanted Black folks to be my only responsibility.

The manager reminded his superiors that his career goals lay elsewhere, but he was not deployed into mainstream personnel. He therefore viewed his movement within the company as promotions "in place," and as evidence that he was not really experiencing mobility in the core corporate structure.

Success is partnered with paradox in this career history: moving up in a racialized corporate area moved this manager further out on a corporate job limb. Because he performed well in an area that was valued in the company at the time, top management rewarded him with higher salaries and kept him assigned to that area. Such rewards, however, excluded him from experiences that would broaden his mastery of more generalized personnel functions. And this lack of generalized experiences further undermined the legitimacy of his claims for promotion to a mainstream personnel job. Therefore, we see a tendency of racialized jobs to sidetrack Black executives. The exchange for establishing an expertise in racialized functions reduced these managers' value and marketability to other areas. People who specialized in racialized roles either lacked, or were perceived to lack, the human capital to compete in mainstream company areas.

The tendency of racialized jobs to marginalize the occupant shows up not only in the case of the frustrated manager. It can be seen, as well, in the case of a company vice president. This executive sought job offers in line management after he completed Sloan's executive training program, but such job offers were not forthcoming, even though the executive program's white cohort received them. The marketplace responded to this man's past stint as an affirmative action manager but overlooked his postgraduate education and success as an MIT-Sloan executive fellow, thus pigeonholing him.

Racialized jobs thus sidetracked careers by siphoning job holders into similar, race-oriented assignments. But doing the job well— ordinarily a desirable trait—created powerful enemies. The frustrated manager indicated that an important part of his job was to identify and correct irregular hiring patterns for which the regional director of personnel was ultimately responsible. When the program to improve minority hiring worked out well, the director of personnel, he said, "was the person who was embarrassed. He was the person who was made to change." Thus, the trade-off for doing his job well—identifying and designing programs to correct hiring biases in the company—was to alienate an important potential mentor, the regional personnel director. The Sloan executive confronted a similar trade-off when a newly appointed executive vice president turned out to be an adversary created during his successful stint in affirmative action.

Racialized jobs, therefore, became mobility traps—dead-end jobs with fancy titles and high salaries—for Black managers who entered white corporations during the 1960s and 1970s. And Blacks who took such jobs confronted a profound career contradiction. On one hand, college-educated African Americans in these jobs in white corporations were "getting ahead." In the case of the frustrated manager, for instance, the job created entrée to Chicago's white business community, a considerably higher salary, and new career vistas. Alternately, however, succeeding in these roles meant that these managers were left behind. The frustrated manager eventually volunteered to be a loaned executive on a citywide corporate project because this route, he said, "represented more training and [potential] mobility." Indeed, as he became known citywide in the early 1970s, he was courted for a personnel job in 10 other companies. He decided to start over with a newly founded computer firm and try, once again, for a personnel director position. Ironically, though, his new job offers involved community work because those companies also were not doing well in the recruitment of minorities.

The comments of a vice president of human resources for a clothing manufacturer also illustrate the trade-offs associated with these positions. In 1967, this man was the first and the only Black professional working for a huge munitions plant in southern Indiana facing intense federal scrutiny. The personnel director approached and offered him the affirmative action job along with a salary he characterized as "a pretty good deal." Yet this man agonized before accepting the position because he was trained to be, and working as, a research chemist. The field of affirmative action depended on the existence of specific public policy. And, like the frustrated steel company manager, he recognized its failure to develop a set of work skills that could branch into nonrace-related personnel areas. He said:

> [Affirmative action] is the kind of field where . . . there's not an awful lot . . . to learn. My biggest concern was I was going to end up becoming the guy who handles all the EEO problems in the corporation. I'm thinking, [even] back in the early 1970s, . . . that if something ever happened to affirmative action, where it wasn't popular anymore, I wouldn't have any other marketable skills.

Indeed, this man's concern about the future labor market for Blacks in racialized corporate roles was warranted. These politically useful jobs in white companies become economically expendable when federal government pressures on companies wane and the problems of Blacks lose importance. For example, in the 1980s, the restrained federal approach to racial issues and the relative political quiescence of Blacks, in conjunction with economic transitions, made these jobs rational targets for companies to dismantle (Collins 1993). Moreover, when racialized jobs erode, there are few places in the company that will absorb the previous job holders (Collins 1993).

Of course, because the role is a contradiction, it works in the opposite way as well. That is, filling racialized jobs also worked to Black executives' advantage. For instance, the vice president/Sloan executive, who also completed postgraduate work in physics and engineering, initially accepted the offer to become an equal employment opportunity manager because, he said, "I wanted to get into management. That was the first and only opportunity that I felt I was gong to get." This man planned to use the job to create a stepping stone rather than to build a permanent oasis. It was, as he put it, a chance "[to] let me get my nose somewhere [and] to get something for myself." Ultimately, he did get something for himself when he resisted the market tendency to continue to slot him into racialized jobs. His training at Sloan positioned him to get broader opportunities in the job market, and he went on to become a vice president in a major firm.

Moreover, a company's dependence on federal contracts, its vulnerability to contract compliance pressures, and initial corporate uncertainty about program development gave racialized jobs value. The same executive noted, "Nobody knew how to do it, but everybody knew it would have to be good." The job, therefore, anointed Black job holders with status in the corporate hierarchy that no other Black person in the company had. As this manager explained, it gave them "a manager title, exposure to the company's inner works, and visibility to the corporation's top people."

Finally, some individuals used racialized jobs to find mentors who could guide and help propel them into core corporate functions. Such was the case of the Sloan executive, who developed an affirmative action program with a company senior executive vice president and who came away with a powerful and active mentor. He said, "He was a white guy who . . . got to know me. Supported a lot of things that I wanted to do. And said, 'You know, you've got a lot of capability and it's a waste to keep you here in EEO.' " Ultimately, occupying a racialized job created a window of opportunity that this man used well.

These careers represent the struggle of Blacks to succeed in a white corporate world where Blacks were anomalies. In this unique context, race worked both for them and against them. Executives were approached for racialized jobs because their visibility brought them to the attention of senior management. Such jobs, in turn, were both potential springboards for, and hazards to, entering mainstream corporate training and competition. With an eye on both factors, these people negotiated their conditions for taking affirmative action and urban affairs positions. In the previous case of the vice president of operations, the racialized job was the vehicle through which he got a new chance, a mentor, and a year of additional specialized and prestigious training.

The contradiction, however, is that racialized roles added to their struggle. This role also pigeonholed executives into affirmative action slots and robbed executives of mentors.

Individual Aspirations versus Group Commitment

There is a second dilemma associated with racialized jobs. The decision to stay in these jobs brought respondents' career aspirations into direct conflict with their racial identity and their commitment to racial group solidarity. Racialized jobs struck a familiar cord with these executives because they addressed social and political issues that permeated Blacks' existence. The problems of Black people were problems that these men both lived and intellectually understood. The majority of these executives were part of the first wave of Blacks in the white private sector to benefit from civil rights pressures. As such, they acknowledged their debt to the decades of struggle and expressed a strong obligation to give something back to the Black community. Thus, when offered a job intended to assist Blacks, some welcomed the jobs as their chance to help channel previously withheld resources (i.e., jobs and contracts) back into the Black community. But, once harnessed to the job by a commitment that linked their sense of group obligation with the administrative interests of a company, executives became pigeonholed and entrenched in a racialized area. The recollections of a 55-year-old director of affirmative action reflect this dilemma.

This individual began his private sector career in catalog operations management for a retail company in the mid-1960s. In 1969, in response to his complaints about the lack of management opportunities for Blacks in the firm, the CEO asked him to set up the equal employment opportunity function. In 1992, he was still head of affirmative action for his third employer. Noting the disparity between where his career started and where it had gone, I asked him why he did not move back into a mainstream function. He noted a variety of factors, including the following:

> I was trained for the operations end of the business but stayed in the
> [affirmative action] end because I felt . . . I had an obligation to do

something [for other Black people] about that time, you know. Prior to that I really wasn't doing anything other than helping myself. But then in the 1960s people became really motivated . . . "Black is beautiful" and the whole concept. And [the job] provided me with an opportunity to make a social contribution and also to continue to be successful in business.

At that time, he idealistically viewed affirmative action as beneficial to the business world because of its potential to change the business environment. He also viewed it as a contribution to the Black community because of its potential to generate resources and opportunities for less advantaged Black people. With pride in his voice, he recalled that he was a member of one of the first Chicago coalitions to address aggressively the issue of hardcore unemployment. He also offered what he considered a critical distinction between his generation of Black managers and the succeeding generations of Black businesspeople. The new wave of Black managers, he argued, "do not have the same sense of social responsibility that we had . . . that is, [they don't feel] an obligation to those back home [i.e., other Black people]." Paradoxically, he also believed that taking the affirmative action function was a misstep in the construction of his career. "If I had to go back and do it all over again," he said, "I would not stay in affirmative action. Them that brings in the dollars is where the most opportunity is. I advise my sons . . . stay out of the staff functions, although those functions are very necessary."

This manager's dissonance raises the question of whether, in the context of corporate culture, some Blacks' sense of solidarity and responsibility worked against individual aspirations and against their mainstream development. Indeed, respondents who did permanently transfer out of racialized areas viewed such jobs as stigmatized in corporate culture. Moreover, to hasten their departures, some quickly pawned their jobs off on Black replacements who, they said, "cared more," or who had, they said, "closer ties to the Black community."

Other respondents commented explicitly on the trade-offs between individual aspirations and community commitment that occurred in accepting racialized jobs. The case of a 45-year-old director of an urban investment program for a major consumer company provides one illustration. Before entering the private sector, this man spent a brief period as a professional basketball player and learned that he enjoyed interacting with people. Consequently, when he was hired in the early 1970s by a large insurance agency, he requested a position in personnel. From that point, his jobs and experiences evolved smoothly in mainstream personnel functions, and he let it be known that his eventual goal was to become a regional personnel vice president.

Several years had passed when a senior vice president in the company offered him a position as division personnel manager. Although the title does not signal a racial component, in fact the job was a specialty position focusing on strengthening the company's affirmative action program. Like the frustrated manager in the steel company, this executive knew that to progress up the corporate ladder in personnel, he needed to remain in—and successfully carry out—a series of mainstream functions. However, he took the racialized job offer. He said, "I felt that if I had to make a choice, affirmative action for me was the most important thing. Because the rest [of the company's personnel functions] were going to take care of themselves." He subsequently moved in and out of racialized positions and occupied one when I first interviewed him.

In his attempt to balance his community commitment and his career goals, he repeatedly made career decisions that he knew worked against his individual interests. He said he knew that "people would perceive me as someone who was not being developed," and that, although he deeply desired it, he said, "[I] probably would never become a regional vice president." After a brief pause, he added, "because I'm Black, the company did probably use me to a certain extent." Yet after this comment, his race consciousness seemed to lead him to a different and (I thought) intriguing conclusion. He said, "But I didn't . . . mind using myself, if I could get more . . . Black folks into the company. So it's hard for me to know what the truth is. Who's using who, and how much?"

Those words sum up this executive's personal and career-defining commitments to use his position to enhance the socioeconomic resources of the group. He was not alone. A majority of executives who stayed in racialized areas also mentioned their sense of obligation to use their presence in the company to make a difference and to give something back to the Black community. For example, an urban affairs director explained that staying in his job was his duty and "my way of civil righting back then." A director of corporate contribution explained his position, saying:

Community affairs had been done in a little different way . . . by two other people who were white community-activist types. They were doing the job as agents of the company. And, while I'm sure people would say that I was doing the same thing, I didn't see it that way. I saw it more as the other direction. And [I] think that [I made] some breakthroughs in that area.

A manager of government affairs noted:

We had a small group of about eight of us that met. We were all community relations managers for major companies. We'd meet informally for lunch because we felt that our role was to facilitate some progress in the community. And we couldn't do that if we didn't talk together and make a solid front.

Present Status versus Future Opportunity

The third dilemma is related to the problem of mobility traps and racialized jobs. This quandary was whether or not to exchange a racialized job for one of less status but more potential for future attainment. Executives in racialized jobs were greatly rewarded because they handled new and unpredictable race-related contingencies facing companies. As a rule, racialized jobs were first created in a company when a respondent filled them. Because these functions were new, top management looked to these executives for guidance and direction in shaping these areas. The ability to provide guidance gave these managers a unique status in companies. For example, managers who filled these jobs were on a first-name basis with corporate CEOs and civic leaders. They also were on a first-name basis with Black nationalists from the streets, and their ability to cross-walk between these conflicting groups made them some of the favorite sons in corporations during the 1960s civil rights era.

A 52-year-old man explained his motivation for staying in racialized jobs. In 1986, this executive worked for the same private sector employer that recruited him from his job at the Urban League in 1967. In both his first job as manpower coordinator and his job as district personnel manager, which he held when I interviewed him initially, his function in the company was, he said, "always something relating to the Black community." He said, "[I] examined issues in the community, [and was] used as a negotiator, [and] fixed problems with Blacks" whenever they existed. Initially, these assignments fit in well with the overall direction he had envisioned for his career. He said:

> My experience, both professional and in life, prepared me for that role in the company. That's what I do best. And I don't want to, didn't expect to, do anything more. The way I cajole myself, perhaps, is that somebody was going to do that job. And I felt that I would do that job with a sense of the community in mind. Not just because it would be a good job to earn money, and get you in and among people of ilk. Although it does. [Question: What do you mean by people of "ilk"?] I'm talking about people with money, and influence, and class.

The executive then paused to chuckle as if reflecting on other incentives that influenced his career deliberations. Perhaps he was struck, as I was, by his use of the term "cajole" as seemingly synonymous with "fooled," and wondered if altruism was the only motivation shaping his decisions. His next comment revealed, both to himself and to me, an equally significant reason he agreed to take the role. He said:

> I made more money than I had ever dreamed of. [And] ordinarily, Sharon, I probably wouldn't have very much to do with [people of ilk]. [Not] if I was in some other kind of job. It is not [my station in life]. Socially, that is not my place. You see, I represent a billion dollar business here when I'm out there. And [there's] not much . . . not many places out there that are not open. Open to me. And that was one of the things that I discovered here. That's why I stayed.

Other executives echoed his sentiments, saying they stayed in racialized jobs, in part, because of the perceived benefits of such jobs. During the 1960s and 1970s, executives viewed such jobs as offering faster mobility, greater freedom and authority, and higher visibility and access to white corporate power brokers than the mainstream jobs of their Black contemporaries. This new and distinctive social status also gave executives an aura of power and prestige in the eyes of their Black peers. The recollections of the 55-year-old

affirmative action director to whom I referred earlier helps to illu-
minate this second point.

I asked this affirmative action director if he ever tried to move
back into the mainstream after he took on equal employment opportunity functions. To my surprise, he said that he turned down a
buyer's job offered to him by a vice president in merchandising with
his first employer. The executive said, "I was stubborn at that point.
No, I didn't want that." Given that buyers were key people in that
organization and that the job was a stepping stone to higher-paying
positions, his refusal signals the attractiveness of racialized positions in companies during the civil rights era. He said:

> Remember now, this [equal opportunity] stuff was exciting and there's
> a trap that you get into. Those of us who are in this kind of area talk
> about it all the time. It's kind of a golden handcuffs trap. We used to
> go on the convention circuit around the country . . . the Urban League
> and the NAACP, promoting our individual corporations. We were
> visible. We were representing the company. We had big budgets. I
> mean, you know, you go to every convention. And [you can] get
> yourself two or three suites and entertain all the delegates. You could
> spend $15,000 or $20,000 at a convention. I never had that kind of
> money to spend, to sign a check, so it was very attractive.

To fully appreciate this manager's perspective, we also should
remember that the economic rewards and social status that accompanied racialized positions were unimaginable luxuries to Blacks—
in this or any employment sector—in the years preceding federal
antibias legislation. Executives who stayed in racialized jobs were
ambitious men who saw themselves doing the best they could do
given the limited job possibilities that Blacks historically had in
white companies. Their process of accounting weighed the jobs'
perquisites against the void in managerial opportunities for Blacks
in white firms. Racialized managerial positions appeared to be a
way to sidestep the career stagnation common among the handful
of Blacks who previously attained management roles but remained
trapped in low-level positions.

These executives thought that racialized jobs were their best
opportunities for social and economic advancement. A 53-year-old
director of corporate contributions said, "That was the place for us

to be." But many now see the downside of that decision. With the benefit of hindsight, the affirmative action director explained, "I believe that had I stayed in operations [I would have] continued to move up and that's where the clout is. But the opportunity just wasn't there [for Blacks] when I first started with that company." After a slight pause he then added, somewhat ruefully, "Things changed, and it is now."

Final Comments on Careers

If these executives had had Black role models, aggressive mentors, or more knowledge about company hierarchies, would they have made different career choices? In other words, did these men need mentors and role models to perceive alternative career options as truly possible? The district personnel manager to whom I referred above may, in retrospect, be satisfied with his career choices, but he now also understands that visibility among white business elites is not the same as having organizational power. The affirmative action manager I wrote about now knows that, in the long run, social commitments are secondary to business decisions and important only in support of a company's profit-generating function.

People who moved into, and stayed in, racialized jobs were as ambitious as those who got out of them. Indeed, and ironically, ambition played a large role in motivating these people to stay where they were. In the 1960s and the early 1970s, racialized jobs represented opportunities for educated, ambitious Blacks to become stars in their companies. Paradoxically, the most attractive features—such as starting titles and salary, freedom, and visibility—also lessened some executives' motivation to move into the companies' mainstream areas.

Because the backgrounds of these people were devoid of exposure to the work world of major corporations, career decision making often was done in a vacuum. Deciphering the rules for upward mobility was a hit-and-miss proposition. Moreover, because they were the shock troops for the future generation of Black managers, they were confronted with open hostility. In the absence of meaningful sponsorship and practical support, they turned to each other for help in making career decisions, which was a case, one man said, "of the blind leading the blind."

References

Collins, Sharon. 1993. "Blacks on the Bubble: The Vulnerability of Black Executives in White Corporations." *Sociological Quarterly* 3:429-48.

Newman, Dorothy K., Nancy J. Amidei, Barbara L. Carter, Dawn Day, William J. Kruvant, and Jack S. Russell. 1978. *Protest, Politics and Prosperity: Black Americans and White Institutions, 1940-1975.* New York: Pantheon.

PART

V

Changes in Ideology and Cultural Myths

AFFIRM EQUALITY,
OPPOSE RACIST SCAPEGOATING

Myths and Realities
of Affirmative Action

STEVEN J. ROSENTHAL

◆◆◆

Item: Richard Herrnstein, co-author of The Bell Curve, with his last racist dying breath proclaimed, "Whatever else this book does, it will destroy affirmative action in the universities."

Peter Brimelow, in *The Bell Curve Debate*, p. 373

Item: In July 1995, the day after Governor Pete Wilson got the University of California Board of Regents to outlaw affirmative action, the *New York Times* reported that the leader of the neo-Nazi Aryan Nations, Richard Butler, praised Wilson for "beginning to wake up" to Aryan views.

Item: The antiaffirmative action crusade in California is being spearheaded by National Association of Scholars (NAS). Over the past few years, the NAS has received millions of dollars from the five leading right-wing foundations: Lynde and Harry Bradley (which also paid "Bradley scholar" Charles Murray to write *The Bell Curve*), Adolph Coors, John Olin, Smith Richardson, and Sarah Scaife.

Affirmative action consists of procedures to identify, recruit, or promote qualified members of disadvantaged minority groups and women in order to overcome the results of past discrimination and to deter employers from engaging in discriminatory practices in the present.

Conservative opponents of affirmative action often deny its achievements, whereas liberal defenders often deny its limitations. A review of the origins and history of affirmative action shows that affirmative action was obtained through militant, multiracial struggle and produced real gains and benefits for working-class and middle-class women and men of all racial and ethnic backgrounds. Affirmative action is a limited reform that was devised and implemented by the government and corporations within the framework of a declining U.S. capitalist system. The history of affirmative action reform demonstrates the inadequacy of reformism and the need for a more revolutionary strategy to destroy racism.

Affirmative action was not designed to alleviate the terrible conditions faced by most Black, Latino, and women workers. For example, the Urban Institute recently estimated that 53 percent of Black men aged 25 to 34 are either unemployed or earn too little to lift a family of four from poverty (Wilkins 1995). Affirmative action has not reduced poverty, reduced unemployment, raised wages, or even kept them from falling. Affirmative action has not prevented capitalists from eliminating jobs, converting full-time jobs into part-time or temporary jobs, or relocating production to low-wage areas. Affirmative action has not prevented politicians and capitalists from cutting school budgets, closing schools, raising tuition, cutting grants while increasing interest rates on loans, and firing teachers. Affirmative action and other antiracist reforms under capitalism demonstrate that reform can barely make a dent in the problem of racism. Revolutionary change is needed to eliminate poverty, provide work and education for everyone, and establish an egalitarian society.

The cry of "reverse discrimination" put forward by racist conservatives is a myth created by politicians and their capitalist backers for the purpose of scapegoating racial minorities. It is capitalists, not Blacks, Latinos, immigrants, women, or "angry white men," who are responsible for the worsening problems that working-class and middle-class people confront.[1]

The capitalist ruling class, the wealthiest one percent of the U.S. population, is the class that controls the economy, both political parties, the mass media, and the universities. Racism is crucial to the ability of the capitalist class to exploit the working class economically and control the working class politically. Ever since the days of slavery, capitalists have depended upon racism to extract maximum profits from the labor of African, Native American, Latino, Asian, and European workers. Ever since the days of slavery, capitalists have fostered and exploited racist divisions as a necessary divide-and-rule strategy for political domination over the working class.

During the 1960s, U.S. capitalists dominated the global capitalist system. U.S. rulers could afford to make small antiracist concessions to head off the growth of a more revolutionary antiracist movement. Since the 1970s, however, U.S. capitalism has declined greatly both internally and internationally. The entire world capitalist system is in a long-term crisis of "overproduction," which means that capitalists are struggling to sell what workers produce. Competition for markets between U.S., European, and Asian capitalists is rapidly intensifying, dissolving the anticommunist alliances of the cold war period.

U.S. capitalists are forced by the crisis of overproduction and sharpening competition to drive down their costs every way they can. They must cut back the welfare state reforms that they set up during the 1930s and the 1960s to undercut the growth of revolutionary communist movements. Corporations have destroyed or weakened labor unions, downsized their work forces, moved operations to low-wage countries, and replaced full-time with part-time and temporary workers. Capitalists are drastically cutting back welfare programs, unemployment insurance, health care, housing assistance, education, environmental protection, social security, and Medicare.

These cutbacks hurt all workers, but most cutbacks have a racist impact and fall most heavily on Black and Latino workers. The capitalists cannot impose these cutbacks without greatly increasing their promotion of racist ideas. Racist ideas justify the cutbacks with stereotypes of undeserving beneficiaries; racist ideas fool some whites into thinking that cutbacks will only hurt somebody else. Racist scapegoating encourages whites to blame Blacks, Latinos, and immigrants for worsening conditions that capitalists are inflicting on the entire working class. Racist ideology justifies police brutality and increased incarceration of minorities, and it justifies the expansion of the police state to suppress future revolt against intensifying racist oppression. The capitalists' attack on affirmative action is a key element in this broader racist offensive. Diverting anger over joblessness and a capitalist system in decline away from the bosses and onto other workers is a crucial aspect of capitalist control over the working class.

During the 1930s, a similar global capitalist crisis and intensification of racism led to the rise of fascism in many countries and to World War II. Fascism is capitalist rule by the most violently racist, nationalistic, sexist, and anticommunist methods. Capitalist rulers abandon their facade of democracy when they need a much more repressive fascist system to drive down the living conditions of the working class and to mobilize society for aggressive war. The United States is in the early stages of fascism and preparation for a third imperialist world war.

To avert this catastrophe requires the building of a mass multiracial movement against racism, fascism, and war. This movement must be multiracial because racist and nationalist divisions are the main weapons used by the ruling class to keep workers weak and make themselves strong. Multiracial and international unity is the main weapon that the working class must forge to defeat the ruling class. The struggle against racism must be guided by a revolutionary anticapitalist strategy rather than a reformist strategy. It is impossible to stop racist attacks on affirmative action merely by calling for a "level playing field." It is an illusion to believe that this capitalist system will ever create a level playing field. Capitalists own the "playing field;" capitalists make the "rules," the laws; and capitalists own and control the "referees," the government. When workers compete with each other on any playing field, capitalists always win and the working class always loses. The working class must level the entire capitalist system, not just the playing field. The only affirmative action that can eliminate inequalities of social class, race, and gender is doing away with capitalism.

Origins and Achievements
of Affirmative Action

During the first phase of the antiracist movement of the 1950s and 1960s, the primarily southern civil rights movement, Black workers and students and their white allies organized massive waves of demonstrations, boycotts, sit-ins, and voter registration drives. They faced beatings, arrests, and murders at the hands of police, sheriffs, and the Ku Klux Klan (KKK). The federal government's inaction exposed the United States throughout the world as a racist society and radicalized civil rights activists. SNCC leader John Lewis tried to give a speech at the 1963 March on Washington condemning the Kennedy administration for its failure to protect civil rights workers in the South, but the march leadership censored the speech (Zinn, 1964:190). Just as workers' sit-down strikes during the 1930s forced the ruling class to recognize labor unions, the civil rights movement forced the ruling class to dismantle its Jim Crow system of legal segregation and to pass civil rights, voting rights, and other legislation.

The second phase was a period of nationwide Black rebellion and revolutionary organization from the mid-1960s through the early 1970s. The civil rights movement had achieved important victories, but the majority of Blacks still faced racist conditions of poverty, unemployment, police brutality, and segregated schools and housing. Urban Blacks rose up in more than 600 rebellions in every major U.S. city between 1964 and 1970. Black parents and students organized militant protests in schools and colleges to demand equal educational opportunities. Black workers and students also participated in massive protests against the U.S. government's imperialist war in Southeast Asia.

The Johnson and Nixon administrations responded to these militant protests with both greater repression and further reforms. Amid racist calls for "law and order," Johnson and Nixon increased the level of repression by sending National Guard and Army divisions into Black communities, developing FBI counterintelligence programs to attempt to infiltrate and destroy militant organizations, and allocating billions of dollars to triple the size of urban police departments, provide riot training, and equip them with everything from tear gas to SWAT teams.

While the ruling class was beefing up this apparatus of repression, it also instituted further reforms. Affirmative action was one of these reforms. It was based on Title VII of the 1964 Civil Rights Act, which prohibited discrimination in hiring for jobs. The Equal Employment Opportunity Commission (EEOC) was formed to administer the act, and in 1968, the EEOC instructed businesses with federal government contracts to take "affirmative action" to increase employment of Black workers. Affirmative action soon was expanded to cover admissions to educational institutions, and separate programs were established to set aside a small percentage of government contracts for minority businesses. In the early 1970s, affirmative action coverage was expanded to include Latinos, Native Americans, women, and handicapped people.

As a result of affirmative action, minority and women workers gained access to jobs from which they had been almost totally excluded. Substantial job gains occurred in the building trades and in city, county, state, and federal government agencies. The percentage of Black firefighters nationwide, for example, increased from 2.5 percent in 1960 to 11.5 percent in 1990. The Los Angeles Fire Department was 94 percent white and 100 percent male in 1973; in 1995, the LAFD is 26 percent Latino, 13 percent Black, 6 percent Asian, and 4 percent women. Affirmative action also increased employment of Black workers in the steel and textile industries. In the steel industry, programs were established that increased access of Black workers to skilled jobs. In the southern textile industry, affirmative action opened up jobs to Black women for the first time. Although concentrated in lower-paying factory jobs, Black women earned three times as much as they had earned previously as domestic workers (Ezorsky 1991).

Studies demonstrate that employment of minority and women workers has increased more at companies that have affirmative action policies than at companies that do not. Moreover, incomes of Black and women workers at affirmative action companies average five to six thousand dollars higher than at nonaffirmative action companies. Minority and women workers are more likely to hold professional and technical jobs at affirmative action companies (Herring 1995:3). Minority enrollment in colleges and graduate and professional schools also increased substantially during the late 1960s and the early 1970s. The percentage of Black adults with college degrees increased from 5 percent in 1960 to 12 percent in 1990. Similarly, the proportion of Black households with an annual income of $50,000 or higher rose from 5.2 percent in 1967 to 12.1 percent in 1991. (Hacker 1992).

Interestingly and significantly, it has been shown that white males have also benefited from affirmative action. The very same studies that show that Blacks and women have benefited from affirmative action also show that the incomes of white males employed at affirmative action companies are higher than the incomes of white males at nonaffirmative action companies. Moreover, studies have shown that "when affirmative action brings whites into greater contact with people of color it enables whites to see that people of color are intelligent and hard working. Indeed, it is white men who work where there are no provisions for affirmative action" who are most racist in their attitudes. In sum, affirmative action has produced "higher incomes, better jobs, and more coworker acceptance" (Herring 1997:11).

White working-class youth have also benefited because affirmative action expanded educational opportunities during the late 1960s and early 1970s. Black college enrollment increased by 95 percent between 1967 and 1972, rising from 370,000 to 727,000. But during that same period, white enrollment increased from 5.9 million to 7.5 million students. In New York's City University system, the majority of the students entering under new "open admissions" policies were working-class whites.

This consistent pattern demonstrates that many Black workers benefited from affirmative action, and that white workers benefited at the same time. These results show that antiracism often has immediately and concretely benefited both Black and white workers. When capitalists cannot use racist divisions to lower wages, all workers benefit. When Blacks and whites work together, white workers and professionals are more likely to discard racist stereotypes and unite in class solidarity with Black workers in a struggle that benefits all workers. Affirmative action thus helps to provide a basis for the multiracial unity that is essential for fighting against any aspect of capitalist exploitation.

Limitations of Affirmative Action and Other Antiracist Reforms under Capitalism

From the very beginning, affirmative action was a reform that was designed and implemented by capitalists and their political servants within the framework of capitalist control over the working class. Affirmative action began in the construction industry, where craft unions belonging to the American Federation of Labor (AFL) were 99 percent white. (By contrast, industrial unions formed under communist leadership during the 1930s by the Congress of Industrial Organizations [CIO] included several million Black workers in their ranks.) In 1969, President Nixon and the big construction companies adopted the "Philadelphia Plan," a plan for increasing Black employment on federally funded construction projects. By expanding the pool of skilled Black construction workers, the Philadelphia Plan increased the percentage of nonunion labor on federally funded projects from 20 percent to 40 percent and substantially lowered construction craft workers' wages and benefits. Politicians increased the number of white and Black workers competing for what soon became a shrinking number of jobs. If white workers had included Black workers in their unions on an equal basis from the beginning, white and Black workers could have united to defend union wages and benefits and to demand enough jobs for all workers. The racist union leadership played right into the hands of the bosses' antiunion strategy (Quadago 1994:61-87).

Since the mid-1970s, affirmative action has been carried out in a declining and decaying American capitalist economic and political system. The capitalists' divide-and-conquer strategy applied under Nixon as the "Philadelphia Plan" has now become part of a plan to incite racist conflict over a shrinking pie.

◆ Since the mid-1970s, median family income for Blacks has declined from 64 percent of white median family income to 58 percent today.

◆ Since the 1970s, real income levels of the working class have declined by 20 percent. Younger production workers' wages have fallen 30 percent.

◆ Throughout these two decades, unemployment rates for Black workers consistently have been two to two-and-one-half times as high as those for white workers, regardless of educational levels.

◆ In the early 1970s, Blacks were only 4 percent of the college professors, 3 percent of the physicians, and 2 percent of the scientists and engineers in the United States, and the percentages are the same today.

◆ Since the beginning of the 1980s, nearly all gains in real income have gone to the richest one percent of the population. This top one percent increased their income by 75 percent during the 1980s, from $312,206 to $548,970.

◆ Within both the white and the Black populations, income distribution has become much more unequal. The rich capitalists of every racial group have gotten richer, whereas the poorest workers of every racial group have gotten poorer. Black workers were particularly hard hit during the early 1980s by Reagan-era cutbacks that targeted programs serving large numbers of Blacks. White workers, including many college-trained white-collar workers, were hard hit during the post-1989 recession by massive corporate downsizing and restructuring (Chideya 1995; Hacker 1992; Edsall and Edsall 1991).

There are other antiracist reforms that politicians and capitalists have transformed into strategies for perpetuating or increasing racism, as indicated by the following examples.

School desegregation was implemented through busing plans that exempted wealthy suburban communities and private schools and desegregated deteriorating, underfinanced urban schools. Racist politicians instigated violent "antibusing" movements and imposed budget cuts for schools and city services. Schools were rapidly resegregated through a combination of tracking programs and "white flight" from urban public schools. When racist politicians in Boston launched a violent antibusing campaign in 1974 to 1975, the International Committee Against Racism (INCAR) organized a multiracial effort to defend integration and to demand better schools.

Desegregation of housing was promised by the 1968 Housing Act, but this act, passed by Congress while soldiers protected them from the rebellions triggered by the assassination of Martin Luther King, Jr., was a political compromise between liberals and conservatives in which no means of enforcement was included in the law (Massey and Denton 1993). Meanwhile, red-lining (bankers drawing red lines on maps to designate white and Black areas of a city) and blockbusting (using racist fears to convert areas from white to Black) made bankers and speculators rich, fleeced both white and Black workers, and created new patterns of segregated communities.

Death penalty laws were declared unconstitutional by the U.S. Supreme Court in 1967 on the grounds that they were applied in an arbitrary and capricious manner (that is, applied mostly to Blacks). Laws were rewritten in most states and approved by the Court, and a handful of whites were executed in the late 1970s to demonstrate that things had changed. Since the early 1980s, states have reverted to the old racist pattern. A majority of the population on death row is Black or Latino, and statistical analysis shows that the death penalty is between 5 and 13 times more likely to be imposed when a Black kills a white than when a white kills a Black or when killer and victim are of the same race. The U.S. Supreme Court acknowledged this statistical pattern in a 1987 case but ruled that it did not matter. Under this criminal justice system, the more things change, the more they remain the same.

These examples show that the ruling class employs many methods to weaken or destroy antiracist reforms: (1) making white and Black workers compete for a dwindling number of jobs; (2) making desegregation of schools and housing merely a transition to resegregation; (3) passing antiracist laws without putting any teeth into them; (4) doing away with racist laws and then replacing them with similar racist laws; and (5) inciting racist "backlashes" against antiracist reforms. All of these methods have been used against affirmative action. The result is that there is very little of affirmative action left.

Affirmative Action Has
Been "Chopped Down to a Stump"

A California proaffirmative action activist accurately wrote that "over the past twenty years the U.S. Supreme Court has already chopped the scope of affirmative action programs down to a stump" (Jones 1995).

♦ The Supreme Court, in the 1978 Bakke case, made "quotas" illegal. The consequences of that decision can be seen clearly from the following fact: "No federal contractor has ever been debarred from doing business with the federal government because it did not meet its goals. In fact, contractors regularly fail to meet their yearly goals" (Giraldo 1995).

♦ The Supreme Court, in the 1989 *Richmond, Virginia versus Croson County* case, declared most "set-aside" programs illegal, even when their intent is to remedy previous exclusion.

♦ The Supreme Court, in the 1989 *Wards Cove Packing Company* decision, shifted the burden of proof of discrimination onto minorities, even when there is a demonstrable disparity in employment. In other words, even when companies have hired no minority workers in the past and are hiring virtually no minority workers in the present, those who are denied jobs have the burden of proving to a court's satisfaction that they were personally discriminated against in order to justify creating affirmative action procedures!

♦ While the Supreme Court was "chopping down" affirmative action, it had plenty of help during the 1980s from Reagan appointees Clarence Thomas, head of the Equal Employment Opportunity Commission, and Clarence Pendleton, chair of the Civil Rights Commission, both of whom were sworn enemies of affirmative action. Thomas drastically cut back class-action suits, reduced staff, shifted the burden of proof from employers to employees, and allowed the backlog of cases to grow to 46,000 and processing time to increase to 10 months. Complicit liberal Democrats did nothing to prevent Thomas from sabotaging the EEOC, just as the liberal Democrats on the Senate Judiciary Committee refused to attack his racist record during his Supreme Court nomination hearings.

Affirmative action today thus cannot require any positive results (quotas); past and present exclusion of minorities cannot be accepted as evidence of discrimination; an impossible burden of proof is on the individual worker or student; and monitoring and enforcement agencies have been virtually destroyed. Under these circumstances, the claim that minority workers and students "enjoy special preferences" at the expense of whites would be laughable if it were not such a dangerous lie!

Refuting the Most Common Arguments against Affirmative Action

Attacks on affirmative action come in many disguises. Below is a critical analysis of the most commonly heard arguments against affirmative action.

1. *People should be hired or admitted to universities on the basis of merit, not racial preference.* This is actually an argument in favor of affirmative action that has been hijacked by opponents of affirmative action.

The "merit" argument is based mainly on the notion that standardized test scores measure who is most qualified for admissions to college and hiring for jobs. Standardized tests, from the SATs and the ACTs used in college admissions to the "blue books" and "red books" used for hiring police and firefighters were created with conscious discriminatory intent and have always been racially and class biased. They do not measure motivation, talent, nor self-discipline, and they do not predict ability to do the work. They have served as racist and class-biased devices of exclusion, perpetuating the inequalities in educational opportunity that minority and working-class students face.

The merit argument also conveniently ignores the university programs of special preference for upper-class children that have existed for centuries. "Legacy" preference for the children of alumni is the true example of special preference for the less qualified. A recent study found that, during the past 40 years, one-fifth of Harvard's students have received admissions preference because their parents attended the school. Affluent white legacies are three times more likely to be accepted to Harvard than other applicants. Similar patterns prevail at other Ivy League schools, such as Yale, Dartmouth, and the University of Pennsylvania.

Although Ivy League administrators had claimed that legacies were well qualified, the U.S. Department of Education's Office for Civil Rights (OCR) found that "the average admitted legacy at Harvard between 1981 and 1988 was significantly less qualified than the average admitted nonlegacy" (Larew 1994:230-1). The OCR study concluded that at most elite universities during the 1980s, the legacy was by far the biggest piece of the preferential pie. "At Harvard, a legacy is about twice as likely to be admitted as a Black or Hispanic student. . . . Marginally qualified legacies outnumbered all Black, Mexican-American, Native American and Puerto Rican enrollees put together" (Larew 1994).

Equally hypocritical were the University of California Regents, who, in July 1995, voted to abolish affirmative action. Whereas they voted to exclude thousands of fully qualified Black and Latino students from the University of California system, they conveniently took no action to end the annual admission of the more than one thousand mostly athlete "special admits." As Tom Hayden and Connie Rice noted, "winning Rose Bowls was important enough to the Regents to merit an exception to their strict academic standards" (Hayden and Rice 1995:264-66).

Two recent studies show that Black workers continue to face the traditional racist pattern of "last hired and first fired." First, "a 1990 Urban Institute study utilizing pairs of Black and white job applicants with identical credentials found that in 476 hirings in Washington, DC, and Chicago, "unequal treatment of Black job seekers was entrenched and widespread, contradicting claims that hiring practices today either favor Blacks or are effectively color blind. In 20 percent of the audits, whites were able to advance further through the hiring process than equally qualified Blacks. . . . A similar study using Hispanic job applicants found them discriminated against 29 percent of the time in San Diego and 33 percent of the time in Chicago" (Wilson 1995:17). Second, a study by the Office of Personnel Management of the federal government found that "Black federal employees were more than twice as likely to be fired than their white, Hispanic, or Asian counterparts." Blacks were 52 percent of the workers dismissed during 1994, according to the study by sociologist Hilary Silver (*New York Times*, April 20, 1995). These studies show that current hiring and firing decisions are based on white racial preference rather than merit and, therefore, demonstrate the continuing need for affirmative action.

2. *Affirmative action has achieved its objectives and is no longer needed.* If an "objective" of affirmative action is to guarantee "equal opportunity," then the studies of hiring and firing cited above demonstrate that this objective has not been achieved. If an objective of affirmative action is to promote greater equality of occupational and educational attainment between Blacks and whites, the facts show that racial inequalities are at least as great as they were during the 1960s.

The federal "Glass Ceiling Commission," in its 1995 report, found that white men, who make up 43 percent of the work force, hold more than 95 percent of all senior management positions. White men are also 80 percent of tenured professors and 97 percent of school superintendents. African Americans are only 4 percent of middle management and college teachers, 3 percent of all physicians and lawyers, and 2 percent of all scientists and engineers. On the other hand, Black workers are 30 percent of nursing aides and orderlies, 25 percent of hotel maids and domestic workers, 23 percent of prison guards and security guards, 22 percent of janitors, and 25 percent to 30 percent of all unemployed workers and "discouraged" workers who have given up on finding a job. Even Black workers with college degrees have an unemployment rate more than twice as great as their white counterparts (Hacker 1992).

Wage gaps between Black and white workers, which narrowed somewhat between the mid-1960s and mid-1970s, have increased steadily since then. Following the same pattern, Black-white differences in college attendance and graduation rates declined from the mid-1960s through the mid-1970s but have been widening for the past two decades. At the same time, as college costs have escalated, the federal government shifted most student aid from grants to loans, which has disproportionately prevented lower income Blacks from attending college. Racial disparities in wages and in college attendance reinforce each other. For the past 20 years, the difference between wages paid to college graduates and noncollege graduates has grown substantially larger.

3. *Affirmative action amounts to "reverse discrimination."* This argument has gotten a lot of publicity, but it has little, if any, substance. A recent report for the U.S. Department of Labor prepared by law professor Alfred W. Blumrosen found fewer than 100 reverse discrimination cases among the more than 3,000 discrimination opinions handed down by federal district and appeals courts from 1990 and 1994. The courts found discrimination in only six cases and provided appropriate relief. The study concluded "that the problem of 'reverse discrimination' is not widespread; and that where it exists, the courts have given relief. Nothing in these cases would justify dismantling the existing structure of equal opportunity employment programs" (*New York Times* 1995). We, therefore, conclude that reverse discrimination is a myth that serves the ideological purpose of scapegoating. It diverts the anger of white men, who have experienced declining economic opportunities, away from the capitalist bosses onto Blacks, Latinos, immigrants, and women.

4. *Affirmative action is divisive.* Affirmative action is not divisive. By integrating workplaces and schools and by concretely demonstrating to whites that minorities and women can do any job that white men can do, affirmative action has historically reduced the divisive racist attitudes of whites and created more of a basis for multiracial unity. Affirmative action is not divisive, but the way that the ruling class has implemented affirmative action in a declining capitalist society that is producing fewer jobs and educational opportunities has been divisive.

A large majority of whites continue to support affirmative action, according to a *New York Times* article, "Affirmative Action and the Voter," by liberal pollster Louis Harris (1995). According to Harris, when California voters were told that the "California Civil Rights Initiative" would abolish affirmative action, only 31 percent supported it, whereas 56 percent opposed it. Many expressed outrage that politicians were trying to fool them with phrases about "preferential treatment."

Those whites who mistakenly think that minorities are receiving unfair advantages and taking away their jobs and educational opportunities have not come to think this way spontaneously. The ruling class is spending a lot of money to try to fool people with the California Civil Rights Initiative (CCRI). The CCRI was initiated by leaders of the California Association of Scholars, the state chapter of the National Association of Scholars (NAS). Over the past few years, the NAS has received millions of dollars from the five foundations that have for decades been the biggest supporters of right-wing racist causes. The Lynde and Harry Bradley Foundation, The Adolph Coors Foundation, the John Olin Foundation, the Smith Richardson Foundation, and the Sarah Scaife Foundation gave $620,000 to the NAS in 1993 alone. These same ruling-class foundations gave millions of dollars to academics Charles Murray and Richard Herrnstein, who advocated in *The Bell Curve* that the government rescind all anti-discrimination legislation and abolish affirmative action (Hernstein and Murray 1994).

It is no accident that some working- and middle-class people do not clearly understand that the capitalist class is to blame for their increasing problems. The ruling class has spent a fortune trying to make sure that angry whites are angry at everyone but the rulers themselves. Therefore, it is misleading to assert that, when there are hard economic times, white people tend to blame Black people for their problems. This view lets the ruling class off the hook and mystifies racism as something white people just have. In fact, in hard economic times, workers are likely to blame their bosses for laying them off, denying them unemployment insurance, closing their schools and clinics, and denying them access to health care. For the ruling class, it is a matter of life and death to get a lot of working- and middle-class people to fall for racist scapegoating. Otherwise, millions of working- and middle-class people will join class-based antiracist and anticapitalist movements.

5. *Affirmative action helps only middle-class Blacks.* This argument is false and is used to discredit affirmative action by implying that it helps those who are already privileged and thus do not need an extra break. Middle-class Blacks commonly experience racist discrimination and mistreatment and therefore need the protection of affirmative action. Most of the Black people who have benefited from affirmative action, however, are working class. They are workers in city, state, and federal governments, construction workers, and other skilled blue-collar and white-collar workers. They are students from working-class backgrounds who would otherwise be excluded from colleges and universities. Only a small minority of the beneficiaries of affirmative action have been lawyers, doctors, and small business people, but their visibility often is used to convey the false impression that affirmative action has mainly helped affluent Blacks.

It is also important to point out that the few highly visible wealthy minorities are neither working class nor middle class but members of the capitalist ruling class. Their attainment of their positions has had little or nothing to do with affirmative action. The ruling class has admitted a few Black capitalists, managers, military officers, politicians, and academics into its ranks in an effort to maintain control over a working class made up increasingly of racial minorities. Ron Brown, Clarence Thomas, and Colin Powell provide a phony facade of fairness and credibility for a racist White House, Supreme Court, and Pentagon, whereas neoconservative academics Thomas Sowell, Glenn Loury, and Stephen Carter and neoliberals William J. Wilson and Cornell West put a Black face on racist arguments against affirmative action.

The ruling class also was forced to increase the number of minorities serving in positions of social control. During the 1960s, the criminal justice system and many other institutions were exposed as racist instruments of repression. The ruling class has modified these institutions so that they can be used to protect the system of inequality and exploitation. In law enforcement, for example, affirmative action almost tripled the number of Black police from 24,000 in 1970 to 64,000 in 1990. Blacks made up 41 percent of all new police officers hired between 1970 and 1990. Demands for more minority or women bosses, politicians, generals, cops, and administrators are not in the interest of the working class. They only help the ruling class control the working class.

6. *Affirmative action helps only white women.* Affirmative action has probably helped white women more than it has helped African Americans, but neither Blacks nor women have even come close to gaining equality with white men. There are three times as many white women in the United States as there are Black people. There are far more white women college teachers, physicians, and other professionals. White women are far more dispersed throughout all social classes than are African Americans, who are concentrated more disproportionately in the most exploited sections of the working class. Half of the capitalist class consists of women, nearly all of whom are white. Because women and men commonly marry each other, women and men are not nearly as segregated from each other as people are by race.

Nevertheless, it is important not to overstate the benefits of affirmative action for white women or to exaggerate the differences between racism and sexism. Although a minority of white women have entered and advanced in previously all-male fields, most white women have experienced an overall decline in their status since the mid-1970s. Sixty percent of white adults who live below the official poverty line are women. Nearly one-fourth of white families are single-parent families headed by a woman. The vast majority of white women workers are segregated occupationally in low-paying sales, office, service, and production jobs, many of them part-time, temporary, and without benefits. Although the "glass ceiling" keeps women out of the highest levels of the corporate hierarchy, the "sticky floor" keeps the majority of white women and women of all races at or near the bottom of the system of capitalist exploitation of the working class.

7. *Affirmative action unfairly stigmatizes qualified minorities.* This is surely one of the most hypocritical arguments invented by opponents of affirmative action. In the first place, racists have always "stigmatized" minorities and regarded them as "unqualified." It is precisely because of such racist assumptions that affirmative action is necessary. Second, white people have been receiving preferential treatment in the United States for hundreds of years without being or feeling stigmatized for it. Wealthy whites do not seem eager to eliminate legacy programs at elite universities or any of the special privileges they enjoy in this capitalist society.

8. *Race-specific affirmative action should be replaced with a class-based form of affirmative action that will have broader support and benefit disadvantaged people of all racial backgrounds.* This has become the line with which people pose as progressive defenders of affirmative action and "champions of the poor of all races" while working to destroy what is left of affirmative action. Therefore, it is the most insidious argument against affirmative action. William J. Wilson (1978, 1987) and the Edsalls (Edsall and Edsall 1991) have been praised by the ruling class for writing books setting forth this argument. University of California, Santa Cruz faculty member Dana Takagi has refuted this argument by explaining why class is not a proxy for race (Takagi 1995:54). Just as there are class differences within every racial group, there are racial differences within each social class. For example, working-class white students score higher on standardized tests than do working-class Blacks and Latinos. Working-class whites score higher than working-class Asians

on the verbal portions of standardized tests. Class-based affirmative action therefore would favor whites over Blacks, Latinos, and most Asians, which is what racist critics of affirmative action desire. Politicians who advocate replacing race with class have no real desire to direct more assistance to low-income people, regardless of race. In fact, they are cutting back all programs that provide such assistance. They may promise that they will take from Black workers and give to white workers, but they will actually take from all workers and give to the bosses. The end result of destroying affirmative action will be just like the end result of every other racist attack. It will hurt Black workers first and hardest, but it will soon hurt the entire working class!

Takagi has also exposed the fallacy of the racist myth of Asian Americans as a "model minority" that has "made it" without affirmative action. Asian Americans face racist exploitation and have not "made it." Many Asian Americans have benefited from affirmative action by gaining access to jobs previously reserved for whites. The "model minority" myth is used to attack affirmative action by claiming that the United States is a "meritocracy" in which everyone has the opportunity to get ahead.

"New" Democrats have been pursuing a political strategy guided by this racist notion of replacing race with class. They argue that Democrats have catered to the "special interests" of Blacks and the underclass by supporting affirmative action, welfare, and other social programs. Democrats can win elections, according to this racist logic, only by appealing to the "forgotten middle class." Democrats have thus embraced the racist ideology put forward for years by the Republicans and have made that ideology the mainstream of U.S. politics. The results are becoming obvious: Republicans and Democrats, who are both financed and controlled by the same capitalist class, disagree only about how severely and how rapidly to make further cuts in affirmative action, welfare, public education, health care, social security, Medicare, and Medicaid.

Why then has President Clinton posed as a defender of affirmative action? He is worried that if he ends affirmative action altogether, it will be virtually impossible to get Black and Latino workers and students to retain any faith in the U.S. system. It will be very hard to convince them to register and vote for Democrats or for anybody. He fears militant revolt and wants to preserve a tiny fragment of affirmative action. Clinton also wants us to continue to regard

Democrats as a "lesser evil" protecting us from the Republicans and all their fascist friends. Liberals will not protect us from fascism and World War III any better than they have protected our jobs, wages, schools, welfare system, neighborhoods, or families. They are only trying to protect the ruling class.

President Clinton, in a July 19, 1995 speech urging that we should "mend, not end" affirmative action, put forward procapitalist reasons for retaining affirmative action that are entirely different from the reasons that workers and students should support affirmative action. Clinton said that affirmative action has made "America stronger." He applauded a "growing Black middle class," claimed that "women have become a major force in business and political life," asserted that "police departments now better reflect the make-up of those whom they protect," and that "a generation of professionals now serve as role models for young women and minority youth."

All of these arguments rest upon illusions. Workers do not benefit by helping American capitalists compete with the bosses of workers in other countries. The Black middle class is not growing but shrinking because of corporate downsizing and Clinton's program of "reinventing government" by eliminating the jobs of government workers. Becoming middle class cannot be the solution for exploited workers. Most workers cannot become middle class under capitalism. Workers cannot solve their problems by rising out of their class but by rising up as a class against their exploiters. A few women have become bosses and politicians, but, like all bosses and politicians, they are enemies of working- and middle-class women. There are more Black police than there used to be, but police departments are still dominated overwhelmingly by racist white cops like Mark Fuhrman, and all cops protect the racist ruling class, not the community. Professional role models are a cruel hoax for a majority of working- and middle-class youth today because the capitalist system offers no opportunities and no future. Professional role models help the ruling class peddle the lie that you can get ahead if you work hard.

The alternative to relying on "lesser evil" Democrats is to build a mass multiracial, antiracist movement. This must be done to oppose further attempts to destroy what is left of affirmative action. It is essential as a matter of principle to oppose all forms of scapegoating. It is important to speak out against the use of racist books and articles in college courses and professors and administrators who spread lies of racial inferiority. In response to calls for "meritocracy," it is important to oppose the use of standardized tests as instruments of racist exclusion. Positive steps that should be advocated include ending tuition for public higher education, restoring funds that have been cut from education budgets, and restoring the primacy of grants over loans, so that students do not accumulate massive debts in order to get a college degree. At the same time, it is also necessary to oppose racist cuts in other social programs, such as AFDC, food stamps, Medicaid, school lunches, environmental protection, Medicare, and social security.

Most important, it is not enough to demand the redistribution of a shrinking number of low-paying, temporary, and part-time jobs, thereby playing into the hands of capitalists who are downsizing and pitting workers against each other. Instead, to unify the working class against the capitalist ruling class, it is necessary to demand jobs with living wages and benefits for minority workers and for all those who need them, and to demand a shorter work day (six hours' work for eight hours' pay) without loss of pay for workers, in order to force capitalist bosses to create millions of new jobs.

Note

1. The "working class" is the class of people that does not own businesses and must work for the capitalist class in order to live. The working class includes both blue-collar and most white-collar workers, as well as part-time, temporary, unemployed, retired, and disabled workers, welfare recipients, and their families. Those who are labeled as "lower class" or "underclass" are not below or under but are part of the working class. The "middle class" is not the working class but the class of people in the middle between the working class and the capitalist class. The middle class consists of small business and franchise owners, managers, supervisors, administrators, planners, and independent and semi-independent professionals, such as doctors, lawyers, research scientists, professors, and engineers.

References

Brimelow, Peter. 1995. "Restoration Man." In *The Bell Curve Debate: History, Documents, Opinions.* New York: Times Books.

Chideya, Farai. 1995. *Don't Believe the Hype: Fighting Cultural Misinformation About African Americans.* New York: Plume Penguin.

Edsall, Thomas and Mary Edsall. 1991. *Chain Reaction: The Impact of Race, Rights, and Taxes on American Politics.* New York: Norton.

Ezorsky, Gertrude. 1991. *Racism and Justice: The Case for Affirmative Action.* Ithaca: Cornell University Press.

Giraldo, Zaida I. 1995, May. "What Everyone Should Know About Affirmative Action." Peaceful Action (e-mail communication).

Hacker, Andrew. 1992. *Two Nations: Black and White, Separate, Hostile, Unequal.* New York: Scribners.

Harris, Louis. 1995, July 31. "Affirmative Action and the Voter." *New York Times on Line.*

Hayden, Tom and Connie Rice. 1995, September 18. "California Cracks Its Mortarboards." *The Nation.*

Herring Cedric. 1995, August. "African Americans, the Public Agenda, and the Paradoxes of Public Policy: A Focus on the Controversies Surrounding Affirmative Action." *Presidential Address at Annual Meeting of Association of Black Sociologists.* Washington, DC.

Hernstein, Richard J. and Charles Murray. 1994. *The Bell Curve.* New York: Free Press.

Jacoby, Russell and Naomi Glauberman, eds. 1995. *The Bell Curve Debate: History, Documents, Opinions.* New York: Times Books.

Jones, Van. 1995, May/June. "What Is the Campaign Against Affirmative Action Really About?" Third Force. (e-mail communication).

Kissack, Glenn. 1995. "The Five Sisters of Right-Wing Philanthropy." (e-mail communication).

Knapp, Peter and Alan Spector. 1991. *Crisis and Change: An Introduction to Marxist Sociology.* Chicago: Nelson Hall.

Larew, John. 1994. "Who's the Real Affirmative Action Profiteer?" In *Debating Affirmative Action,* ed., Nicolaus Mills. New York: Delta Books.

Massey, Douglas and Nancy Denton. 1993. *American Apartheid: Segregation and the Making of the Underclass.* Cambridge: Harvard University Press.

Mills, Nicolaus, ed. 1994. *Debating Affirmative Action.* New York: Delta Books.

New York Times On Line. 1995.

Quadagno, Jill. 1994. *The Color of Welfare: How Racism Undermined the War on Poverty.* New York: Oxford University Press.

Steinberg, Stephen. 1995. *Turning Back: The Retreat from Racial Justice in American Thought and Policy.* Boston: Beacon Press.

Takagi. Dana. 1995, May. "We Should Not Make Class a Proxy for Race." *Chronicle of Higher Education,* 5:54.

Wilkins, Roger. 1995, March 27. "Racism Has Its Privileges." *The Nation,* 409-16.

Wilson, Reginald. 1995. "Affirmative Action: Yesterday, Today and Beyond." Washington, DC: American Council on Education paper.

Wilson, William J. 1978. *The Declining Significance of Race.* Chicago: University of Chicago Press.

———. 1987. *The Truly Disadvantaged.* Chicago: University of Chicago Press.

Zinn, Howard. 1964. *SNCC: The New Abolitionists.* Boston: Beacon Press.

CONSERVATIVE RELIGIOUS AND IDEOLOGICAL PERSPECTIVES

Sources and Consequences for Public Policy for the Poor

CHARLES JARMON

The perception of the nature and causes of poverty is more likely to have a greater impact on the formulation of public policies for government intervention than are the absolute needs of the poor. This is because such policies depend on social and cultural legitimation. Historically, the sources of legitimation have inhered in religious and ideological components of the American core culture to which proponents of both sides of the debate on antipoverty reform appeal in debating the issues of poverty. Much of the debate on poverty has been driven by the criss-crossing conflicts present in this core of values and beliefs (e.g., note discussions in Cook 1979; Sachs 1983; and Herrnstein and Murray 1994). It is in grasping the nature of religious and ideological conflicts that we understand the underlying bases of support and opposition against the different programs identified with antipoverty reform movements, particularly when we may feel compelled to single out such factors as regional, racial, class, and special group interests.

In few areas of national life are the debates more sharply differentiated than at the level of party politics, where the capacity for mobilizing support to influence public policy depends on how well these cultural meanings are advanced by a particular political party. The respective leaders, if not true believers, are often swayed to adopt significant viewpoints from the party line to prove or demonstrate loyalty and commitment to party interests. This makes periodic elections one of the important ways in which the level of debate on the issue of poverty is raised, one that results in ritualistic and continual reinforcement of images of the poor in American public opinion.

Renewed interest in issues related to poverty may occur because of unpredicted changes in certain sectors of the society or by the unexpected outbreak of demonstrations and riots by the poor themselves, a subject to which I refer later. With respect to the former, the issue of poverty loses or gains intensity from time to time—for example, diminished or increased by profound changes in the economy as occurs when critical lags appear between the technical skills required of a changing economy and those possessed by a large segment of the labor force. Such lags result in massive unemployment among the least educated and poorest of the working class. In general, because African Americans are located disproportionately at the bottom of the class hierarchy, this situation has a greater impact on the African American community. Once into a protracted state of unemployment, those in this group of displaced workers are frequently ascribed labels that might have no association with the cause of their plight. They become the object of the mass media, the popular press, and the public referenda as the debate continues on what government should do about their needs.

In the current electoral climate, we can observe political leaders engaged in a power struggle over decisions related to welfare reform, and much of the fight revolves around fundamental definitions and symbolic assertions about the poor. The current archetype of this phenomenon is evident in the recent successes of the Republican Party (see Gingrich 1995), where the primary players have been the Christian Right, white males, and a variety of conservative think tank organizations. The purpose of this conservative movement is to remake the federal government, with the objectives of this movement embodied in the "Contract With America," the blueprint for the Republican conservative reform. Those on the left, the liberal and moderate Democrats, proponents of liberation theology and so on, have appeared impotent against the conservative movement.

For this study, I limit the discussion to the conservative side of the debate on poverty and concentrate on the historical development of religious and ideological traditions that have accounted for much of the resistance toward reforms for the poor. As a caveat, I do not attempt to deemphasize the fundamental importance of structural economic imperatives that underlay patterns of inequality but to address poverty from an angle that will make it possible for us to focus on an important range of questions that might further our understanding of their connection with social and cultural factors.

Three Questions and Assumptions

Three questions are particularly important in the development of the present work. First, why is it that in a nation where so many economic goods are produced and subsequently wasted that the principal conditions that continue to place the poor at an extreme disadvantage remain substantially unchanged? This question requires an economic or class frame of reference, which, according to whether it be derived from a Keynesian, Marxist, or other economic model, could reasonably explain the imperative of persisting structural inequality in wealth, income, capital, or land. There is no dearth of scholarly efforts in the social sciences to explain the economic bases of inequality, and therefore, there is no attempt to provide the details of the various perspectives here. Second, how is the continuing poverty of the poor legitimated? Unlike the first, the approach to this question must involve the role of cultural phenomena in limiting the upward mobility of the poor—that is, in this case, institutionalized religious and ideological beliefs about the poor. The important assumption is that structural inequality must be buttressed by, or must be accompanied by, social and cultural bases. Three, what is the significance of this interaction with reference to the development of public policy for the poor? This question assumes that action without imposed sanctions generally follows creed, such that, under the present conceptual framework, core religious and ideological values are sources from which negative perceptions about the poor are drawn and subsequently acted upon. The negative images fuse into the popular discourse, making it easier to distort the reality of life as experienced by the poor. Distorted images militate against public support of policies for govern-ment intervention. Given the vigorous debates that surround the issue of poverty, how historical and structural levels of the society interface to influence contemporary responses to poverty warrants significantly more attention by sociologists. Much can be learned from the acrimony, partisanship, and polarization between the groups that are actively in opposition on the issue of welfare reform.

These questions, then, bring us to the examination of two cultur-ally based theories about the nature of poverty and about the low standing of the poor with respect to social policy as well. The remainder of the discussion focuses on the social historical analysis of conservative religious and ideological thought and concludes with new questions for research on contemporary poverty and public policy with respect to the African American community.

The Invisibility of the Poor Theory

Many Americans would like to ignore poverty, closing their eyes to its reality. Most have little personal experience or contact with the poor. In this sense, poverty—as observable reality—has little visibil-ity, or meaning, beyond the immediate environment of the poor themselves, and therefore attracts very little empathy from the general public. This inhibits the development of sufficient general public support for issues addressing economic, housing, health, and educational conditions related to poverty.

The invisibility of the urban poor is beyond all else a function of economic disparity, but it is manifested in their relative isolation, concentration, and disproportional distribution in poverty areas of big cities. According to recent census reports, nearly 78 percent of the poor among African Americans live in central cities, and the majority (71 percent) reside in highly concentrated poverty areas (U.S. Bureau of the Census 1991). This pattern is also observed for poor Hispanic Americans and poor whites, with 66 percent of poor Hispanics and 50 percent of whites residing in highly concentrated poverty areas, respectively. These demographic circumstances make them strangers to the higher economic classes, who perceive them to think, feel, and act differently. The poor, because of this condition, are likely to be seen as a natural group rather than as a group essentially socially constructed and arising from the complex politi-cal economy (Katz 1989). The concentration factor of poverty has become so observable that some social scientists even espouse de-concentration as one of the solutions to improving the condition of the poor (Massey 1994).

By understanding the nature of this invisibility, caused mainly by the separation of neighborhoods by class and race, we understand why average, mainstream Americans possess limited knowledge of the poor. This limitation predisposes them to be influenced easily by myths and stereotypes of the poor. For example, the average white American grows up with only superficial observations of the life experienced by poor blacks, given the historical patterns of neighborhood separation and racial segregation that continue to polarize Americans by class and race. These observations usually have occurred in random fashion—as happen with commuters traveling between central business districts and suburban communities—or through what is cursorily seen, heard, or read in journalistic media coverage. The geographic separation, along with the lack of adequate knowledge of the life of the poor, reinforces the invisibility.

Liebow (1967) and Harrington (1962, 1984) have identified the condition of invisibility as one of the factors that increases the vulnerability of the poor in society, because most Americans do not develop a keen sense of the perniciousness of poverty. The national consciousness to such reality has proved to be responsive to political agitation, as was demonstrated in the 1960s and 1970s when Harrington and others launched the "politics of moral outrage" and "middle-class guilt" by bringing the condition of the poor into sharp focus (Butler and Kondratas 1987). In the 1990s, it happened again when the national consciousness regarding the condition of poverty was heightened by the Los Angeles riots.

Politicians, generally aware of the negative sentiments of the majority population toward reforms (e.g., the resistance to using taxes to pay for social services), typically act accordingly by supporting bills to spend less money on welfare programs. They tend to demonstrate more sensitivity to issues concerning the poor when extraordinary events such as riots or quadrennial elections occur. In effect, they avoid the issue of urban poverty until faced with a pressing need to do so, such as during the time of riots; when the need is to reintegrate the poor into the community for the good of the "social order" (Piven and Cloward 1971); or to enhance their own legitimacy, that of a political leader, or of the political party during local and national elections.

Heightened awareness to needs of the poor also depends on the interest expressed by the mass media. This was a factor in the rise of the popular press as it took strong opposition against the conservative position in the 1960s and 1970s. For example, when Harrington (1962, 1984) brought national attention to the invisibility of the rural and urban poor, the mass media followed with extensive coverage of the living conditions of the poor and captured the public's attention. The rapid rise in public interest in the poor not only became a catalyst but an important basis for legitimating the Great Society programs of the Kennedy-Johnson administrations in the 1960s, and also for the Civil Rights movement, which transfigured the hopes of African Americans as well.

However, as the public polls disclose, this progressive movement was short-lived and not sufficient to sustain the legitimacy for public support for the poor. Cook's (1979) review of survey research of public opinions reveals that the proportion of respondents in nationwide surveys favoring federal support to help the needy went as high as 60 percent between 1961 and 1963, whereas the previous high (45 percent) came just after World War II. However, after the peak was reached in 1963, there was a precipitous decline to 18 percent in 1964, and the low level of public support for the poor remained below 25 percent for the next decade. Currently, according to the Gallup Poll (1993), only 35 percent of the American public favor the government doing a great deal to help the poor, which is 25 percent fewer than in the early 1960s.

The precipitous decline in the public's favorable attitude toward government intervention suggests how deeply entrenched conservative beliefs about the role of the government are in the mind of the public, especially with reference to providing social services for the poor. Some scholars might reasonably argue that such entrenchment may reflect strongly held attitudes toward the principle of laissez faire, but this argument would not explain why much of the opposition to supporting social services invokes negative and distorted images of the poor.

The Stigmatization Theory

Stigmatization has several negative consequences. First, it debases the inner-city poor, whom some scholars now refer to as the underclass. The debasement is further intensified by the higher prevalence of social problems—for example, unemployment, inadequate housing, homelessness, crime, hunger, poor schools, single female householders, and high infant mortality rates—in depressed urban areas than in nonpoor urban areas and suburbs. Second, it militates against the development of a context for understanding underlying racial, economic, or other social and structural conditions linked to poverty. Third, it helps to foster marginalization, disparagement, and repressed anger, which contribute collectively to the disaffection among this segment of the population in ways that reinforce their poverty. A thorough exploration of these consequences would go beyond the scope of this chapter.

Suffice it to say that studies consistently show that in the minds of many Americans, poverty, particularly inner-city poverty, is identified with attributes of the poor themselves (e.g., Katz 1989, 1993; Kluegel and Smith 1986; Ryan 1972; Goodwin 1972). The reality, however, is that poverty results from a configuration of diverse political and socioeconomic causes. For example, scholars have identified it with several principal causes (state transformation, Quadagno 1992; political economy, Cazenave 1990 and Katz, 1989; economy and community dislocation, Wilson 1987; race, Hill 1989; political ideology, Murray 1984; intelligence and IQ, Herrnstein and Murray 1994; social control and welfare, Janowitz 1977; race and class, Jarmon 1976; income and ideology, Huber and Form 1973; situational factors, Valentine 1968; and the family, Moynihan, Barton, and Broderick 1965). This means that the question of poverty itself has evoked different orientations toward public policy, a subject to which I devote attention later.

I argue that failure of public policy for the poor is strongly associated with widespread negative perceptions of the poor that emanate from culturally embedded religious and ideological ideas. Both the ideas and the negative symbolism that derive from them must be understood if we are to understand the complexity of attitudes that justify and legitimate the low standing of an estimated 36 million poor (U.S. Bureau of the Census 1996). Under the present capitalistic system, which benefits from the existence of economically vulnerable classes, this situation is functional and expected. That is, whereas the dominant expectation is that one's life chances should be associated ultimately with one's individual qualities, the lesser expectation is for the government to provide equal access to the essential ingredients for the development of the requisite individual qualities. In this regard, consider the resistance to removing the long-standing patterns of inequality that have suppressed the status of blacks in the American society.

The Social Historical Approach

There are persisting historical linkages between the culture in which the poor live and deeply entrenched societal perspectives that bear on social and economic forces affecting their lives. Research has demonstrated the importance of understanding this connection with respect to the public policy process from a variety of angles (Gans 1991; Kluegel 1990; Oropesa 1986; Duncan 1984; Wilensky 1975; Huber and Form 1973). For example, Huber and Form argued that widespread adherence to dominant ideological beliefs is a stable feature of American thought about the permanent nature of inequality. Yet Duncan argues the need to move beyond such perspectives— that is, to a consideration of periods or cycles in which individual families receive public support, giving poverty a less permanent face. Even between different leading industrial countries, Wilensky found that differences in dominant ideological legacies accounted for differences in public policies regarding poverty. Notwithstanding the disparate approaches to poverty, it remains clear that public opinion generally is a dominant social factor that inhibits support for reform or distributive issues.

Does emphasizing selected conservative aspects of the American culture as part of the problem in addressing the issue of poverty contradict what we know about the past history of reforms that have occurred in America? Not if we accept the premise that most reforms came into existence because of the need to cope with national catastrophes or to plan for changes associated with major transformation in modern society itself. This, for example, constitutes the basis for the programs identified with the Social Security Administration Act of 1935. In such cases, the near universality of need in the national population diminishes the propensity to isolate groups for invidious comparisons. This position is also supported by findings that the moral classification of the poor even survived the Great Depression (see Katz 1989), with the idea of relief for the poor remaining pejorative and degrading. That these views were able to endure is significant to understanding the difficulty of instituting planned change in the institutions that control the lives of the poor.

This work is part of the larger scholarly effort to make the belief-value-related constraints on public policy more explicit, with special attention paid to problems peculiar to the inner-city poor. The emphasis here on the coexistence of religious and ideological symbolism as sources of antecedent values and beliefs is not to propose a monolithic cultural framework that holds that the central problem of the poor resides in the cultural sphere; rather, it is to draw attention to this sphere as a neglected dimension of the broader issue between poverty and public policy. In effect, it is to address this dimension as one of the factors that contribute to the complexity involved in attempting to reduce poverty.

How does the present approach differ from many contemporary contributions to the social historical literature on poverty? The primary difference is the emphasis put on the need to understand the deeper patterns of thought about the poor in American society. For example, one of the significant works in this area is Katz's work on the intellectual foundation of the War on Poverty. His chronicled history of the facts about poverty and changes in the postindustrial city provides only cursory discussion of the orthogenetic sources of ideas regarding the poor in Western culture. His purpose, however, was different. He set out to explain how the American society, as a wealthy nation, lacked the political will to move toward a welfare state committed to transforming the conditions associated with poverty. Thus, he emphasized the dialectical bases for understanding the War on Poverty of the late 1960s and early 1970s and the conservative reaction to it. His was an effort to explain an "episodic moment in history," during which public policy was the outcome of shifting political fortunes of the major principals involved on one side or the other of the dialectics between reform and reaction. The political diversity on these issues ranges from the differences existing between the liberal intellectuals and progressive political groups allied with the Democratic party to the religious right and the conservative political opposition groups allied with the Republican party. This approach departs by explaining how the conservative elements in American society justify their position on antipoverty reforms, such as current conservative proposals for making changes in Medicaid, education spending, and job training. I argue that neither of the two sides (facilitated by well-recognized think tanks) has had to invent new ideas for conceptualizing the poor; each simply updates old ideas, although many of them have been greatly weakened by the currents of social and economic changes.

The Poor—Images of the Undeserving

The notion that Americans tend to blame the poor for their poverty and to ascribe to them such stereotypes as dishonesty, laziness, improvidence, deviance, immorality, and worthlessness is consistent with recent findings (e.g., Feagin 1975; Waxman 1983; Kluegel and Smith 1986). Such images are also expressed in descriptive language meant to stigmatize the urban poor and enforce the perception of them as undeserving. For the poor in the African American community, for example, many have been placed in pejorative categories—for example, chiseling "welfare queens" and "Cadillac daddies"; immoral "welfare mothers," with no qualms about having their "welfare babies"; idle "corner boys"; and criminal "street hustlers." Such images present the poor as preferring to receive government benefits over being gainfully employed. Not surprisingly, this picture masks the findings of most researchers that most poor people actually prefer to work, or the fact that at least 40 percent of the poor get along without any government benefits at all (Butler and Kondratas 1987). Exaggerated misperceptions make it easier for leaders opposed to reform to write off the condition of the poor as hopeless as the leaders lobby and vote against government programs for the poor.

Such typescripts, as mentioned here, do not hold for the majority of inner-city poor, a point that is supported by the significance of other social, economic, cultural, and situational factors that have been recognized in the literature (e.g., see Blum and Rossi 1969; Moynihan et al. 1965; Ginsberg 1983; Harvey 1984; Wilson, 1987).

Construed as a deviant social category, the "undeserving poor" serve as a negative reference group, and their subjection to negative sanctions brings before society the boundaries and definitions that reflect the need of the capitalistic system to maintain at least minimal commitment of the nonpoor to the work ethic. Thus, from time to time, the question is raised as to whether stigmatization of the poor is done without some underlying notion of this function, independent of the religious factor as a source of ideas for legitimizing it. Notwithstanding such concerns, negative symbols of the poor impede the development of meaningful social policies for the poor by sustaining an image of them as misfits in the American capitalist system.

The Poor in Christian Symbolism

Religion derives its force from its cosmological property—its specification of definitions and meanings that human groups associate with their social environments. In this sense, it is a source of legitimacy for much of the meaning that Americans traditionally have accorded to social and cultural life, with poverty being only one dimension. The most immediate religious history of mainstream America is identified with Judaic and early Christian influences connected with the rise of Western civilization in Europe and their subsequent transformation and contribution to American culture.

Many of the views of the poor today can be seen in ancient and more recent Christian conceptions of the poor, reflecting a deep religious base, but one that has not been without some important changes.

The Poor in Pre-Reformation Christianity

The biblical reference to pre-Reformation Christianity can be divided between the period preceding the birth of Jesus Christ (Before the Common Era) and after his birth (the Common Era). The history of the first is chronicled in the Old Testament, and that of the second is recorded in the New Testament, the two representing both influences from Judaic origins and the rise of Christianity itself. Pre-Reformation Christianity, as I have deduced from these two sources, fostered four paramount themes pertaining to the poor: (1) the inevitability of the existence of the poor in society, (2) the expectation of charity and generosity toward the poor, (3) the exhortations for and triumph of justice for the poor, and (4) the locus of culpability for the poverty of the poor.

Inevitability. Two important points emerge in reference to perceiving the poor as an inevitable part of society. First, this theme advanced the notion that the poor occurred naturally and, in turn, constituted a permanent element in society. The verse, "The Poor shall never cease out of the land" (Deuteronomy 15:10-11), conveys this perception. Second, the theme legitimizes the poor as a social category. In this sense, Lenski (1966) asserts that in the early stages of Christianity, the place of the poor was part of an organic hierarchy over which religious and wealthy elites held divine rights. It is unlikely that this conceptualization could be dismissed easily by either religious or political leaders of the pre-Reformation era.

Charity and generosity. Both charity and generosity were held as imperatives and were considered to inspire the grace of God. Although the rich were not condemned for their wealth, it was their sacred duty to be generous toward the poor in order to attain salvation. The following verse reflects this theme: "Those who have given to the hungry, the sick, the stranger, and prisoner will inherit the Kingdom of God, while those who have not will be doomed to suffer everlasting punishment" (Matthew 25:42-46). This theme not only defined expectations with respect to providing support for the poor, but it also offered positive outcomes for the wealthy and even an ascetic way of life for the "perfect Christian." The perfect believer in Christianity should be inspired to "go sell what you possess and give it to the poor and you will have treasure in Heaven" (Matthew 19:21).

Justice. Justice represented a special concern for ethical dealings with the poor in daily life and would embody a sense of divine intervention for the poor, whose justice would proceed to its inevitable conclusion after death in the sacred Kingdom. This latter is an inference suggested in the following covenant: "Blessed are you poor for yours is the Kingdom of God" (Luke 6:20). We might also infer that this provides a teleological basis for the poor to accommodate themselves to their position in this world by offering the prospect that their suffering would end with their ascension to grace and salvation in the next world. Some biblical scholars indeed go as far as to associate justice for the poor with the genesis of Christianity itself. Miranda (1974), for example, makes the argument that the intervention of God in history might be interpreted to have occurred because of the need to achieve justice for the poor and the oppressed.

Culpability. Ascription of culpability for the poverty of the poor expressed a moral imperative for all able-bodied individuals to engage in productive activity. This imperative, interlocking both providential and behaviorist bases for poverty, differentiated between the poor whose situation originated in unique circumstances beyond their control, such as widows, orphans, and slaves, and the poor whose condition was perceived to have originated from imprudent lifestyles. The differentiation can be seen in this admonition: "If any would not work, neither should he eat" (2 Thessalonians 3:3-2). We can infer that this moral condemnation, in tandem with others, creates the basis for moral categories and establishes the basis for defining the undeserving poor, a conception portrayed in much of the contemporary literature about the poor.

In sum, the images of the poor in early Christian thought emerged from a providential design, which spelled out the relation of the poor to the rest of the community, especially to the wealthy. Saint Augustine (Augustinus 1950) expressed this point clearly in his argument that the existence of the poor was a part of a greater design in which the will of the poor was to be understood in terms of a divine providence. However, as Christianity underwent profound changes, images of the poor changed.

The Poor in Protestant
Reformation Thought

In considering the Protestant Reformation, we cannot dismiss its impact on England, the country with the greatest historical relevance for its diffusion into American culture. During most of the 16th-century in England, the growth and spread of Protestantism produced changes in religious ideas and in the traditional economic and political position of the Church. Radical ideas, arising out of opposition to Catholic Christianity, promoted popular uprisings and revolts against religious doctrines. This turmoil also involved challenges against maligned Church economic and political power, because it was the largest landowner in many sections of the country (Clark 1977). In effect, the Protestant movement was the seedbed out of which radical religious and secular changes converged to transform English provincial society. We focus here on the transformation of ideas concerning perceptions of the poor.

The Protestant Reformation brought about three important changes in the way the poor were perceived: a reversal of the moral obligation of the wealthy to be charitable and generous to the poor, a reversal of the idea that the poor were assured salvation in an afterlife, and a reversal of the attribution of culpability for one's

TABLE 8.1 Differences in Perceptions of the Poor in Pre-Reformation
and Post-Reformation Christianity

Theme	Pre-Reformation	Post-Reformation
Inevitability	+	+
Charity and Generosity	+	-
Justice and Salvation	+	-
Culpability	-	+

poverty. As shown in Table 8.1, three of the four principal themes
were affected by the rise of Protestantism. The poor would continue,
however, to be perceived as a permanent part of society. In effect,
these reversals were connected with transformations in ideas about
making a living, particularly those that inspired a religious basis for
the acquisition of profit, which constituted one of the most fundamental differences in religious ideas of the 16th century and the
pre-Reformation era of Christianity (Heilbroner, 1961:16).

Under the Protestant doctrines, as most were founded on Luther-
anism and/or Calvinism, the three reversals were expressions of
radical changes in religious thought. First, the wealthy would no
longer be subjected to a moral obligation to be charitable; the strong
emphasis in Calvinism against charity extolled the virtues of individual responsibility. Montagu (1971) argued that this development
represented a sharp departure from the Catholic Church's history
of abrogating to itself responsibility for the poor. Second, the idea
that the poor were assured salvation in an afterlife was obviated by
the teachings of predestination, which highly favored members of
the upper strata for whom economic success itself was a sign of
salvation. Through the work ethic, man was seen as dutifully fulfill-
ing his calling (Tawney 1926; Weber 1958). Third, the reversal in the
idea of culpability denotes a loss of divine imminence of the poor in
Christianity. The poor, in contrast, were condemned for their presumed lack of character and unwillingness to work, signs of their
providential exclusion from the privileged classes. This is not a
comprehensive picture of the Protestant Reformation or of the extent of its impact on the West, but suffice it to say that many of the
ideas fundamental to the religion were transplanted to America and
permeated its cultural traditions. This is evidenced by the Puritani-
cal tradition that developed in the eighteenth and nineteenth centuries. For example, Weber (1958) used the writings of Benjamin

Franklin to show its broad influence in American society as well as to make note of its spread among the Protestant churches, where an increasing secular orientation and penchant for autonomy in church affairs could be observed. These ideas helped to shape an American core of values, which included strong value orientations toward individual achievement, material success, freedom, and morality. However, there are scholars who argue that secular changes in American society have weakened the impact of the Protestant ethic, particularly the work ethic (see Hammond and Williams 1976).

The Poor in Natural Law Paradigms

As alluded to earlier, profound secular developments had an impact on images of the poor. Social and economic changes, which had accompanied nineteenth- and early twentieth-century America, weakened the Protestant ethic, but they also came dressed in their own set of ideological dogma, defining and sustaining the emerging industrial order. In the sense that this body of thought extends the base for conservative ideas, it is important to explore it for understanding the persistence of negative images of the poor. For this reason, I focused on the natural law paradigms.

For this purpose, the beginning point of the discussion remains England for the same reasons cited in our consideration of the Protestant Reformation. In the 18th century, the proponents of this tradition were seeking answers to explain the sharp increase in the number of the poor in a rapidly expanding urban population, which was both a consequence of the migration of peasants from the feudal countryside and the nascent development of commercial and industrial economies in cities. In nineteenth-century America, the prototypical large industrial city began to rival cities in England as well as those in other parts of Europe. American cities became magnets for both international migration, drawing poor rural peasants to their centers from southern Europe, and for internal migration, drawing poor blacks from the southern states in this country, African Americans seeking to escape discrimination and poverty. For both situations, the conservative response tended to be characterized not only by the similarity of the explanations for the persistence of poverty but also by the similarity in the justifications used to argue against social intervention on behalf of the poor.

These justifications came clothed in their own ideologies—natural law. The major English proponents of the natural law paradigm—Joseph Townsend (1786), Thomas Malthus (1798), Charles Darwin (1859), and Herbert Spencer (1892)—coincided in their principal views of the poor. In effect, these proponents would argue that neither the government nor the rich should be held responsible for the condition of the poor. Innately inferior either in mental capacity or character, the poor were assumed to be less able to adapt in the struggle for existence in the competitive market economy. Government intervention on behalf of the poor was understood to only increase the numbers of poor in society.

These same ideas were used by American writers. Although the discussion of the natural law issues goes back further than the nineteenth century, it can be found in the writings of such prominent scholars as George Fitzhugh (1854), William Graham Sumner (1883), and Richard Herrstein and Charles Murray (1994). African Americans were especially debased in the writings of Fitzhugh and Herrstein and Murray, where race became a specific issue. Let us give brief attention to how these ideas were used by Fitzhugh in the middle of the nineteenth century and continued at the end of the twentieth century by Herrstein and Murray.

George Fitzhugh

George Fitzhugh, an apologist for the American slave system, transformed the natural law paradigm into a justification of slavery and argued that it was a better system for blacks than the factory systems were for the massive wave of urban migrants in the big cities of the Northeast and for those in the big, industrial cities in European countries. The central point of Fitzhugh's (1854) *Sociology of the South* was in his argument that African slaves lacked the mental ability to compete in a free, capitalistic society; slavery protected them from open competition with whites and served their personal and physical needs. Freedom for slaves would be tantamount to consigning them to a condition worse than slavery. Whereas the focus of European writers mentioned earlier had emphasized inferior constitutional factors, proclivities for vices, or poor work habits, irrespective of particular groups, Fitzhugh invoked race as the primary factor. The racial theme continues to surface as an explanation for poverty among the African American population.

Charles Murray

Charles Murray, one of the most prominent proponents of the natural law paradigm among contemporary American scholars, continues the debate on the significance of inherited intelligence for explaining variations in human behavior, a school of thought inspired by the classical Darwinians. In *The Bell Curve*, he, along with Herrnstein, argues that intelligence is the key component missing in public discussions on poverty (Herrnstein and Murray 1994). His argument is that the public has been misled about the direct relationship between intelligence and poverty, and until this relationship is adequately understood, public policy to help the poor will continue to be inadequate. This conclusion clearly has greater applicability to and suggests greater differentiation among the disparate groups of whites who constitute the mainstream American population but who have vastly different levels of economic achievement than exist in the black community. In his analysis of the National Longitudinal Survey of Youth data, for example, during which he consciously focused first on whites, he discloses that only 2 percent of very bright whites in the sample were poor, whereas 30 percent of the very dull were, a rate 15 times greater than the former. The overall average for the sample, 7 percent, reflecting the weight of the rate of poverty (6 percent) for the larger group of whites whose intelligence fell within the "normal" range, provided the baseline from which to view the extremes of intelligence in relationship to being poor. Intelligence truly appeared to have had a compelling influence, but because Murray felt that it overrode other factors whose influence we already accept, such as parents' educational background and single parenting, he urged that greater national attention be given to the influence of IQ on poverty.

Murray's analysis runs into difficulty when he attempts to explain why African Americans fall disproportionately toward the bottom of the economic ladder, particularly within the context of the controversy involving black/white IQ differentials. His view can be illustrated by the following syllogism: Poverty is a problem associated with low IQ; the prevalence of below-average IQs is greater among blacks than whites; therefore, there exists a disproportionate number of low-IQ mothers in the African American community, who give birth to a disproportionate number of black children that grow up living below the poverty line. This approach is flawed. As an explanation for poverty in the black community, it does not consider the fact that IQ itself is greatly influenced by poverty. The reality, then, is that both heredity and socioeconomic (SES) factors contribute to the development of the IQ of individuals.

Moreover, the confluence of both historical and contemporary economic inequality is a central factor contributing to the complexity of poverty. When an attempt is made to reduce the issue of poverty to the single factor of IQ, it distorts the problem. It understates or omits the significance of other explanatory factors. It leads to the assumption that the IQ differential, as measured by standardized tests, is a reflection of natural racial differences in intelligence. No doubt this occurs because scholars have not answered fundamental questions about the specific relationship between IQ and heredity, socioeconomic circumstances, and culture.

Although census data affirm that the rate for blacks living in poverty continues to be higher than for whites—currently 33.1 percent and 12.2 percent, respectively—it is noteworthy that Murray's NLSY data disclosed that, at every level of intelligence, more blacks than whites were found living in poverty. Conversely, proportionately fewer of the brightest among blacks were found to be as wealthy as the brightest among whites. When such findings are disclosed by research, it should be a reasonable deduction that the intelligence factor is not the single compelling explanation for why disproportionately higher rates of poverty exist in the African American community. But too much of this kind of evidence about the unreliability of IQ scores as predictors of behavioral outcomes is not taken seriously. For example, the Army beta tests that were given during World War II to American soldiers, which included blacks, whites, and other ethnic groups, demonstrated the importance of social and environmental factors. These intelligence tests showed that blacks from several northern states (e.g., Illinois, Pennsylvania, Ohio, New York) ranked higher on the tests than did whites from several southern states (e.g., Alabama, Kentucky, Mississippi, South Carolina). Half a century has passed without much advancement on this question. Clearly, the existence of evidence about the role of nonhereditary factors has not deterred the minds of many conservatives. Murray's work, therefore, represents a salient example of how old ideas may be revived from the core culture and how they may significantly influence debates on important contemporary social issues. In this case, it is the idea that nothing much can be done by the government to change the situation of the poor because the problem connected with their poverty is their low IQ. For Murray, the masses of poor, both black and white, are mentally inferior.

Two Limitations

Let me raise two limitations involving the use of religion and ideology as bases for deriving explanations about meanings and perceptions about the poor. First, they pose questions of definition, meaning, relativism, and objectivity (Huber and Form 1973), all of which a heterogeneous society (class, race, age, occupation, etc.) makes inevitable. However, I argue here that the relevancy of these questions has not been explored sufficiently. These questions are not only relevant but are demonstrated in the persistent, dominant genre of images about the poor that exists in the collective mind of the American public. Furthermore, I argue that similar subjective explanations have been sustained across generations. This is a paramount consideration for seeking insights from the directions of religion and ideology, where clear conceptions of the poor are established and have strong associations with the present existence of stigmatization, or patterns of stereotyping the poor. In effect, these constitute definitions and meanings in terms of the dominant cultural belief/value system. To entertain these subjective elements, as I have attempted here, is not to dismiss approaches that emphasize that the material conditions of poverty have a strong association with the low standing of the poor, or that define their position as a derivative of recurrent economic imperatives; nor does it dismiss approaches that consider the continuous interaction of the above two approaches. I will comment briefly on the latter approach before proceeding to the second limitation.

Research by Newman (1988) makes us aware of the possible interaction between the approaches. For example, in examining the question of symbolic attributions of the poor as aspects of the core culture, and as bases for defining the relationship between the poor and nonpoor, she finds that the ideas found in the dominant belief system form a symbolic universe, one that is taken for granted because it exists as a part of the second nature of the more privileged groups in society. This universe appears to be consistent and is held comfortably until a personal experience (or compelling episodic event) raises troublesome contradictions about forces affecting their own well-being. Her study raises the significance of understanding the views of workers who unexpectedly find themselves in a situation of long-term unemployment that has resulted from conditions such as job displacement, plant closings, or corporate downsizing. Its importance becomes obvious in that many such individuals are now downwardly mobile and, as a result, find that they must endure a personal struggle against the stigma reserved for the poor. However, it is telling that there is still a strong tendency for them to hold on to the same beliefs of which they have become objects.

Second, there is an inherent limitation in primarily focusing on the conservative side of the debate. This is true even if we allow for the validity of the argument evoked by the premise that the changes attributed to progressive movements have tended to be more beneficial to the poor when they have incorporated benefits for larger segments of society. On the other hand, there is a need to understand the role that liberal views have played in shaping particularistic policies for the poor, and scholars have devoted their attention to it (e.g., Vedder and Gallaway 1992; McMurry 1991). The question "Do antipoverty programs benefit the poor?" is quintessential in the arguments of conservatives who seek to answer it by pointing to the failure of such programs (e.g., Murray 1984); in contrast, liberal scholars seek to answer it by calling attention to the inadequacy of the government or to repressive forces in the political economy (e.g., Feagin 1975). This latter side of the debate deserves attention; a proper discussion of it here, however, is impossible within the present framework.

Conclusion

Finally, this discussion has advanced the idea that public policy for the poor occurs in a social and cultural context, which is inextricably connected with America's religious and ideological history. In a period when the federal deficit approaches nearly five trillion dollars, and the accompanying escalation of pressure to cut back on spending for federal programs for education, medical care, and child support, as well as the recent arguments in the public policy arena for the devolution of responsibility for social services from the federal government to states, there is not a better time than now to consider the relevance of the ideas developed here for understanding the significance of this context. The line has been drawn between and among competing office holders and their constituencies; the apologists have taken their sides on the issues of poverty;

and the arguments being raised are the familiar ones that follow party lines.

The increasingly worsening condition of the poor in the African American community makes it necessary to scrutinize the intellectual arguments found on the conservative side of the debate, whether within or outside of the social sciences. In this regard, the present effort was undertaken to explain significant questions about why the poor in general, and African Americans in particular, remained poor in an affluent society. Why, in other words, is there great popular resistance to an array of programmatic policy initiatives—e.g., Head Start, Aid to Families with Dependent Children, Medicaid, Federal Food Stamp Assistance, Section VIII Housing, Enterprise Zones, Negative Tax Incentives, Affirmative Action, Pell Grants? In this light, why is there less resistance to building new prisons to incarcerate criminal offenders, most of whom will come from poverty areas in the African American community? I conclude that such initiatives may be condemned or given very little attention as a result of persistent stereotypes, or because of conservative ideas defining the poor. The complexity of poverty demands that the origin of such conceptions be understood. That has been the purpose of our focus on core religious and ideological ideas as neglected components in discussions to clarify conceptions of the poor in a proclaimed free market society.

Simple awareness of the perceptual problem concerning the poor is not likely to change the fundamental relation of the poor to the economic system. However, it can be a catalyst for inspiring positive action, debunking myths, and paving the way for a more favorable climate for the kind of decision-making that will foster more realistic national priorities for reducing the level of inequality experienced by the poor.

Economic reforms will only be meaningful if the poor are imbued with a new aura of legitimacy. This is a national issue. The nation must be pressed to do it. Scholars and activists must take the lead in bringing about this transformation. Without their involvement, the concentration of wealth and the distribution of the country's resources will continue disproportionately to favor those in the higher socioeconomic strata. For example, in political decisions involving budget cuts, tax redistribution, tenant rights, and the like, the interests of the poor will not be represented, and their position in society will worsen. Unfortunately, many conservatives in the general populace in turn will continue to see their condition as the natural order of things, an order that should not be changed by the government's intervention with public policies.

References

Augustinus, Aurelius. 1950. *City of God.* New York: Dutton.

Blum, Zahava D. and Peter Rossi. 1969. "Social Class Research and Images of the Poor: A Bibliographic Review." In *On Understanding Poverty,* ed. Daniel Moynihan. New York: Basic Books.

Butler, Stuart and Anna Kondratas. 1987. *Out of the Poverty Trap.* New York: Free Press.

Cazenave, Noel A. 1990. "North Philadelphia: Demographic Transition, Economic Change, Public Policy, and Social Consequences Two Decades After the Riot of 1964." *National Journal of Sociology* 4:201-26.

Clark, Peter. 1977. *English Provincial Society from the Reformation to the Revolution.* Cranberry, NJ: Associated University Presses.

Cook, Fay L. 1979. *Who Should Be Helped? Public Support for Social Services.* Beverly Hills, CA: Sage.

Darwin, Charles. [1859] 1965. *The Origin of Species.* New York: Norton.

Duncan, Greg J. 1984. *Years of Poverty, Years of Plenty: The Changing Economic Fortunes of American Workers and Families.* Ann Arbor: Institute for Social Research, University of Michigan.

Feagin, Joe R. 1975. *Subordinating the Poor: Welfare and American Beliefs.* New York: Prentice Hall.

Fitzhugh, George. 1854. *Sociology of the South.* Richmond, VA: A. Morris.

Gallup, George. 1993. *The Gallup Poll Public Opinion 1993.* Wilmington, DE: Scholarly Resources Inc.

Gans, Herbert. 1991. *People, Plans and Policies: Essays on Poverty, Racism and Other National Urban Problems.* New York: Columbia University Press.

Gingrich, Newt. 1995. *To Renew America.* New York: HarperCollins.

Ginsberg, Leon H. 1983. "Changing Public Attitudes About Public Welfare Clients and Services Through Research." In *Applied Poverty Research,* ed. Richard Goldstein and Stephen M. Sach, 241-52. Totowa, NJ: Rowman and Allanheld.

Goodwin, Leonard. 1972. *Do the Poor Want to Work?* Washington, DC: Brookings Institution.

Hammond, Philip E. and Kirk R. Williams. 1976. "The Protestant Ethic Thesis: A Social-Psychological Assessment." *Social Forces* 54:579-89.

Harrington, Michael. 1962. *The Other America.* New York: Macmillan.

———. 1984. *The New American Poverty.* New York: Holt, Rinehart & Winston.

Harvey, David. 1984. "On Planning the Ideology of Planning." In *Planning Theory in the 1980's: A Search for Future Directions,* ed. Robert W. Burchell and George Sternlieb, 213-33. New Brunswick, NJ: The Center for Urban Policy Research.

Heilbroner, Robert L. 1961. *The Worldly Philosophers.* New York: Time, Inc.

Herrnstein, Richard J. and Charles Murray. 1994. *The Bell Curve.* New York: Free Press.

Hill, Robert B. 1989. "Economic Forces, Structural Discrimination and Black Family Instability." *Review of Black Political Economy* 17(3):5-23.

Huber, Joan and William H. Form. 1973. *Income and Ideology.* New York: Free Press.

Janowitz, Morris. 1977. *Social Control of the Welfare State.* New York: Elsevier.

Jarmon, Charles. 1976. "Ideology, Structural Constraints and the Dilemma of Black Youths." In *Afro-Americans: A Social Science Perspective,* ed. Rutledge M. Dennis and Charles Jarmon, 89-101. Washington DC: University Press of America.

Katz, Michael. 1989. *The Undeserving Poor: From the War on Poverty to the War on Welfare.* New York: Pantheon.

———. 1993. *The Underclass Debate: Views from History.* Princeton, NJ: Princeton University Press.

Kluegel, James R. 1990. "Trends in Whites' Explanations of the Black-White Gap in Socioeconomic Status, 1977-1989," *American Sociological Review* 55:512-25.

Kluegel, James R. and Eliot R. Smith. 1986. *Beliefs and Inequality.* New York: Aldine.

Leibow, Elliot. 1967. *Tally's Corner.* Boston: Little, Brown.

Lenski, Gerhard. 1966. *Power and Privilege.* New York: McGraw-Hill.

Malthus, Thomas R. [1798] 1926. *An Essay on the Principles of Population.* New York: Macmillan.

Massey, Douglas S. 1994. "Migration, Segregation and Geographic Concentrations of Poverty." *American Sociological Review* 59:425-45.

McMurry, Dan. 1991. "The Several Faces of Hunger: A Review of the Types of Information Available to the Public on Domestic Hunger, 1967-1990." *National Journal of Sociology* 5:91-110.

Miranda, Jose. 1974. *Marx and the Bible: A Critique of the Philosophy of Oppression.* New York: Orbis.

Montagu, Ashley. 1971. Foreword. In *A Dissertation on the Poor Laws,* by Joseph Townsend. Berkeley: University of California Press.

Moynihan, Daniel P., Paul Barton, and Ellen Broderick. 1965. *The Negro Family: The Case for National Action.* Washington, DC: Office of Policy Planning and Research, U.S. Department of Labor.

Murray, Charles. 1984. *Losing Ground: American Social Policy.* New York: Basic Books.

Newman, Katherine. 1988. *Falling from Grace: The Experience of Downward Mobility.* New York: Free Press.

Oropesa, R. S. 1986. "Social Class, Economic Marginality, and the Image of Stratification." *Sociological Focus* 19:229-43.

Piven, Francis F. and Richard Cloward. 1971. *Regulating the Poor.* New York: Pantheon.

Quadagno, Jill. 1992. "Social Movements and State Transformation: Labor Unions and Racial Conflicts in the War on Poverty." *American Sociological Review* 57:616-34.

Ryan, William. 1972. *Blaming the Victim.* New York: Vintage.

Sachs, Stephen M. 1983. "Toward a Political Economy of Poverty Research: A Critique from Right to Left." In *Applied Poverty Research,* ed. Richard Goldstein and Stephen M. Sach, 14-28. Totowa, NJ: Rowman and Allanheld.

Spencer, Herbert. [1892] 1969. *The Man versus the State.* Caldwell, ID: Caxton.

Sumner, William G. 1925. *What Social Classes Owe to Each Other.* New Haven, CT: Yale University Press.

Tawney, Richard H. 1926. *Religion and the Rise of Capitalism.* New York: Harcourt, Brace.

Townsend, Joseph. [1786] 1971. *A Dissertation on the Poor Laws.* Berkeley: University of California Press.

U.S. Bureau of the Census. 1991. "Poverty in the United States." *Current Population Reports,* P-60, No. 181. Washington, DC: Government Printing Office.

U.S. Bureau of the Census. 1996. "Poverty in the United States: 1995." *Current Population Reports,* P-60, No. 194. Washington, DC: Government Printing Office.

Valentine, Charles. 1968. *Culture and Poverty.* Chicago: University of Chicago Press.
Vedder, Richard and Lowell Gallaway. 1992. *The War on the Poor.* Lewisville, TX: Institute for Policy Innovation.
Waxman, Chaim I. 1983. *The Stigma of Poverty.* New York: Pergamon.
Weber, Max. 1958. *The Protestant Ethic and the Spirit of Capitalism.* New York: Scribner.
Wilensky, Harold L. 1975. *The Welfare State and Equality: Structural and Ideological Roots of Public Expenditures.* Berkeley: University of California Press.
Wilson, William J. 1987. *The Truly Disadvantaged: The Inner City, the Underclass, and Public Policy.* Chicago: University of Chicago Press.

AFRICAN-AMERICAN FAMILIES AND PUBLIC POLICY

The Legacy of the Moynihan Report

JUAN J. BATTLE
MICHAEL D. BENNETT

The conclusion from these and similar data is difficult to avoid: During times when jobs were reasonably plentiful . . . the Negro family became stronger and more stable. As jobs became more and more difficult to find, the stability of the family became more and more difficult to maintain. . . . The impact of poverty on Negro family structure is no less obvious, although again it may not be widely acknowledged. (Moynihan 1965:21)

It is no secret that the major problem facing African-American families is that a disproportionate number of them suffer from poverty and joblessness. However, this fact, brought to public attention in an undeniable way by the Moynihan report in 1965, sometimes has been overshadowed by a widely believed cultural myth that also rose to prominence through Moynihan: the theory that the Black "underclass" is the victim of its own decimated family structures and failed morals. Since its publication 30 years ago, some have used the Moynihan report's findings about the untenable economic situation faced by a large portion of African-American families to argue for government action aimed at alleviating the poverty that is the root cause of the problem. Others have drawn on the report's speculation about the "tangle of pathology" inherent in the "matriarchal" African-American family to blame these families for a long list of supposedly debilitating symptoms. This dual legacy of the Moynihan report still functions to distort public policy efforts to confront the crises facing the Black family by confusing fact and fiction.

One would think that the facts, in this case, would speak for themselves. In 1965, Moynihan was shocked that the latest employment statistics showed that the white unemployment rate was 4.7 percent and the "nonwhite" unemployment rate—composed almost entirely of "Negroes"—was 8.7 percent (p. 66). Since then, the picture has grown much worse. Beginning in the 1980s, Black unemployment climbed to more than 14 percent, higher in some urban areas, and higher still for young African-American males (U.S. Bureau of the Census 1994:396). Even more disturbing is the increased divergence between Black and white wealth. After decades of closing the income gap between Black and white, rich and poor, the breach widened enormously in the 1980s. In 1983, the median wealth of white families was 11 times greater than that for nonwhite families; by 1989, the ratio had grown to 20 times (Woolf 1995). If, according to Moynihan, Black unemployment and poverty were the "root cause" of crisis in the mid-1960s, who could deny that those roots have grown even deeper in the mid-1990s?

In spite of common knowledge about the problems confronting millions of African-American families, public policy in the 1980s and 1990s has been much more likely to focus on a virulent form of "blaming the victim" than on making proactive efforts to remedy the situation. The tendency has been to worry about the supposedly self-defeating behaviors of the Black poor, not poverty itself, and to be concerned more about the moral improvement of African-American families than about their economic deprivation. As we approach the twenty-first century, the facts of African-American unemployment and poverty have been buried beneath myths about the implosion of Black family structures.

The roots of this tragedy extend from the distaff branch of Moynihan's theory, the part of his legacy that has been used to ascribe the problems confronting poor African-American families to internal social and cultural failings. The use of the term *culture of poverty* to describe this myth that the very poor live in a qualitatively different culture than the nonpoor was not employed by Moynihan. The term was coined by Oscar Lewis in the 1960s to describe certain behaviors of very poor communities in Mexico and Puerto Rico. However, the subsequent history of the term in the public policy arena has more to do with Moynihan's notion of the "tangle of pathology" inherent in poor African-American families than it does with Lewis's research.

Only a subterranean presence in the 1970s, "culture of poverty theory" resurfaced with a vengeance in the 1980s as a tool to discipline African-American families. Conservatives like Charles Murray, with his book *Losing Ground: American Social Policy, 1950-1980*, put an insidious twist on such theories by suggesting that not only did government intervention not make a dent in the culture of poverty, federal programs actually fed the problem by making poor Black families dependent on the government. According to the conservative argument, social programs only reinforced the pathological behavior of poor families who became permanently locked in the underclass—a class no longer defined by inadequate resources but by cultural deficiencies.

The notion of the underclass as a legitimate academic category was given credence by Ken Auletta (1982), who portrayed the urban poor as the victims of individual pathologies rather than as the prey of larger social and political forces. Although a chorus of scholars responded that the category of the underclass had no academic standing, some agreed with James Q. Wilson (1992) that

> it is nonsense to pretend that such a group does not exist or is not a threat. The reason why it is called an underclass and why we worry about it is that its members have a bad character: They mug, do drugs, desert children, and scorn education. (p. 103)

This dubious formulation promulgated by conservative academics has risen to prominence with the collusion of misleading reports in the mass media. In his recent column, William Raspberry (1993) assisted in resurrecting the most insidious part of Moynihan's formulation of the "range of pathologies we have in mind when we say 'underclass.' " Raspberry was particularly concerned about the damaging effect of female-headed households. Without a shred of evidence, Raspberry suggests that "children need both parents—not just two breadwinners, but two parental roles. Two-parent homes are a protection not merely against poverty but also against a variety of emotional insecurities." This exemplified the shift in the 1990s from a general assault on African-American families for being mired in a loosely defined culture of poverty to a disdain specifically for female-headed households.

A month earlier, *Newsweek* devoted most of an issue to the topic of "A World Without Fathers: The Struggle to Save the Black Family." In the lead story of that *Newsweek* feature, Michele Ingrassia (1993) claimed that "by every measure—economic, social, education—the statistics conclude that two parents living together are better than one" (p. 21). Of course, the reporter went on to provide no such statistics other than census figures indicating that the children of single mothers are more likely to be poor than the children of married couples. In what comes to a typical evasion of pathology theory, the analysis is deflected from exploring why these women are poor to blaming them for being single. Rather than citing a single reliable study about the "damage" caused by single-parent homes, Ingrassia quotes psychiatrist James Comer's groundless speculation that "the exploding population of African-American children from single parent homes represents 'the education crisis that is going to kill us' " (p. 21). The article degenerates into stereotyped claims about the need for fathers and the failure of mothers—for example, "Fathers typically encourage independence and a sense of adventure, while mothers are more nurturing and protective" (p. 21).

Unfortunately, the distortions of the mass media have been aided by supposedly more credible academic sources. McLanahan and Booth (1991) review recent research that argues that the children of mother-only families are more likely than the children of two-parent families to perform poorly in school, drop out, marry early, divorce, commit crimes, and abuse drugs and/or alcohol. Some have traced these alleged pathologies to the absence of a male adult role model.

The Moynihan report occupies a strange position in the history of the debate between those who see the problems confronting poor African-American families as self-inflicted (the results of the culture of poverty and matriarchal structures) and those who look at poverty itself, and particularly joblessness, as the causative factor. Although Moynihan (1965) himself does not use the phrase "underclass" or "culture of poverty," he does, as we have seen, identify the fundamental problem confronting the Black community as the "tangle of pathology" associated with a matriarchal family structure. But at the same time, Moynihan traces the cause of this problem to the unemployment of Black men. Contemporary research has unraveled this seeming paradox by showing that it is a lack of economic opportunity, and not insufficient moral fiber, that tears apart many African-American families.

In his long-standing efforts to dispute the "pathological" elements of Moynihan's theory while agreeing with its emphasis on the blight of joblessness, William Julius Wilson has shown conclusively that the greatest source of pressure on African-American families comes not from internal weakness but from external pressure. Wilson (1987) notes that in the 1960s, this view was readily accepted until "in the face of the overwhelming focus on welfare as the major source of Black family breakup, concerns about the importance of male joblessness have receded into the background" (p. 90). Wilson's massive research indicates that the underlying cause of "social problems in the ghetto" are "changes in the urban economy, which have produced extraordinary rates of Black joblessness" (p. ix).

To an extent, W. J. Wilson's emphasis on the "problems of male joblessness" may be myopic. Wilson (1987) argues that the single greatest factor accounting for the large number of female-headed African-American families is the unavailability of " 'marriageable' (i.e., economically stable)" African-American men (p. 91). It may be true that decreasing African-American-male joblessness would increase dual-parent families, but Wilson is operating on the implicit assumption that dual-headed families are inherently desirable and even normative. If the assumption is that the most desirable outcome is not necessarily a particular family configuration but a family (of whatever configuration) with adequate resources to raise its children, then perhaps the focus should be expanded to include African-American *female* joblessness and underemployment. In addition to indirectly lifting African-American families out of poverty by emphasizing job programs that would provide more "marriageable" African-American men, why not directly attack the problem by pushing for public policy aimed at lifting the families *already in existence* out of poverty as well?

This criticism notwithstanding, one of the reasons that Wilson's (1987) research is so persuasive is that the conservative counterarguments about the moral failings of the underclass are, as he points out, weakened because of a lack of direct evidence and because they seemed to be circular in the sense that cultural values were inferred from the behavior of the underclass to be explained, and then these values were used as the explanation of the behavior. (p. 15)

In other words, the conservative argument is less the product of social science research than of the kind of "thought experiments" beloved by Charles Murray and his ilk. The problem with the unflattering picture of the urban poor painted by conservatives like Murray is that, as Michael Katz (1995) argues, the "underclass" is "not really a sociological term but a convenient metaphor" for middle-class fears of the urban "menace" (p. 65). To be a meaningful term of analysis, the "underclass" should have definable parameters and historical specificity, but it has neither. Katz notes that as far back as 1854, Charles Loring Brace (1855), of New York City's Children's Aid Society, was arguing that the "bad tendencies" of an "ignorant, debased, and permanently poor class in the great cities" was the "greatest danger" facing America. Brace went on to provide a description of the urban poor that echoes even more closely the modern descriptions of the underclass: "The members of it come at length to form a separate population. They embody the lowest passions and the most thriftless habits of the community. They corrupt the lowest class of working-poor who are around them" (p. 3). Almost a century and a half later, public policy is still being shaped by such hysterical claims rather than by a considered analysis of the facts at hand.

Another major hole in the argument that the problems confronting African-American communities can be traced to the deficiencies of the Black family is that the measures said to indicate such deficiencies—such as divorce rates and the rate of single parent families—have no inherent value as measures of anything. Parental configuration—whether a family is a dual- or single-parent household—has no demonstrable affect on children when the effect of socioeconomic status is controlled (Battle 1996). Furthermore, although African-American families are more likely to be headed by one parent than are white families, all ethnic groups have undergone dramatic—and roughly equal—increases in rates of divorce and single-parent configurations. So the question is not "Why have Black family structures failed?" but "What social forces are pushing all families in a similar direction?" This trend provides further evidence that it is socioeconomic forces, not individual morals or ethnic characteristics, that are putting pressure on all families, and especially on lower income families—which in U.S. society are disproportionately African American.

Yet many policymakers continue to believe the myths about poor Black families in spite of the available evidence. They are quick to agree with James Q. Wilson's delineation of the characteristics of the "underclass" and their presumed propensity to commit crimes, do drugs, abandon families, and scorn education. It is important to get the message across that the preponderance of social science research indicates precisely the opposite.

Rather than increasing along with the numbers of urban poor, crime rates actually have decreased in American cities over the past decade. Between 1980 and 1990, the crime rate decreased from 116.3 per thousand to 93.4 per thousand. In the mid-1970s, the crime rate was even higher: 128.9 per thousand. Violent crime also has gone down from 32.8 per thousand in 1975 to 29.6 per thousand in 1990 (U.S. Bureau of the Census 1994:203). The social costs of the street crime measured by these statistics, although magnified by the media and conservative demagogues, are greatly overshadowed by the debilitating effects of corporate crime. Jeffrey Reiman (1995) estimates that in 1991, white-collar crime cost the United States in excess of $197 billion. He goes on to note that this figure

is almost 6,000 times the total amount taken in all bank robberies in the United States in 1991 and more than eleven times the total amount stolen in all thefts reported in the FBI Uniform Crime Reports for that year. (p. 111)

Based on these numbers, one can only imagine the economic benefits that would accrue for local, state, and federal government if the law seized all the assets of those convicted of white-collar crimes just like it does for street crimes like drug trafficking. The potential income, which could be used to bolster the conservative agenda of cutting taxes and the deficit, far outweighs Republican efforts to save money by eliminating job programs and decreasing welfare and Medicaid benefits. Despite this fact, it is the "underclass," not the "overclass," that is depicted as the major drag on our society. Given the available data on the cost of white-collar versus blue-collar crime, any rational public policy would focus less on the pathology of poor African-American families than on the pathology of rich white families.

Another myth centered around African-American families is drug use; although overrepresented in the African-American community, the average drug abuser in the United States is not Black, but white. Of those arrested for drug abuse violations in 1992, 39.6 percent were Black and 59.4 percent were white (U.S. Bureau of the Census 1994:205). So, despite the stereotype, drugs are less likely to cause the downfall of a poor Black son raised by a single mother on the streets of the ghetto than they are to seal the fate of a white male product of suburban nurturing.

But the crux of the recurrent arguments about "Black pathology" is the image, conjured by J. Q. Wilson (1992) and others, of the self-inflicted ignorance of fractured Black families. Although Wilson raises the specter of crime and drugs, most contemporary inheritors of the "social pathology" theory have been most haunted by the sight of single-parent families that supposedly produce maladjusted children and underperforming students. These claims have reached their highest pitch in recent assaults on single mothers.

However, all of the research upon which the assault is based suffers from one fatal flaw—it fails to consider that the behavioral differences between one- and two-parent families are fundamentally differences of economic resources. In other words, the problem is not that single parents are somehow more incompetent than dual parents; the problem is that they are much more likely to be poor. Andrew Cherlin (1981) notes that "the most detrimental aspect of the absence of fathers from one-parent families headed by women is not the lack of a male presence but the lack of a male income" (p. 81). The poverty rate among single-parent families is six times higher than that among two-parent families because the women who usually head these families are more likely to be either divorced—and so reentering the job market after a long absence—or already in the job market at the bottom tier traditionally reserved for women. Many single mothers are also victims of the fact that half of the men who owe child support fail to pay all that they owe, and another quarter do not pay at all (see Eitzen and Zinn 1994). These trends are magnified for African-American women who live in the more strained economic situations that produce higher rates of divorce, less education, less access to jobs paying a living wage, and more difficulties with acquiring child support.

No one disputes that contemporary African-American families are much more likely to be headed by females than are their European-American counterparts; the question is whether this arrangement is pathological or merely one result of the various cultural adaptations made by Black families ever since slavery. A large body of research suggests that for more than 300 years, Black family structures have been a source of strength for generations of African Americans. In a direct response to the Moynihan report's efforts to trace Black family "pathologies" to the debilitating effects of slavery, Herbert Gutman (1976) provided conclusive evidence that slavery did not break apart and destroy the Black family; rather, he argues, slavery was "an oppressive circumstance that tested the adaptive capacities" (p. xxi) of such families and, in so doing, provided resilient family structures that functioned admirably long after emancipation. Although slavery's legacy of racism and the economic deprivation of African Americans certainly have put pressures on Black families up to the present, Gutman and Jones (1985) have shown that family resiliency has been equally long lasting. The larger synthetic social histories of Gutman and Jones have been supported by more narrowly focused scholarship on the survival strategies of "underclass" families in nineteenth-century New York (Stansell 1986) and twentieth-century Chicago (Stack 1974).

The most important attribute of a family is not its composition but whether or not it functions. A large body of research suggests that the extended kinship structures of many African-American families headed by single mothers may be a better strategy for the urban poor than the nuclear family structure often held up as the norm (see Jaynes and Williams 1989; Stack 1974). In fact, Willie (1993) suggests that the egalitarian pattern of extended Black families is uniquely suited to the needs of a "subdominant" group whose greatest hope lies in change rather than stability.

The most important fact to communicate to public policy makers about African-American families is that the overwhelming preponderance of contemporary research indicates that African-American families are victimized by socioeconomic exclusion, not by pathologies arising from an "underclass" mentality or "matriarchal" family structures.

A test case of this fact is provided by evidence concerning the effect of family structure on the educational achievement of Black youth. A superficial investigation of census data reveals that as more African-American children were raised in single-parent families, fewer of them dropped out of school. In 1970, 31.5 percent of African-American children lived with one parent; however, by 1991, that number had climbed to 57.5 percent. During this same time period, trends in dropout rates for African-American students significantly declined. More specifically, for 16- to 17-year-olds, 12.8 percent were high school dropouts in 1970, but by 1990, that number had declined to 6.9 percent (*Progress and Peril* 1993). In an effort to interpret such data, there has been an enormous amount of research investigating the effects of family configuration on the achievement of students (see Schneider and Coleman 1993) and, especially, African-American youth.

Battle's (1996) work found that although some research concerning the exact effect of single- versus dual-parent households on the academic achievement of African-American students supports the widely held belief that dual-parent families are inherently more conducive to the child's academic success, others have argued that family configuration has little or no effect on student achievement for African-American youth. Furthermore, research indicates that although family configuration may be important for white students' achievement, such is not the case for their African-American counterparts. Battle's research went on to show that contrary to public opinion, when socioeconomic status is controlled, the much-assaulted single-parent family configuration has no detrimental effect on children's school performance. More specifically, at the lowest levels of socioeconomic status, African-American children in single-parent households actually *outperform* their peers in dual-parent households.

Unfortunately, these facts and research have not been able to penetrate the social construction of urban poverty that all-too-often functions independently of objective data in formulating public policy geared toward African-American families. The result has been a history of public policy running parallel with the successes of the New Deal and Great Society programs that has robbed well-intentioned programs of ultimate success. At the same time as the federal government took an active role in responding to actual poverty with some remedies, the government also launched an assault on inner-city, mostly African-American and Hispanic families in an effort to assuage the fears of a mostly white and suburban population. Michael Katz (1995) indicates that beginning in the 1930s, the government undertook a series of policy initiatives that proved destructive for African-American families: introducing redlining into mortgage appraisals, which starved inner-city neighborhoods of capital for home ownership; building highways that destroyed housing and sealed off most African Americans from the suburbanizing white middle class; and, in general, colluding "to transform much public housing into stigmatized, segregated, underfunded ghettos" (p. 83). In other words, the government has given with one hand and taken away with the other. The result, Katz concludes, is that "government actions have intensified both the spread of poverty and the decline of formerly great cities" (p. 82).

These trends were magnified during the Reagan-Bush years when, from 1980 to 1990, grants to cities were cut in half and several programs crucial to the stability of many African-American families were terminated: the jobs program of the Comprehensive Employment and Training Act; the nontargeted funds of general revenue sharing; funds for redeveloping cities from urban development action grants; and most initiatives for constructing public housing (see Katz 1995). As a result, the percentage of city budgets derived from the federal government declined from 14.3 percent to 5 percent between 1980 and 1992 (Dreier 1992). The problems confronting the urban poor thus have not been the result of cultural deprivation but of planned economic deprivation. In the words of Eitzen and Zinn (1994), "federal government policies have supported and encouraged suburbanization, metropolitan deconcentration, corporate and job flight, and disinvestment patterns that have contributed to the decline of U.S. cities" (p. 128). These cuts disproportionately affect Black families because, in 1989, African Americans comprised 56 percent of the poor in central city poverty areas. Eitzen and Zinn make the implicit explicit by arguing that the rape of cities is actually an assault on African Americans; they argue that "cities and urban have become metaphors or euphemisms for race" (p. 130) in public policy forums. There is no disputing that public policy has bled inner cities dry and, in the process, transformed the environments of many African-American families into pockets of unremitting poverty.

The renewed interest, during the Clinton administration, in welfare reform and the problem of "illegitimacy" provides further evidence of the coded language of bad public policy. As Katz (1995) argues, "When most of those dehumanized as 'illegitimate' are African Americans, a group formerly denied full humanity by law, the racism underlying the rhetoric of welfare reform loses its technocratic and bureaucratic facade" (p. 85). In other words, contemporary public policy has given a Black face to welfare, illegitimacy, and, in fact, the typical inhabitant of the make-believe categories of the culture of poverty and the underclass. The racialization of poverty has made it easier for conservatives to convince mostly white voters that it is better to blame African-American families (the victims of regressive social policy) for their own difficulties than to go to the socioeconomic roots of the poverty that confronts many families—Black and white.

The sad history of racist public policy aimed at punishing the urban poor for their supposed failings perhaps has never been more cruelly exploited than in the Republicans' "Contract With America." Aptly renamed the "Contract on America" by its critics, this legislative agenda includes the "Taking Back Our Streets Act," which perversely responds to the fiction of urban (read: Black) depravity while contributing to the fact of urban poverty. The act expressly cuts social spending aimed at the root causes of crime to attack the symptoms by building more prisons and hiring more police officers. The contract also includes the misleadingly titled "Personal Responsibility Act," which not only blames women, and especially single women, for their own poverty but actually adds to their problems by restricting access to and severely cutting welfare programs.

Although the contract has succeeded largely in reinforcing the linkage between welfare and illegitimacy in the public imagination and arguing that welfare cuts will thus decrease out-of-wedlock births, almost a decade ago W. J. Wilson (1987) pointed to research that indicates that "welfare receipt or benefit levels have no effect on the incidence of out-of-wedlock births" (p. 81). Based on a thorough review of the historical record, Katz (1995) notes that despite supposed good intentions, welfare reform has usually "served as a synonym for cutting benefits to poor people" (p. 19). His review also indicates that rather than providing the real measures needed to end welfare dependency—education and a living wage—cutting welfare rolls has forced poor families to subsist on temporary jobs that keep them below the poverty line and, all too often, condemn them to life on the streets.

Democrats would do well to remember that the way they won the votes of African Americans and the urban poor was by enticing them away from the Republican party with the first comprehensive welfare policy in the United States. The Democrats capitalized on these gains during the Johnson administration by launching the so-called War on Poverty. Although subsequent partisan critics, such as Presidents Reagan and Bush, claimed that the "loss" of the War on Poverty was a lesson in the limitations of big governments, the facts indicate otherwise. Katz demonstrates that the programs launched in the Kennedy and Johnson administrations cut poverty among the elderly by two-thirds, expanded public housing, improved nutrition, and increased medical assistance to the poor. He concludes that far from showing the "impotence of the federal government" and the limits of its "competence," the War on Poverty showed that "the federal government remains potentially the most powerful weapon in the anti-poverty arsenal" (p. 72). In other words, history proves that the ability of concerted government action to redirect resources can have a profound impact on levels of joblessness and poverty. In short, a renewal of the War on Poverty, not preaching to African-American families about their reputed moral shortcomings, is what is needed to revitalize economically ravaged Black communities.

Based on the accumulated research of the past 30 years or more, it is safe to conclude that the "Contract on America" is precisely the wrong public policy. It would be difficult to formulate legislation more diametrically opposed to the dictates of reason given the overwhelming evidence that poverty and joblessness, not immorality and deviancy, are at the root of the problems confronting African-American families. The tack taken by those who wish to avoid responsibility for the havoc that social policy has wrought on Black families uses every excuse to displace the fact of the socioeconomic exclusion of African Americans onto an ideology of cultural inferiority. As Stacey (1994) concludes in her analysis of the excesses of conservative rhetoric about family values:

> The centrists have it backward when they argue that the collapse of traditional family values is at the heart of our social decay. The losses in real earnings and in breadwinner jobs, the persistence of low-wage work for women and the corporate greed that has accompanied global economic restructuring have wreaked far more havoc on Ozzie and Harriet Land than have the combined effects of feminism, sexual revolution, gay liberation, the counter culture, narcissism and every other value flip of the past half-century.

The gruesome irony is that the attack on illegitimacy launched by conservatives on behalf of "family values" is precisely the rhetoric that most damages many African-American families.

Those who bear the brunt of the failure of public policy to address the real needs of single-parent families are the children in these families. Again, this is especially true of children in African-American families, almost half of whom live below the poverty line (two-thirds in single-parent families), as opposed to 16 percent of white children (see Eitzen and Zinn 1994 and Jaynes and Williams 1989). Being true to the elements of his report that traced Black poverty to socioeconomic structures (and not personal failings), Daniel Patrick Moynihan (1988) has noted that the federal government can help alleviate the economic difficulties faced by children in single-parent families in one of two ways: Aid to Families with Dependent Children (AFDC) or the Survivors Insurance (SI) program that is part of Social Security. Moynihan goes on to point out that whereas SI has "been rising five times as fast as average family income since 1970," AFDC has actually decreased by 13 percent since 1970. It is hard to find a clearer example of how policymakers have been willing to intervene on behalf of white families while sabotaging African-American families and blaming them for socially engineered failures. The dividing line between the legacy of the Moynihan report is too often the color line—white families are granted the status of victims of occasional flaws in the system while Black families are blamed for their individual failings. A similar inequity is displayed in the tendency to blame single mothers for their own poverty while offering sympathy (though little else) to dual-parent families mired in poverty.

Social research and public policy that focus on this problem between dual- and single-parent families are giving more attention to the individual behavior—especially of women—as opposed to the structural factors that perpetuate poverty in single-parent families. The answers to the problems faced by single mothers have very little to do with scolding them for their wanton ways or lecturing on the problems of "bastardy," and everything to do with providing them with what they need. If policy makers really want to help single mothers, they should provide them with institutional support—education, job training, employment programs, a minimum wage capable of lifting a family out of poverty, affordable day care, accessible health care, and programs to extract payments from deadbeat dads.

In fact, Battle's (1996) research indicates that efforts to force poor single mothers to marry—whether as a requirement of welfare payments, stigmatization of out-of-wedlock births, or by whatever means necessary—would be counterproductive at lower levels of socioeconomic status, where having two parents in poverty seems to put even more stress on children and adversely affect their schooling. Once again, the bottom line in determining whether a family is most likely to be stable and successful is not whether a family has one or two parents but whether a family has enough income to meet basic needs.

In this light, the problem faced by African-American families is not a culture of poverty—a myth that implies a collection of specific behaviors transmissible between generations and permanently shaping alternative values and preferences—but poverty itself—the fact that lack of capital and employment possibilities, poor education, and overstressed social networks are not conducive to stable families. We concur with the findings of the Committee on the Status of Black Americans which, on behalf of the National Research Council, undertook the task of surveying the voluminous research on "the changing position of Blacks in American society since 1940" (Jaynes and Williams 1989:x). With regard to the status of African- American families, they concluded that the culture of poverty arguments for the existence of pathological behaviors among the poor are "not supported by empirical research" (Jaynes and Williams 1989:25). On the contrary, the "primary correlates of poverty are macroeconomic conditions" (p. 25). This conclusion rejects the portion of the Moynihan legacy based upon speculations about matriarchy and pathology to focus on the long-standing counterlegacy that traces the problems of African-American families to joblessness and poverty.

Just as the best elements of the Moynihan report helped to spur the first War on Poverty, so the legacy of Moynihan's macroeconomic analysis of the roots of Black poverty can help launch a new War on Poverty. However, this renewed War on Poverty should not replicate the mistakes of its progenitor. Despite the many successes of Johnson's program, his War on Poverty backed away from initial plans to focus on the labor market and democratization of welfare mechanisms; instead, the program focused on a supply-side solution to poverty through job training delivered via a hierarchical bureaucracy (see Weir 1992). Rather than creating another level of well-intentioned bureaucrats imbued with the liberal-managerial mindset of helping the poor through external discipline and management, we need a democratized mechanism for delivering services to poor African-American families that are in accord with their actual needs.

The vestigial mechanisms for democratic control of the initial War on Poverty programs need to be developed rather than sabotaged. There are a number of welfare rights groups nationwide that have campaigned for direct control of those organizations that seek to control them. One such group that is based in Boston, ARMS (Advocacy for Resources for Modern Survival), speaks for the concerns facing so-called "welfare mothers":

> Women who are already in crises do not need the added stress of conflicting policies among the services that are ours by right. We are strong, capable, and often wise beyond our years. We demand that we be allowed to have some control over our own lives. No governor, president, general, or legislators should be able to dictate to us where we live, what we eat, or where, or even whether we should work outside the home when we are already taking care of our children. (Dujon, Gladford, and Stevens 1995:288)

One of the great failings of social science and public policy in the 1960s was to define the poor, and particularly the "Negro Family," as passive and degraded. Acting from this assumption, even the most well-intentioned policies helped feed the notion that the poor were somehow inferior and in need of uplift, rather than merely poor. Thus the terrible irony was that the misguided part of Moynihan's legacy (pathology theory) undercut the impetus of the report: to help the Black family through concerted government action. America's heritage from this mistake is the tendency to offer poor families therapeutic advice when they need economic resources and political mobilization. The new War on Poverty cannot afford to make this mistake.

It may strike some as odd that in suggesting public policy options best suited to serve the needs of African-American families, we have bypassed race-based solutions to push for a more universal sociopolitical program. Along these lines, William Julius Wilson (1987) has persuasively argued that antidiscrimination legislation is not enough to help those African-American families most at risk because the problems they face have to do with structural shifts in the economy. This means that the next War on Poverty needs to focus less on race-based programs—which are not terribly successful when dealing with the very poor and which alienate a large part of the electorate—and more on restructuring the economy as a whole (via universal programs that have a broad appeal, such as those aimed at revitalizing cities and increasing the availability of quality education, health care, and employment).

The best policy options are clear. The question is whether policy-makers can sort out the facts from the fiction in the dual legacy of the Moynihan report's prescription for African-American families— the fact of African-American underemployment and poverty or the fiction of the "tangled pathology" of Black matriarchy. The paradox is that despite 30 years of accumulated research, the current Congress prefers to make policy on the basis of the latter rather than the former.

References

Auletta, K. 1982. *The Underclass*. New York: Random House.

Battle, J. 1996. "The Relative Effects of Single- versus Dual-Parent Families and Socioeconomic Status in Explaining the Educational Achievement of African American Middle Grade Students." Under review.

Brace, C. L. 1855. *Second Annual Report of the Children's Aid Society of New York*. New York: Children's Aid Society.

Cherlin, Andrew. 1981. *Marriage, Divorce, Remarriage*. Cambridge, MA: Harvard University Press.

Dreier, P. 1992. "Bush to Cities: Drop Dead." *The Progressive* 56(July):20-23.

Dujon, Diana, Judy Gladford, and Dottie Stevens. 1995. "Reports from the Front: Welfare Mothers up in Arms." In *Race, Class, and Gender: An Anthology*, ed. M. L. Anderson and P. H. Collins, 281-88. Belmont, CA: Wadsworth.

Eitzen, D. S. and M. B. Zinn. 1994. *Social Problems*. 6th ed. Boston: Allyn and Bacon.

Gutman, H. and J. Jones. 1985. *Labor of Love, Labor of Sorrow: Black Women, Work and the Family from Slavery to the Present*. New York: Basic Books.

Gutman, H. G. 1976. *The Black Family in Slavery and Freedom, 1750-1925*. New York: Vintage.

Ingrassia, M. 1993. "Endangered Family." *Newsweek* August 30:16-27.

Jaynes, G. D. and R. M. Williams, Jr. Eds. 1989. *A Common Destiny: Blacks and American Society*. Washington, DC: National Academy Press.

Katz, M. B. 1995. *Improving Poor People: The Welfare State, the "Underclass," and Urban Schools as History*. Princeton, NJ: Princeton University Press.

McLanahan, S. and K. Booth. 1991. "Mother-Only Families." In *Contemporary Families: Looking Forward, Looking Back*. Ed. A. Booth, 405-28. Minneapolis, MN: National Council on Family Relations.

Moynihan, D. P. 1965. *The Negro Family: The Case for National Action*. Washington, DC: Office of Policy Planning and Research, U.S. Department of Labor.

———. 1988. "Our Poorest Citizens—Children." *Focus* 11(Spring):5-6.

Murray, C. 1984. *Losing Ground: American Social Policy, 1950-1980*. New York: Basic Books.

Progress and Peril: Black Children in America. 1993. Washington, DC: The Black Community Crusade for Children, coordinated by the Children's Defense Fund.

Raspberry, W. 1993. "Nothing Beats Having Two Parents." *York Dispatch* Sept. 28:A4.

Reiman, J. 1995. *The Rich Get Richer and the Poor Get Prison: Ideology, Class, and Criminal Justice.* 3d ed. New York: Macmillan.

Schneider, B. and J. Coleman. 1993. *Parents, Their Children, and Schools.* Boulder, CO: Westview.

Stacey, J. 1994. "Dan Quayle's Revenge: The New Family Values Crusaders." *The Nation* (July 25/August 1):119-22.

Stack, C. B. 1974. *All Our Kin: Strategies for Survival in a Black Community.* New York: Harper & Row.

Stansell, C. 1986. *City of Women: Sex and Class in New York, 1789-1860.* New York: Knopf.

U.S. Bureau of the Census. 1994. *Statistical Abstract of the United States.* 114th ed. Washington, DC: Government Printing Office.

Weir, M. 1992. *Politics and Jobs: The Boundaries of Employment Policy in the United States.* Princeton, NJ: Princeton University Press.

Willie, C. V. 1993. "Social Theory and Social Policy Derived from the Black Family Experience." *Journal of Black Studies* 23:451-59.

Wilson, J. Q. 1992. Redefining Equality: The Liberalism of Mickey Kaus. *Public Interest* 109:101-8.

Wilson, W. J. 1987. *The Truly Disadvantaged: The Inner City, the Underclass, and Public Policy.* Chicago: University of Chicago Press.

Woolf, E. N. 1995. *Top Heavy: A Study of the Increasing Inequality of Wealth in America.* New York: Twentieth Century Fund Press.

PART

VI

Race and Educational Segregation

RACE RELATIONS AND CAMPUS CLIMATE FOR MINORITY STUDENTS

Implications for Higher Education Desegregation

GAIL E. THOMAS

◆◆◆

The decade of the 1960s is probably what comes to the mind of the average American citizen regarding an era of wide-scale racial unrest, turbulence, and social protest in U.S. society. However, in the late 1980s and throughout the 1990s, the resurgence and continuing occurrence of racial and ethnic conflict and violence, largely on predominantly white college campuses, constitutes the new image concerning racial unrest for most Americans. Reports from the National Institute Against Prejudice and Violence (Pendergast 1990) indicate that in 1989, one-fifth of all minority students at predominantly white colleges and universities experienced race-related verbal or physical harassment. One in four students perceived considerable racial conflict on their campuses during this time (Hurtado 1992), and 115 U.S. colleges and universities reported racial incidents. In commenting on the resurgence of racial conflict and confrontation on college campuses, Altbach and Lomotey (1991) noted the following:

> Racism is a problem of all of American society, not of higher education alone; yet higher education is now on the front lines of the conflicts as were once the buses, the lunch counters, the city streets, the factory employment offices. (p. viii)

On the surface, it would appear to be a taboo that an "enlightened" place like higher education, with a cadre of "enlightened" or potentially "enlightened" people, would be the stage for racial hostility and conflict. However, a deeper assessment of the situation—especially given (1) the increase in minority and nontraditional students' presence in higher education and society; (2) the decrease in financial aid; (3) the increase in political conservatism and strong challenges against affirmative action; and (4) the persistent and increasing degree of racial and ethnic segregation in elementary and secondary schools (Parsons 1990; Orfield, Schley, Glass, and Reardon 1993), in housing (Tienda and Lii 1987) and in society in general (Tienda 1990)—suggests that one could readily predict and expect racial conflict and unrest on today's college campuses.

Research addressing minority students on predominantly white campuses consistently indicates that following the Adams mandate to desegregate higher education, most predominantly white institutions—especially those that experienced rapid increases in minority student enrollments—were not prepared to accommodate minority students or meet their needs. Thus, the lack of fit between most minority students and what they bring to the white college environment, coupled with the traditional culture and composition of these institutions, are sources of potential conflict. Second, prior to college enrollment, whites, Blacks, and Latinos are less likely to encounter each other in elementary and secondary schools and in their residential communities. In 1991-1992, 66 percent of Blacks and 73 percent of Latinos attended predominantly minority schools; and in the Northeast alone, almost half of the Latino and African American students attended schools with 90 percent to 100 percent minority enrollments (Orfield et al. 1993). Thus, many white public college students are encountering U.S. minority students in larger numbers for the first time.

Studies show that minority and especially majority students have very little knowledge and appreciation for each other's cultures

(Banks 1988; White and Sedlacek 1987). Farrell and Jones (1988) noted that today's minority college students, primarily from low-income, working-class communities, are among the most assertive students. They frequently reject the traditional norms and values governing predominantly white colleges and universities. In addition, working-class, low-income white students (many of whom are highly vocal and racially intolerant) are entering higher education in increasing numbers. Both low socioeconomic status minority and majority students are entering higher education at a time when financial aid, especially in the form of grants and scholarships, is diminishing in availability, amount, and duration. Thus, these students are compelled to compete for scarce resources.

All these factors—the decreasing availability of aid; limited respect, knowledge, and tolerance for racial and cultural differences; and the first-time encounter of assertive minority and majority students in higher education—may very well explain the recent increase in conflict and racial disturbance on college campuses. The American Council on Education's 1989 survey of academic administrators indicated that only one out of four administrators at U.S. colleges and universities believed that their campus provided a "very good" to "excellent" climate for Black students (Hurtado 1992). Only 21 percent believed that their campus provided a supportive climate for Hispanic students. Hurtado (1992) noted that "if these issues have been left unattended since the influx of minorities in higher education in the 1960s, it is no wonder that campuses continue to deal with racial tensions" (p. 541).

Although campus racial conflict can be explained by a number of factors, including the increased presence of minorities in higher education (Blalock 1967; Hurtado 1992), "cultural ignorance, intolerance and isolation" (White and Sedlacek 1987; McClelland and Auster 1990), and increased competition between majority and minority groups (Farrell and Jones 1990), these factors do not shift the responsibility that American colleges and universities have to provide a broader and more diverse quality education to students. Chickering (1969) and, more recently, Banks and Banks (1993) noted that a major need for all U.S. college students involves developing an increased tolerance and respect for individuals with different backgrounds and cultures. Given its major role in society, higher education is also compelled to take the lead in reducing racial tension and discrimination and in successfully achieving racial and cultural diversity.

Past and current research on campus climate indicates that although administrators at some institutions have invested time and resources in minority programs and services and increasing minority student enrollments, many have not effectively addressed campus race relations, racial conflict, and the voluntary patterns of segregation that are still prevalent at many of these institutions (Hurtado 1992; Jones, Terrell, and Duggar 1991; Farrell and Jones 1988; Loo and Rolison 1986).

This chapter reviews existing literature on campus race relations and racial conflict at U.S. colleges and universities. In addition, it discusses observations regarding campus race relations and the status of minorities based on recent site visits to four public U.S. colleges and universities within states previously operating de jure systems of segregation. The chapter concludes with recommendations for improving campus race relations and diversity in public higher education. First, a brief account of student racial demographics on predominantly majority (i.e., white) and minority campuses is provided given the relative increase in students of color in U.S. colleges and universities and the impact of changing demographics for these institutions and society.

Predominantly White and Traditionally Black Institutions and Their Minority Students and Faculty

There are more than 2000 predominantly white two- and four-year U.S. public institutions (Carter and Wilson 1994). During the mid- and late 1970s, after court-mandated higher education desegregation, the number of Blacks, Hispanics, and other underrepresented racial minorities in these institutions increased drastically. Two-year colleges absorbed most (i.e., more than 50 percent) of Black and Hispanic enrollment in predominantly white colleges during this time and continue to do so (Mingle 1981; Olivas 1986; Carter and Wilson 1994). These groups remain underrepresented in predominantly white four-year colleges and comprise less than 4 percent of the total enrollment in these institutions (Carter and Wilson 1990). The faculty at predominantly white institutions remain largely white at approximately 90 percent (Carter and Wilson 1994). Black faculty comprise less than 3 percent of the faculty in white colleges and universities, and Hispanic faculty less than 2 percent (Jackson 1991; Reyes and Halcon 1990).

Currently, there are 106 historically or traditionally Black colleges and universities in the United States. Initially, these institutions were established for the sole purpose of educating Blacks who were denied access to white institutions. Thus, up until the 1973 Adams mandate, Black colleges enrolled and granted degrees to virtually all Blacks in American higher education (Thomas and Hill 1987; Jackson 1991). Approximately one-eighth of the students enrolled in traditionally Black institutions (TBIs) are white (Nixon and Henry 1992). The number of whites obtaining degrees from TBIs has increased 5.2 percent per year since 1976 (*New York Times* 1993). Five of the 106 TBIs have more than a 50 percent white student body, and nine others are approaching white student status (Nixon and Henry 1992).

Most white students in TBIs are enrolled in state institutions in the South. These students are largely attracted to TBIs because of low tuition costs, lower admissions standards, and certain course offerings. A 1990 report by the Southern Regional Education Board (SREB) indicated that white students at TBIs are two to three times more likely to be upper-level or graduate students, and older, married, and enrolled in evening classes on a part-time basis. In addition, most white students live off campus, have better finances (because of outside employment), and better grades than Black students (Southern Regional Education Board [SREB] 1990). In contrast to predominantly white institutions (PWIs), the average Black and non-Black students at TBIs enter these institutions with lower finances and lower academic credentials (Astin and Cross 1981; Fleming 1981; SREB 1990). Also, the budgets and funds at TBIs are far less than similar resources at PWIs (Scott 1981; Thomas and Hill 1987; Carter and Wilson 1990). In 1984, the average TBI had a faculty that was 39 percent white (Thomas and Hill 1987), and in 1991, about 31 percent white (Nettles 1994a).

Snapshot of the Current Educational Status of Black and Hispanic Students

Race relations and the nature of racial climates at U.S. colleges will affect the future higher education participation and success of Blacks, Hispanics, and other underrepresented minorities. Even if this reality did not exist, the future of higher educational access and success for these groups would still remain dismal. The reason is that although Blacks and Hispanics are becoming a larger percentage of the school and college-age populations, their present high school graduation, college participation, and completion rates continue to show a greater disparity between their aspirations, their potential, and their actual educational success.

Since 1984, Blacks have not experienced a gain in high school completion primarily because of the decline in the rate of high school graduates among Black males. Also, high school graduation rates have not increased substantially for Hispanics since the 1970s and are the lowest compared to whites and Blacks (Carter and Wilson 1990). In 1989, among high school graduates (i.e., 18- to 24-year-olds), 38.8 percent of the whites versus 30.8 percent of the Blacks, and only 28.7 percent of Hispanic Americans, enrolled in a two- or four-year college. More recent data by Nettles (1994b) on patterns of persistence for minority and majority undergraduates in public four-year colleges in selected states indicate that in general, Blacks are more likely than whites to drop out of college and progress more slowly, and they are less likely to attain either an associate or bachelor's degree. Olivas (1986) and Carter and Wilson (1990) have shown similar trends for Hispanic students.

Problems of social and cultural adjustments and the lack of fit between the predominantly white college environment and the expectations, values, and culture of Black and Hispanic students have been identified as factors that explain the relatively lower levels of higher education success of these students (Farrell and Jones 1988; Allen 1990; Hurtado 1992; Thomas, Clewell, and Pearson 1993). Given their lower levels of success in higher education (especially in predominantly white institutions) coupled with problems of poor adjustment and isolation in many colleges and universities, it is essential to examine more closely the status and conditions of minority students in higher education—especially on predominantly white campuses. What follows is a review of the literature on these topics.

Campus Climate and Race Relations at White and Black Colleges

The California Postsecondary Education Commission (1992) defined campus climate as "the formal and informal environment—

both institutional and community-based—in which individuals learn, teach, work, and live in a post-secondary setting" (p. 9). The commission argued that a major goal of every educational institution should be to ensure an equitable environment for all students; that an assessment of campus climate (especially institutional policies, programs, attitudes, and expectations that affect the educational achievement of all students) would facilitate this. The commission further noted that the primary gauge of the effectiveness of a college or university should be its success in providing an equitable educational environment for all students.

In its findings on racial climate at Stanford and Berkeley, the commission reported that a large percentage of students from historically underrepresented backgrounds believed that (1) racial stereotyping influences their interaction with faculty; (2) subtle forms of prejudice and devaluation were common experiences in their daily lives; (3) most white students were against affirmative action and viewed it as a zero-sum game in which they would lose; and (4) upon arrival, it was desirable and necessary to associate with other minority students from their same background.

The observations of the California Postsecondary Education Commission have been cited frequently in other literature on campus racial climate. For example, a report on campus climate by the National Association of Independent Colleges and Universities and National Institute of Independent Colleges and Universities (1991) summarized the following conditions that were cited repeatedly by minority students and staff members as primary sources of racial stress and conflict on college campuses: ignorance on the part of whites about other ethnic groups and insensitivity about their circumstances, feelings, and needs; isolation and alienation of minority groups from the larger campus community; stereotyping by whites about minority group attributes and behavior; too few faculty role models for minority students; inclination of institutions to address minority needs and concerns through a single office, rather than broadly and systematically throughout the institution; the separation/integration dilemma of students of color—the strongly felt need for a dormitory, special group, or association of their own as a support base, which tends to compound the problem of separateness; and bewilderment, confusion, and sometimes resentment and anger on the part of white students over what they perceive as the excessive sensitivity of minority students and their tendency to ascribe racist motives to actions that arise more from lack of knowledge or perplexity.

Nixon and Henry (1992) reported that one-fifth of all minority students at PWIs experience verbal or physical harassment. The National Institute Against Prejudice and Violence documented that between 1986 and 1987, racial, religious, ethnic, and homophobic violence occurred on 130 campuses (Farrell and Jones 1988); it occurred on another 115 campuses in 1989 (Nixon and Henry 1992). These incidents included racial epithets, verbal threats, hate flyers, humiliating jokes, graffiti, and physical assaults (Ehrlich 1990). They occurred largely between Black and white students at PWIs (Farrell and Jones 1988). Allen (1990) and others (Willie and McCord 1973; Farrell and Jones 1988; Thomas et al. 1994) reported that of all the problems and challenges faced by minorities at PWIs, those of isolation, alienation, and a lack of peer and faculty support are perceived by these students as the most severe.

Regarding racial isolation and alienation, Farrell and Jones (1988) reported that many minority students find it necessary to engage in "voluntary segregation" as a major mechanism to survive the college experience. White students often interpret the behavior of minority students as unfriendly and racist (Loo and Rolison 1986). Studies show that even on relatively calm campuses, there is considerable social distance among students of different racial and ethnic backgrounds (McClelland and Auster 1990). Green (1989) reported that minority students often feel marginal and isolated as a result of the scarcity of minority students, faculty, and administrators, and they feel an absence of minority contributions and focus in the curriculum.

In a study of sociocultural and academic satisfaction among minority students (Thomas et al. 1993), alienation and dissatisfaction were significantly greater for these students than for whites. Forty percent of the minority students in the study indicated that the university did not reflect their values at all, or only to a limited extent. Black and Chicano students reported feeling a lack of integration into the university. One-fourth of the Blacks and Chicanos did not feel integrated, and 37 percent of them felt socially isolated. This is corroborated further in a previous study by Madrazo-Peterson and Rodriguez (1978) and Mayo, Murguia, and Padillo (1992) regarding Blacks and Chicanos. Their findings indicated that social isolation on predominantly white campuses created mental stress and anxiety for these minority students, and that informal and formal social integration of these students with faculty and nonminority students at these institutions was critical for retention and academic achievement.

Minority students in studies by both Thomas et al. (1993) and Madrazo-Peterson and Rodriguez (1978) reported experiences of racism, prejudice, and discrimination on campus and in the local community. These students also reported being singled out in class and asked to give not only their opinion, but an opinion that represented all minorities. Most students responded to stress by self-imposed withdrawal, by associating primarily with other minority students, by leaving the university, or by total immersion in the educational process. Madrazo-Peterson and Rodriguez stated that physical withdrawal often can result in emotional distancing and could reinforce feelings of isolation.

Faculty Perceptions and Differential Treatment

In addition to contending with negative majority student perceptions, minority students also struggle with debilitating faculty perceptions and differential treatment. Trujillo (1986) found that professors interact differently with minority than with nonminority students and had significantly lower academic expectations of undergraduate minority students than of nonminority students. Trujillo further noted that some minority students indicated that they perceived unequal treatment by professors and a lack of adequate oral feedback as compared to nonminorities. Thomas et al. (1993) reported similar findings from their study of Black and Hispanic graduate students in predominantly white graduate schools at the departmental level. These students asserted that many of their white professors held stereotypical views of them and awarded them a B or B+ when they felt that they had done A work. The students also perceived white faculty as having lower educational expectations of them than of white students.

Very few studies encountered by the author focused on the experiences of Hispanic students in predominantly white institutions. However, Madrazo-Peterson and Rodriguez (1978), and Patterson, Sedlacek, and Perry (1984) reported less social isolation in these institutions expressed by Puerto Rican students than by Black students. They also noted that Blacks find predominantly white campuses less receptive than Hispanics do. Loo and Rolison (1986) reported that 63 percent of whites in their survey of minorities on white campuses perceived their university as supportive of minority students versus only 28 percent of Black and Chicano students. They also noted that 80 percent of Chicanos and Blacks lived in segregated housing on campus.

In their review of racial incidents on predominantly white campuses, Farrell and Jones (1988) identified the following as "risk factors" prevalent at campuses that are likely to experience racial conflict: (1) large white enrollments on campus with a predominantly white surrounding residential community; (2) campuses located in isolated college towns; (3) unclear rules for student conduct and weak and/or nonexistent sanctions for racist/sexist behavior; (4) substantial numbers of low-income, working-class majority students whose previous residence has been in majority or nearly majority cities and towns; (5) weak leadership and commitment at the central administrative level of the university with respect to racial and gender equity and diversity; (6) failure by the university administration to act swiftly and decisively once a racial incident has occurred; (7) ineffective minority student support programs; (8) small numbers of minority faculty and staff at the institution; and (9) lack of university initiatives to bridge the cultural and social gap between majority and minority students.

The authors concluded that given the presence of these factors on campuses that have experienced racial conflict, the question is not whether there will be other incidents involving racial conflict but rather where they will occur next and how they will be addressed.

Site Visits of Minority and Majority Students on Predominantly White and Predominantly Minority Campuses

To obtain an updated and first-hand assessment of racial climates for minority undergraduates at predominantly white and predominantly Black institutions, the author, with the assistance of three SEF Task Force members, conducted two-day site visits of four public institutions within 3 of the 10 original Adams states. Two of the institutions were predominantly white (one a comprehensive research institution with an 82 percent predominantly white student body at the time of this investigation; the other a large urban campus with a 78 percent predominantly white student body at that time); and two were predominantly minority institutions (one a traditionally Black college with an 87 percent Black student enrollment during this study; and one a predominantly Hispanic institution with a 62 percent Hispanic student enrollment at the time of this study).

The two minority institutions were selected primarily because of their success in enrolling and graduating Black and Hispanic undergraduates in general and especially in engineering. The predominantly white urban institution was selected given its strategic location in an urban setting that is predominantly Black, a state population that was 20 percent Black and an on-campus student population that was 22 percent minority (of which 14 percent is Black) at the time of this investigation. This institution was also selected because of new and progressive leadership in central administration that was observed and commented upon frequently at this university. The comprehensive research institution is known nationally for its research. It consists of 16 colleges and universities. This institution was selected primarily because of the high levels of racial conflict that had taken place on its campus within the past two years and the relatively large concentration of Blacks (22 percent) within the state in which it is located.

Informants (both minority and nonminority) were asked what they perceived as the greatest challenge for minority students at their institutions. The most frequent responses at each institution were as follows: At the comprehensive institution—(1) financial aid; (2) subtle and overt racism; (3) minority students being able to retain their identity; and (4) having the confidence that they can "make it." At the traditionally Black institution, the challenges for white students and some international students were as follows: (1) mixing with Blacks and taking full advantage of the university beyond coming to class and going home; (2) appreciating and respecting Black culture; and (3) attending this school despite the pressure and negative advice and feedback from family, friends, and high school counselors about attending. At the predominantly white urban campus, the challenges identified were (1) retaining Black males and Black students in general; (2) being ignored or denigrated by white faculty in the classroom; and (3) racial separation and isolation. At the predominantly Hispanic campus, the most important challenge entailed reducing and, on a more long-term basis, eliminating bias against Mexican nationals.

At the end of the interviews, informants provided recommendations for improving race relations on their campuses. The responses by institutions were as follows: At the comprehensive institution— (1) more assertive and committed leadership at the top; (2) greater financial aid to attract and retain minority students and faculty; (3) more diversity awareness education and workshops; (4) greater racial diversity among faculty and staff; (5) greater involvement and mentoring of minority students by white faculty; and (6) more attention to nonacademic factors affecting minority students' attrition. At the urban white institution—(1) greater financial aid to attract and retain minorities; (2) more programs to involve faculty in improving diversity; (3) more guidelines and efforts to diversify the curricula and the campus; and (4) more personalized counseling of students to possibly identify racial problems. At the traditionally Black institution—(1) provide more opportunities for non-Black students to engage in nonacademic activities; (2) provide more on-campus housing for non-Black commuter students; (3) become more active in creating diversity and in supporting non-Black students; (4) create a more structured approach to recruiting non-Black students; (5) create more social organizations for white and international students; and (6) address issues of cultural awareness and diversity more extensively during student orientation programs. At the predominantly Hispanic institution—(1) address problems between Mexican American students and Mexican nationals; (2) stress the cultural and racial ties between these two groups; and (3) incorporate these ties into the curriculum.

The recommendations that informants made regarding improving campus race relations and diversity are consistent with those reported in the research literature (Willie and McCord 1973; Loo and Rolison 1986; Madrazo-Peterson and Rodriguez 1978; Farrell and Jones 1988; Livingston and Steward 1987; Hurtado 1992; Thomas et al. 1994; SREB 1990; California Postsecondary Education Commission 1990). For example, Loo and Rolison (1986) recommended the following:

(1) creating and supporting residential, social, and academic communities within the university that provide culturally supportive environments for minority students; (2) increasing the proportion of

ethnic minority representation among students and faculty; (3) strengthening student support services for minorities; (4) countering racism among administrators, faculty, and students to create a more comfortable learning environment for ethnic minority students. (p. 13)

Of all the various recommendations in the research literature, and from recent campus site visits, the following are most compelling and should be considered by colleges and universities to improve campus race relations and to increase the access and success of minority students and faculty:

1. *Strong, committed, and systematic leadership at the president and provost level coupled with greater shared commitment by deans, department heads, and faculty throughout the university.*

Adequate and "real" leadership at the top and throughout colleges, departments, and academic affairs must be a central and continuing part of institutional leadership and commitment. To encourage greater college- and faculty-level involvement, university and state officials must be willing to more adequately and more visibly reward individuals, programs, and departments that have a positive impact on improving diversity and campus race relations. They must also create effective financial and nonfinancial incentives for individuals who are less inclined to support diversity and a positive racial climate. One mechanism for achieving this is to establish campus diversity and positive race relations as "sacred cows" comparable in stature and consequences to research and teaching productivity. Thus, accomplishments in diversity would become an equally important part of the tenure and promotion process for faculty and a major criterion for allocating funds to universities, colleges, and departments.

2. *Adequate and sustained financial aid to recruit, enroll, and retain minority students and faculty, and to support and reward diversity efforts.*

Financial aid to students should consist of grants and fellowships that are adequate in amount and duration to compensate housing and living expenses. In addition, set-aside monies should be made available to (1) support, continue, and expand effective diversity efforts and programs; and (2) implement innovative and experimental programs in diversity.

3. *Establishment of positive race relations and racial diversity as top institutional priorities that are reflected in policies and practices at every level and throughout the entire university.*

Hurtado (1992) reported that traditional notions of institutional quality based on reputation and resources and top institutional priorities based on these traditional criteria are associated with high racial tension on campuses. She noted that commitment to diversity was usually weak or ambivalent at institutions that employed and were bound by traditional standards of college quality. Hurtado further argued that strong institutional commitment and a more "student-centered" campus (i.e., in terms of priorities) can substantially improve minority and white students' perception of campus race relations.

4. *Broad-based, ongoing, and effective programs to recruit and retain minority students and faculty.*

Some of the literature indicates that passive, "wait and see who applies" recruitment efforts and approaches, as well as recruitment by word of mouth, are much more common practices at predominantly white institutions than are formal, well-established recruitment programs (Swoboda 1990; Thomas et al. 1993). Many of these institutions also "cast their net" very narrowly, rather than broadly, thereby restricting their recruitment search for students to the "talented tenth" among minority students and to superstars among minority faculty (Thomas et al. 1993; Mickelson and Oliver 1991). In its report, members of the University of Wisconsin (1990) noted that when recruiting faculty candidates, nonsupportive departments take the view that "We're only looking for certain people, in certain narrow subspecialties, at certain times." They concluded that this approach, coupled with narrowly written position descriptions, tend to exclude rather than include applicants with new pedagogies, specialties in race- or gender-related issues, and interdisciplinary expertise.

5. *Achievement of a greater racial representation and balance among students and faculty.*

Institutions, both white and nonwhite, must increase U.S. minority representation beyond tokenism or beyond what may be perceived as "too many" or the "threatening tipping point." Until more meaningful racial representation and balance are achieved in colleges and universities and in society, existing patterns of "voluntary segregation" and alienation on college campuses will persist.

6. *Universitywide curricula assessment, expansion, and reform.*

Systemic and systematic curricula assessment and reform must occur, with the primary goal of having racial and cultural diversity represented within all departmental curricula and throughout the university. These curricula must adequately reflect the contributions, perspectives, and cultures of U.S. minorities on campus, in the state, and in the nation. What exists currently on many campuses are isolated minority studies programs or weak and sporadic course offerings and requirements. Diversity must not necessarily replace courses but should be integrated into current course materials.

7. *Implementation of ongoing university-, college- and departmentwide diversity training and prejudice reduction workshops.*

The literature and our site visits consistently revealed the prevalence of cultural ignorance, insensitivity, and prejudice that many students and faculty bring to the college environment. Thus, cultural appreciation, respect for differences, and prejudice reduction must become a more serious and sustained part of the learning process on all college campuses. Given the current state of campus race relations, this education must be just as mandatory as are college course requirements in mathematics, science, and the liberal arts.

8. *In-depth, systematic self-assessment of campus climate, diversity, and race relations.*

Ongoing and in-depth assessments are needed to better determine the status and progress of colleges and universities regarding campus climate, diversity, and race relations. Data on student, faculty, and staff attitudes regarding these issues, and their perception of quality of life on campus, are also needed to help improve race and human relations. Results from the data should be disseminated widely and discussed among students, faculty, and staff.

9. *Immediate and effective mechanisms to address racial-ethnic harassment and racial misconduct.*

More progress has been made in addressing sexual harassment on college campuses than racial misconduct (Farrell and Jones 1988; Wilson 1990). However, given the strained state of human and race relations in colleges and universities, racial and sexual misconduct should have the same consequences as academic failure, which is prompt dismissal.

10. *More systematic and better collection and reporting of data on the admissions, recruitment, performance, and retention of minority and majority students and faculty.*

Having placed greater emphasis on recruitment and enrollment than on retention, many colleges and universities remain "record poor" on minority student and faculty retention data (Thomas et al. 1993; University of Wisconsin 1990). Therefore, states must hold colleges and universities accountable for these data, and colleges and universities must hold all departments, colleges, and programs within universities more accountable.

11. *Expansion of adequate and centrally located housing for minority students.*

Set-aside funds to support new experiments in reducing housing segregation and to encourage and reward students to engage in cross-racial residential living will be necessary to help reduce voluntary segregation and racial isolation on college campuses. Special perks, including more attractive housing stipends, housing supplements, and reducing housing costs, might be considered. Successful programs should be publicized and supported more extensively.

Until or unless state and college and university officials heed and implement many of the consistent and persistent recommendations to improve campus race relations and minority access and success, the business of higher education desegregation will remain unfinished. In addition, the U.S. Supreme Court's dockets will expand, and intergroup tension and violence on American college campuses may become a greater issue. More important, all segments of society will increase in polarity around the issue of race and cultural diversity. The latter is inevitable in the absence of more positive and assertive leadership from American colleges and universities and from society in general regarding these issues.

References

Allen, W. 1990. "College in Black and White: Black Student Experiences on Black and White Campuses." In *In Pursuit of Equality in Higher Education* ed. A. S. Pruitt. Dix Hills, NY: General Hall.

Altbach, P. G. and K. Lomotey. Eds. 1991. *The Racial Crisis in American Higher Education.* Albany: State University of New York Press.

Astin, Helen S. and Patricia H. Cross. 1981. "Black Students in Black and White Institutions." In *Black Students in Higher Education,* ed. Gail E. Thomas, 30-46. Westport, CT: Greenwood.

Banks, J. 1988. *Multiethnic Education.* Boston: Allyn and Bacon.

Banks, J. and C. A. McGhee Banks. 1993. *Multicultural Education.* Boston: Allyn and Bacon.

Blalock, H. 1967. *Toward a Theory of Minority-Group Relations.* New York: Wiley.

California Postsecondary Education Commission (CPEC). 1992. *Assessing Campus Climate: Feasibility of Developing an Educational Equity Assessment System. Commission Report 92-2. Sacramento, CA: CPEC.*

Carter, D. J. and R. Wilson. 1990. *Minorities in Higher Education: Ninth Annual Status Report.* Washington, DC: American Council on Education.

———. 1994. *Minorities in Higher Education: Thirteenth Annual Status Report.* Washington, DC: American Council on Education.

Chickering, A. A. 1969. *Education and Identity.* San Francisco: Jossey-Bass.

Ehrlich, H. J. 1990. *Campus Ethnoviolence and the Policy Options.* Baltimore: National Institute Against Prejudice and Violence.

Farrell, W. C., Jr. and C. K. Jones. 1988. "Recent Racial Incidents in Higher Education: A Preliminary Perspective." *Urban Review* 20:211-26.

Fleming, John E. 1981. "Blacks in Higher Education to 1954: A Historical Overview." In *Black Students in Higher Education,* ed. Gail E. Thomas, 9-17. Westport, CT: Greenwood.

Green, M. F. 1989. *Minorities on Campus: A Handbook for Enhancing Diversity.* Washington, DC: American Council on Education.

Hurtado, S. 1992. "The Campus Racial Climate: Contexts for Conflict." *Journal of Higher Education* 63:539-69.

Jackson, K. 1991. "Black Faculty in Academia." In *The Racial Crisis in American Higher Education,* ed. P. G. Altbach and K. Lomotey, 135-48. Albany: State University of New York Press.

Jones, A. C., M. C. Terrell, and M. Duggar. 1991. "The Role of Student Affairs in Fostering Cultural Diversity in Higher Education." *NASPA Journal* 28(2):121-27.

Livingston, M. D. and M. A. Steward. 1987. "Minority Students on a White Campus: Perception is Truth." *NASPA Journal* 24(3):39-49.

Loo, C. M. and G. Rolison. 1986. "Alienation of Ethnic Students at a Predominantly White University." *Journal of Higher Education* 57:58-77.

Madrazo-Peterson, R. and M. Rodriguez. 1978. "Minority Students' Perceptions on a University Environment." *Journal of College Student Personnel* May:259-63.

Mayo, Judith R., Edward Murguia, and Raymond V. Padillo. 1992. *Social Integration and Academic Performance Among Minority University Students.* College Station, TX: Race and Ethnic Studies Institute Research and Policy Report (1:3).

McClelland, K. E. and C. J. Auster. 1990. "Public Platitudes and Hidden Tensions: Racial Climates at Predominantly White Liberal Arts Colleges." *Journal of Higher Education* 61:607-42.

Mickelson, R. A. and M. L. Oliver. 1991. "Making the Short List: Black Candidates and the Faculty Recruitment Process." In *The Racial Crisis in American Higher Education,* ed. P. G. Altbach, 149-66. Albany: State University of New York Press.

Mingle, J. 1981. "The Opening of White Colleges to Black Students." In *Black Students in Higher Education,* ed. G. E. Thomas. Westport, CT: Greenwood.

National Association of Independent Colleges and Universities and National Institute of Independent Colleges and Universities. 1991. *Understanding Campus Climate.* Washington, DC: ERIC Clearing House. (ERIC Document Reproduction Service No. ED 342 864)

Nettles, Michael T. 1994a. "Minority Representation among Public College and University Degree Recipients, Faculty and Administrators." Commissioned paper, Southern Education Foundation, Atlanta.

———. 1994b. "Student Achievement and Success after Enrolling in Undergraduate Public Colleges and Universities in Selected Southern States." Commissioned paper, Southern Education Foundation, Atlanta.

Nixon, H. L. and W. J. Henry. 1992. "White Students at the Black University: Their Experiences Regarding Acts of Racial Intolerance." *Equity & Excellence* 25:121-23.

Olivas, M. A. 1986. *Latino College Students.* New York: Teachers College Press.

Orfield, G., S. Schley, D. Glass, and S. Reardon. 1993. *The Growth of Segregation in American Schools: Changing Patterns of Separation and Poverty since 1968.* Cambridge, MA: National School Board Association.

Parsons, J. 1990. "Inner City Schools—Poverty and Segregation: Has the Picture Changed since 1967?" In *U.S. Race Relations in the 1980s and 1990s,* ed. G. Thomas, 65-76. Washington, DC: Taylor-Francis.

Patterson, A. M., Jr., W. E. Sedlacek, and F. W. Perry. 1984. "Perceptions of Blacks and Hispanics in Two Campus Environments." *Journal of College Student Personnel* 25:513-18.

Pendergast, J. 1990. "Racial Climate Chilly on College Campuses." *Cincinnati Enquirer* June 3:A1, A12.

Reyes, M. and J. J. Halcon. 1990. "Racism in Academia." In *Facing Racism in Education,* ed. N. M. Hidalgo, C. L. McDowell, and E. V. Siddle, 69-83. Cambridge, MA: Harvard Education Review.

Scott, G. 1981. "The Financial Status of Black Colleges." In *Black Students in Higher Education,* ed. G. E. Thomas, 226-32. Westport, CT: Greenwood.

Southern Regional Education Board. 1990. *Black and White Students' Perception of Their College Campuses.* Atlanta: SREB.

Swoboda, M. 1990. *Retaining and Promoting Women and Minority Faculty: Problems and Possibilities.* Madison: University of Wisconsin System's Office of Equal Opportunity Programs and Policy Studies.

Thomas, G. E., B. C. Clewell, and W. Pearson, Jr. 1993. *The Role and Activities of American Graduate Schools in Recruiting, Enrolling, and Retaining United States Black and Hispanic Students.* Graduate Record Examination Board Research Report No. 87-08.

Thomas, G. E. and S. Hill. 1987. "Black Institutions in U.S. Higher Education." *Journal of College Student Personnel* Nov. 28:6.

Tienda, M. 1990. "Race, Ethnicity, and the Portrait of Inequality: Approaching the 1990s." In *U.S. Race Relations in the 1980s and 1990s,* ed. G. E. Thomas, 137-58. Washington, DC: Taylor-Francis.

Tienda, M. and D. T. Lii. 1987. "Minority Concentration and Earnings Inequality: How Blacks, Hispanics and Asians Compared." *American Journal of Sociology* 93:141-65.

Trujillo, C. M. 1986. "A Comparative Examination of Classroom Interactions between Professors and Minority and Non-Minority College Students." *American Educational Research Journal* 23:629-42.

University of Wisconsin. 1990. *Retaining and Promoting Women and Minority Faculty Members: Problems and Possibilities.* Madison: University of Wisconsin System.

White, T. J. and W. E. Sedlacek. 1987. "White Student Attitudes Toward Blacks and Hispanics: Programming Implications." *Journal of Multicultural Counseling and Development* 15:171-91.

Willie, C. V. and A. S. McCord. 1973. *Black Students at White Colleges.* New York: Praeger.

Wilson, R. 1987. "Recruitment and Retention of Minority Faculty and Staff." *American Association of Higher Education Bulletin* (Feb).

Wilson, R. 1990. "Black Colleges Shift to Racial Mix." *Christian Science Monitor* 82(50):12-13.

Wilson, William J. 1987. *The Truly Disadvantaged.* Chicago: University of Chicago Press.

AFROCENTRIC EDUCATION

*Understanding the
Effects of Black Academies
on Academic Achievement*

KERRY ROCKQUEMORE

The education of inner-city youth has become a major problem in the United States. The failure to attain educational equity and excellence for poor and minority students is evident in the low standardized test scores, high dropout rates, and low graduation rates existent in the major cities around the country. The problems of inner-city schools begin with their outdated goal: facilitating the present and future assimilation and integration of the children of disparate ethnic, language, racial, and economic groups into the political, social, and economic system of society.

For many, the social integration goal has lost its appeal and its effectiveness. As the central cities have undergone major transformations, the face of their public school populations has changed dramatically. Currently, they are almost entirely socially, ethnically, and racially homogenous, with Black, Hispanic, and poor White children overrepresented (Watson 1980). The direct effects of this demographic shift are a changing of educational goals and objectives, expectations, curriculum, teaching strategies, and preparation of teachers (Kapel and Kapel 1982). Specifically, inner-city schools suffer from a host of social problems that manifest in low test scores, increased drug abuse, heightened levels of adolescent suicide, changes in the value attributed to schooling, violence in schools, conflicting value systems, economic change, and inadequate funding.

Because of the increasing perception that schools are not meeting the needs of African American children, reformers in Detroit have founded three African-centered academies (which will be referred to throughout the chapter as Black Academies). Similar projects have been proposed and/or implemented in New York City; Milwaukee; Washington, DC; Brooklyn; Baltimore; and Chicago. The stated purpose of Detroit's Black Academies is to "address the unique needs of disadvantaged urban youth, particularly low academic achievement, poor self concept, and the lack of skills to function adequately in an increasingly complex society" (Moore 1994). Detroit's Black Academies have recently undergone their third-year evaluation, which has three major conclusions: (1) Students' achievement was higher at the Academies than in selected comparison groups of students at similar public schools, (2) students at the Black Academies increased standardized test scores from their previous year at the Academy, and (3) students at the Black Academies increased daily attendance rates from the previous year and were above the comparison group. The independent report concludes that academic achievement of Black students at Detroit's Black Academies has increased (Moore 1994: 1).

Although this report gives some indication of these schools' success, it fails to examine how the Academies are accomplishing this goal. Evaluating the success of these institutions is critical. However, if that evaluation is devoid of an explanatory component, policy implications are inconceivable. Therefore, this chapter will establish a theoretical model, using the education literature, to explain how the Black Academies in general, as innovative organizations, work to increase the achievement of Black students. Detroit's Black Academies will serve as a case study for the purpose of discussion. The specific aim is to analyze how the unique social relations and structural features associated with the Black Academies, working through the mechanisms of increased motivation, self-esteem, and an internalized locus of control, increase the average level of academic achievement for Black students. This model will provide a foundation for future research and the basis for discussion of major policy issues involved in the Black Academies movement.

Detroit

The city of Detroit is replete with many of the problems of major metropolitan cities. These problems are mirrored in its public schools. Residential segregation has resulted in a central-city student population composed overwhelmingly of poor and African American students. Crime and violence run rampant in the schools, necessitating the presence of metal detectors and security guards in school buildings. High unemployment, combined with increasing availability of lucrative opportunities in illegal activity, has left students perceiving few incentives to continue their education.

Academic achievement is typically lowest in schools with low-income minority students (Orland 1990), and Detroit is no exception. At the secondary level, the state of Black males in Detroit's city school district is disturbing. Detroit Public Schools Research and Evaluation Department reports that for the 1989-1990 school year, more than half of the Black male students in this district were Chapter 1 eligible, giving an idea of the poverty among Detroit's urban Black males. Notably, 66.4 percent of these students experienced suspensions, and only 39 percent graduated. This illustrates the high level of disciplinary problems that exceed the most important measure of academic success.

Suspensions and dropouts directly harm individuals and their opportunities by decreasing functional literacy, marketable job skills, and, ultimately, employment possibilities. Simultaneously, they have a negative effect on the greater metropolitan area. These individuals consistently engage in deviant behavior, violent crimes, gang activity, drug abuse, and other actions that lead to self-destruction and the deterioration of the community. The outlook for inner-city Black males in Detroit is one of recurrent deviant behavior that overshadows academic success and ultimately stagnates socioeconomic mobility.

The proposal for a group of Black Male Academies was motivated by these alarming statistics. Granted a school charter from the state of Michigan, three Black Academies (the Malcolm X Academy, the Paul Robeson Academy, and the Marcus Garvey Academy) opened in the 1991-1992 school year. These public elementary schools are unique in that their chartered status allows for autonomy concerning all financial, curricular, and personnel matters. This has allowed the originators to fundamentally restructure the organization of the school and remake the educational experience for Black students.

The Academies are continually growing. The total enrollment in Detroit's Academies has nearly doubled from their inception, increasing from a total of 453 students in the 1991-1992 school year to 1273 students in 1993. This seems to be indicative of the community support and interest in the education offered by these institutions. Each Academy has extended the grade levels offered from the previous year. Finally, in response to various legal challenges, the Academies have continued to admit 15 percent to 19 percent female students. Given this general background of Detroit's Academies, we can now turn to the issue of developing a conceptual explanatory model.

Theoretical Model

In the private sector, some success has been found for Black students in Catholic schools located in urban centers. Many of these schools have shown high levels of academic achievement among their predominantly poor and minority student populations. Research has proposed that this is due to their unique organizational structure. Contemporary Catholic schools are proposed to be communal organizations (as opposed to bureaucratic organizations). This type of organizational environment, grounded in a Catholic mission, seeks to develop students' personal and academic growth. Communal organization has been cited as a determinant of the higher levels of academic achievement in Catholic schools, as compared to public schools (Bryk, Lee, and Holland 1993).

It is this author's belief that the organization of Detroit's experimental schools strongly resembles the communal organization of Catholic schools, replacing the fundamental Catholic mission with an Afrocentric ideology. This alternative approach has gained the support of parents, teachers, and administrators who are increasingly frustrated with the deteriorating condition of urban schools. Therefore, an exploration of communal organization as it manifests in the Black Academies is warranted.

Communal Organization

Schools as organizations can be conceptualized from two distinct sociological perspectives: (1) the rational-bureaucratic perspective and (2) the schools as "small societies" perspective (Lee, Bryk, and Smith 1993). The first perspective regards schools as bureaucratic organizations in which authority is defined by roles rather than people. There exists in these organizations a strict division of labor where teachers act as subject matter specialists. Additionally, specific rules define behavior with minimal personal discretion. Comprehensive public high schools, specifically as depicted by Powell (1985), typify this bureaucratic structure (Lee et al. 1993).

In contrast, the communal perspective views schools as small societies. This type of organization emphasizes informal social relationships. Schools operate under unique sets of values (instead of rules) that members support. Adult roles are diffuse, rather than specialized, and there exists a minimal division of labor (Lee et al. 1993). Contemporary Catholic schools are representative of this small society view and are referred to as communal organizations (Bryk et al. 1993).

Bryk and his colleagues have posited that, conceptually, the level of communal organization of a school is determined by (1) the nature of the social relations, (2) the extent of shared activities, and (3) the degree to which values are shared. These components are asserted to have a combined effect in determining the level of communal organization in a particular school. Specifically, Bryk asserts that no single component is sufficient to create this type of organization. Shared values, shared activities, and intimate social relations are mutually reinforcing and create a unique school experience for students.

How, then, can the idea of communal organization be applied to the Black Academies? Furthermore, how do these components increase achievement for Black students? Figure 11.1 is a schematic representation of the conceptual theory, which will enable us (1) to consider how this organizational arrangement takes form in Black Academies and (2) to understand how psychological mechanisms mediate the relationship between communal organization and average levels of Black achievement. The three aspects of communal organization will be discussed in turn, as will the mechanisms through which they effect achievement.

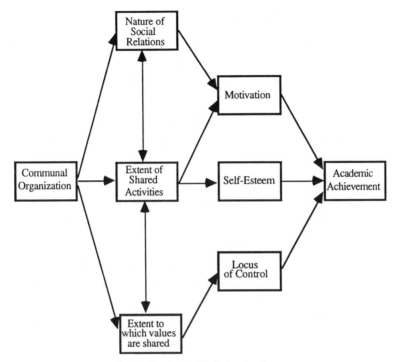

Figure 11.1. Communal organization in Black Academies.

The Nature of Social Relations

One component of a communal organization is a set of intimate social relations among members, the degree of which may vary according to the context. One way these social relations are manifested directly is in diffuse teacher roles. Teachers within a communal organization have broad responsibilities beyond their classroom duties. These multiple responsibilities include advisor (of extracurricular activities), coach, counselor, and adult role model. This variety of activities allows for multiple opportunities for student-teacher interaction on a personal level. Teachers express personal interest in students and their lives, and these relations may even extend to the home. Relationships outside the classroom allow for students to view teachers as individuals, rather than exclusively in the traditional capacity of educator or disciplinarian.

The extended roles of teachers are grounded heavily in the mission of the school. In the Catholic context, these roles are asserted to be "a deliberate enactment of the principle of Christian personalism, set in the context of the larger social justice mission of the school" (Bryk et al. 1993). Teachers in Catholic schools are thought to have consciously chosen their role in this environment and often view it as a "mission" or "calling." In a general sense, then, teachers in a communal organization have varied responsibilities that extend outside of the classroom. They recognize that the goals of schooling include not only the intellectual but the personal and social development of their students.

It is the cumulative effect of these various social relationships that aid in the development of internal motivation. Motivation has been posited to be a crucial determinant of learning and its outcomes, as expressed in academic performances. Although there are many aspects of motivation, this chapter is concerned with the increase in intrinsic motivation. Children are motivated intrinsically when learning and performing at school are goals in and of themselves. This is the opposite of extrinsic motivation, which is the performance of an activity for the purpose of gaining material or other rewards that are not related to school or learning (Malone and Lepper 1987). When students are in a daily environment that fosters intimate relations between students and teachers, and when they are continually inspired by the people who are stressing the importance of their academic development, they are more likely to be motivated and engaged in learning activities and, therefore, are more likely to achieve in the academic arena.

The role of teachers in the Black Academies is crucial, given the at-risk population that they serve. There can be little doubt that Black children growing up in the inner cities are in desperate need of role models, one of the important roles assumed by teachers in the Black Academies. Single female-headed households have risen to more than 50 percent in Detroit, indicating that only half of Black children have a traditional father figure in the home to serve as a primary model. Steinburg (1987) has found that children from single-parent households are more susceptible to peer influences to engage in antisocial behavior. Additionally, Fischer (1977) asserts that poor urban males develop strong peer subcultures that value behaviors that generate social problems. Combined with the effects of long-term poverty and negative environmental factors, Black children (especially Black male children) require positive adult male role models, which are in short supply.

Long-term poverty, hopelessness, and alienation from mainstream society and its institutions have given birth to a sense of despair in the inner cities. Anderson (1990) has established that it is pervasive enough to have seeded an oppositional culture (or street culture) whose norms are opposed to those of mainstream society. Street culture is distinct from Black culture. In actuality, Anderson defines it as a set of values and rules governing life and behavior within many poverty-stricken Black neighborhoods. According to Anderson, all the residents are aware of the rules—termed the codes of the streets—but they have varying investments in the street culture. Trends have shown that young people have the largest investment in this oppositional culture.

Ogbu (1985) shares the belief in the street culture and defines its effects on Black youth in terms of cultural inversion. He suggests that African American inner-city residents "tend to define Black culture, competence, and behavior in opposition to White culture, competence, and behavior" (p. 66). Commonly among Black children, success in school is frequently defined as "White" behavior. The codes of the streets dictate that personal respect, or "juice," has the highest social value. This respect is not won by academic distinction but rather by public displays of hardness, violence, or general disrespect through deviance from white cultural norms.

In schools, this cultural inversion leads students to use linguistic, cognitive, and behavioral styles that conflict with expectations of typical school staff. Street-specific behaviors such as strutting, rapping, woofing, playing the dozens, using selective slang, and/or wearing expressive clothing (highly valued in street culture) are viewed as threatening, rude, arrogant, intimidating and negative. They lead to the excessive suspensions of Black male students and are believed to be nonconducive to learning (Billson and Majors 1992). To succeed in school, students must give up such traits and adopt (or mimic) the white middle-class culture of schools. Students achieving academically are then rejected by their peers for "acting white." Black students, then, must become "raceless" to be academically successful (Fordham 1988). Therefore, the development of Black masculinity and academic success are in opposition.

Teachers at the Black Academies are role models and active agents in counteracting the cultural inversion process by demonstrating positive alternatives and, in effect, delegitimizing the street culture. When teachers are strongly in agreement with the Afrocentric ideology of the school, their commitment is to students' holistic development. This is manifested in the extent to which they participate and feel responsibility for their extended roles. Teachers command students' respect (get their juice) through their professional competence as educators, their demonstrated commitment to students outside of the classroom, and a strict disciplinary code. These roles also allow for teachers to convey nurturance and personal guidance to students. Furthermore, there is a conspicuous absence of the behavior displayed by negative influences in their neighborhood (i.e., violence or a "hard" attitude). Instead, teachers provide an opportunity for students to see people of their own race in positions of legitimate authority, reinforcing the value of hard work in traditional Black culture. Teachers at the Black Academies are then able to establish varying levels of intimate social relationships with students.

The street culture typically provides the most widely recognized means for gaining status among Black students. It has, in fact, provided an avenue for achievement that is recognized by students' peers and in the students' nonschool environment. In general, street culture (as differentiated from Black culture) devalues academic achievement. Students feel social pressure to either (1) accept the codes of the streets, gain their respect from deviant behavior, and do poorly in school; or (2) accept the school's culture and face the social consequences among peers. The extended roles of teachers seemingly shatter this either/or polarity by making school a place where student culture and academic achievement coexist and are mutually reinforcing. Therefore, the teacher-student relationships nourish an environment in which Black students can be engaged in learning activities without experiencing negative consequences. Furthermore, the environment created allows for alternative avenues of achievement (status) in which students can invest their finite energy. Within this context, learning is supported, motivating students to be engaged in their academic activities. These positive relationships increase intrinsic motivation by allowing students to increase their investment in their education. By extension, this increase in intrinsic motivation is manifested in higher academic achievement.

Shared Activities

Another component of a communal organization is a set of shared activities (Bryk et al. 1993). These activities can be academic and/or nonacademic, and they can serve a variety of functions, including (1) socializing members into the school norms; (2) empowering community members (faculty, parents, and students); (3) increasing the personal relationships of community members; and (4) increasing the participation of all actors.

Academic Activities

Traditionally, academic activities refer to the standard curriculum as it is experienced by all students. In Catholic schools, where minimal tracking exists, Bryk et al. (1993) argue that academic activities "afford a common ground that facilitates personal ties and socializes members to school norms" (p. 277). These authors argue that academic activities, in which students have limited choice in their program, are a particular form of ritual. Each student, through his or her coursework, shares a common experience with others in the school, and this shared experience increases student engagement.

This aspect of communal organization takes on a different twist when applied to Black Academies, where the shared academic activities revolve around an Afrocentric curriculum. This alternative to the standard curriculum has as its goal the recentering of knowledge and academic material to focus on and be reflective of the students in the school. This pedagogical shift proposes that Black students center their view and evaluation of the world within their own historical and ontological framework (Asante 1980). Through this means, every student in the school is exposed to relevant Black-centered political, economic, historical, cultural, and environmental experiences and materials. The symbolic purpose of a reflective curriculum is the legitimation of Black culture. The role of the shared curriculum, which is nonstandard and directly tied to racial uplift, has an increased importance in this context.

It is proposed that cultural legitimation through the Afrocentric curriculum empowers Black students and increases their self-esteem. Self-esteem is defined theoretically as a positive or negative orientation of oneself. A student with low self-esteem "lacks respect for himself, considers himself unworthy, inadequate, or otherwise seriously deficient as a person" (Rosenberg 1979:54). Alternatively, a student with high self-esteem perceives himself to be a person of worth. Through the traditional school curriculum, the Black student is placed on the margins of intellectual activity. The only people of his or her race that have contributed to society are the traditional figures, such as Martin Luther King, Jr., Malcolm X, and Sojourner Truth. The students' history is celebrated in February as something unique and outside the typical school curriculum. Most important, the understood perspective and norm of overall subject matter is that of the middle-class White male. This indirectly tells the student that he is a member of an inferior race that has done little more historically than serve the dominant culture, with few notable exceptions. The standard curriculum, then, stigmatizes the child and reinforces what he or she sees consistently in the popular media— that Black people are inferior. Although this is not a process that happens in a short amount of time, the consistent, subtle devaluation of Black culture confirms students' individual feelings of inadequacy, unworthiness, and deficiency directly related to their racial category.

Conversely, proponents of Afrocentric education assert that children who are presented with a reflective curriculum see themselves and their people at the center of the information presented in the classroom. In literature, history, politics, and art, students develop an orientation grounded in this perspective. This does not mean replacing all things European, but instead expanding the dialogue to include African American information (Asante 1980). The philosophy of Afrocentrism asserts that education based on European and Euro-American subject matter is so deeply racist that only an Afrocentric theory of education can mitigate the effects of racism on the psyches of Black schoolchildren. This counters the negative images that a child constantly sees and, if it is consistent over time, the child will begin to see him- or herself as part of a rich history and view his or her racial category as distinct from, but not less than, the majority culture. This fosters feelings of personal worth that infer positive self-esteem free from superiority, arrogance, or contempt for others.

Nonacademic Activities

Nonacademic activities are the second aspect of shared activities within a communal organization. These activities serve the function of developing adult-student personal relationships and increase the participation of all actors. Extracurricular activities work to increase students' academic achievement through the mechanisms of increased self-esteem and intrinsic motivation. In the Black Academies, nonacademic activities tend to be centralized around the Afrocentric nature of the community.

One example is the daily morning 30-minute Harambee at the Paul Robeson Academy. The purpose of this activity (as stated by the principal) is to "reinforce the sense of community in the school" (Moore 1994:63). Harambee means "coming together and sharing" in Swahili. Each morning, the entire school has a general assembly at which students participate in meditations, self-affirmation, and recognition of special achievement. Visitors are encouraged to attend these sessions and participate in a receiving line with teachers and other staff. Students pass through the receiving line as they exit for their morning classes.

It is this type of shared, nonacademic activity that continually instills in students the values of the school community and deepens the interpersonal relations of community members. Because the values of the school are centered on learning and academic achievement, the students are continually exposed to these ideals. It is then conceivable that students will internalize these values and develop a strong intrinsic motivation that will result in increased academic achievement.

Students' self-esteem is also affected by the nonacademic activities. There exist many studies on the development of self-esteem of Black children (for an overview, see Taylor 1976). Self-esteem arises through the interaction of an individual with society, especially parents, teachers, peers, and other representatives of society's institutions (Erickson 1968). It has been asserted that Black students experience cultural rejection within schools that causes them to reconsider what they may be able to achieve or produce, reconfiguring their identity along the way. The devaluation of Blackness that typically takes place in the child's sociocultural environment, especially in the schools, can lead to negative racial self-identification, self-hatred, and low self-esteem (White and Johnson 1991). The nonacademic activities that take place in the Black Academies provide students with the opportunity to experience, in their formative years, an environment that validates their Black identity. This reinforces the value of their culture and education through extensive interaction with the community.

Overall, shared activities support students' self-esteem. They receive positive input and influences throughout the school during the time they are required to attend. Additionally, they receive consistent input through nonacademic activities and from a variety of members of the school community. Students can internalize their possibilities for success through education and feel positive about who they are. This increase in self-esteem empowers students to work hard academically and, consequently, increases their academic achievement.

Shared Values

The final component of a communal organization is a set of shared values. Shared values are common understandings among members of the organization. These understandings include the level of consensus by adults about the school's purpose, teachers' beliefs about student capabilities, and beliefs about the behavior of students and teachers. Bryk and his colleagues (1993) assert that these types of educational concerns are a direct reflection of fundamental beliefs about the nature of the individual and society. Therefore, not any set of values will do. A high level of communal organization requires a strong commitment by various adult members to the basic values and goals of the school as articulated by its leadership.

This component of a communal organization seems to be most crucial in that it underlies the school's social relations and shared activities. Furthermore, it provides the ideological foundation in which the other components are grounded. It is in this component of a communal organization that there lies the danger of particularization—specifically, an ideological drawing that implies closure to the outside (Lee et al. 1993). Indeed, the success of the organization in functioning as a community, without closure, may very well be dependent on the degree to which values are shared by members, particularly by teachers.

Students in a communal organization, experiencing a cohesive set of shared values, ideally will internalize these values. When there exists a high degree of consensus about school values, students' academic achievement will increase through the mechanism of an internalized locus of control. This mechanism can be conceptualized as an individual's perceived sense of power in directing the course of his or her life, which can be on a continuum of internal to external (Findley and Cooper 1983). Ideally, the shared values of the school propose to create an environment that is a mini-society, not necessarily a reflection of our society as it is, but rather as it should be. If, then, these underlying values are empowering to students, particularly if the students are socially disadvantaged, this creates a school environment that is a "safe space" in which students are valued as individuals and can assume a meaningful role in that mini-society. This, then, drives students' perceptions of control over their lives internally because they learn that they do possess the power to direct their future through their education.

The Black Academies were established by the Detroit public schools for the purpose of addressing the unique problems of disadvantaged urban youth. These problems were particularly articulated as low academic achievement, poor self-concept, and the lack of skills to function adequately in an increasingly complex society (Moore 1994). As stated, the Academies are geared toward addressing both the academic and social development of urban students. This however, does not entirely encompass the mission and the goals of the Academies. They all have explicitly stated that they are Afrocentric in ideology, meaning that they are attempting to increase students' academic achievement and self-concept as they are related to their Black identity. It is this fundamental belief that informs the selection of staff, the school environment, the curriculum, and parents' decisions about sending their children to one of the Academies.

The Coleman report (Coleman 1966) found that Black students, in general, had an external locus of control. White students, by comparison, typically had an internalized locus of control. Coleman and his colleagues found this particular social-psychological variable to be a significant determinant of academic achievement. Locus of control can be defined as an individual's perceived sense of control over events throughout his or her lifetime (Findley and Cooper 1983). The two types of loci of control are internal and external. If people have an internal locus of control, they will view themselves as the means of achieving their desired ends; they are in control of directing the course of their lives. People with an external locus of control perceive themselves as having no control over their lives, and that, in fact, strong factors keep them from achieving their desired ends. Research continues to explore Black students' locus of control (for an overview see Banks, Ward, McQuarter, and DeBritto 1991). One can hypothesize, then, that for this highly at-risk student population, an environment that is structured and informed by a fundamental mission that validates and values racial identity will affect its students. If interactions and activities are informed by this empowering ideology, students will be immersed in an environment that is controlled by people of their own race. This school environment, as a mini-society, should then foster an internalized locus of control. Furthermore, with a central focus on academic achievement, students should then use their empowered status to become increasingly engaged in their schoolwork and increase their academic achievement.

Discussion

It has been the aim of this chapter to discuss the newly emerging institutions known as Black Academies, using Detroit as a case study to examine how these schools are increasing the academic achievement of Black students. The use of the communal organization model, originally created to describe Catholic schools, provides us with a conceptual tool through which the Black Academies can be discussed. Furthermore, the model enables us to theoretically link the organizational variables, through social-psychological mechanisms, to understand their effects on average levels of achievement. Although the Black Academies evaluation report may supply an indication of their success, rigorous research is clearly necessary to explore its findings and to empirically test the conceptual model laid out in this analysis.

With the failure of school integration, there remains, however, a fundamental question. If the Black Academies are successful in raising academic achievement, why do they remain such highly contested terrain? It would seem that if these emergent institutions are increasing achievement, then they must be considered as viable alternatives to the overwhelmingly unsuccessful traditional school model for Black students. However, this is not the case. Detroit's efforts in establishing the Black Academies were disputed from the outset and continue today. From court battles questioning constitutionality to swastikas painted on the doors and bullets sprayed across the playground, Detroit's Black Academies, and the Black Academy movement in general, are questioned and challenged even in the face of successful evaluation.

The paradox of public policy is clearly illuminated in the case of the Black Academies, and specifically in the case of Detroit. That paradox revolves around the fact that schools are acculturating institutions. It would seem, then, that the very concept of an Afrocentric school questions the assumptions that underlie public education in the United States. The underlying assumption, that schools operate to facilitate assimilation using and valuing white middle-class culture, is not only being questioned but rejected by proponents of the Black Academies. A school that is organized and operated by Black people from an ideology that puts African Americans at its intellectual center and uses Black culture as the normative focus cannot function from an assumption of assimilation. Therefore, that assumption is discarded.

Reform efforts are typically encouraged and implemented when they pose no threat to the very nature of the institution. Black Academies, however, are perceived as challenging the institution of public education. In actuality, it may be that the idea of Afrocentric education fundamentally appeals to a Black community that is fed up with inadequate public schools. That interest is then translated into enormous energy and momentum that creates the communal school organization and facilitates its effectiveness. However, because the shared values of the communal organization are not Catholic but racially based (specifically Afrocentric in ideology), it will continue to be highly contested. Specifically, research implies that the communal organization model can be applied to public schools to increase minority achievement. However, the Afrocentric value system that is used in this case as the shared values of the community is politically controversial. It is precisely this controversy that has stagnated the dissemination of this alternative school model, despite its success.

The presence of Black Academies calls for not only an examination of the state of education for African American children but also, in effect, a reexamination of the fundamental conflict in America's public schools: that between the middle-class white culture of schools and the diverse cultures of the growing minority populations. The presence of these Academies seems to illustrate that Black educators and parents in specific metropolitan areas are no longer willing to stand by and passively accept the assimilation goal in public schools. Instead, they are demanding that public schools be recreated and be culturally reflective of their own communities.

References

Asante, M. K. 1980. *Afrocentricity: The Theory of Social Change.* Buffalo, NY: Amulefi.
Anderson, E. F. 1990. *Streetwise: Race, Class, and Change in an Urban Community.* Chicago: University of Chicago Press.

Banks, W. C., W. E. Ward, G. V. McQuater, and A. M. DeBritto. 1991 "Are Blacks External?: On the Status of Locus of Control in Black Populations." In *Black Psychology,* (3rd. ed), ed. R. Jones, Berkeley, CA: Cobb and Henry.

Billson, J. and R. Majors. 1992. *Cool Pose: The Dilemmas of Black Manhood in America.* New York: Lexington Books.

Bryk, A. S., V. E. Lee, and P. B. Holland. 1993. *Catholic Schools and the Common Good.* Cambridge, MA: Harvard University Press.

Coleman, J., E. Q. Campbell, C. J. Hobson, J. McPartland, A. M. Mood, F. D. Weinfeld, and R. L. York. 1966. *Equality of Educational Opportunity.* Washington, DC: U.S. Department of Health, Education, and Welfare, Office of Education.

Coleman, J. S. 1966. *Equality of Educational Opportunity.* Washington, DC: Government Printing Office.

Erickson, E. 1968. *Identity, Youth, and Crisis.* New York: Norton.

Fischer, C. S. 1977. *Networks and Places: Social Relations in an Urban Setting.* New York: Free Press.

Findley, Maureen J. and Harris M. Cooper. 1983. "Locus of Control and Academic Achievement: A Literature Review." *Journal of Personality and Social Psychology* 44:419-27.

Fordham, S. 1988. "Racelessness as a Factor in Black Students' School Success: Pragmatic Strategy or Pyrrhic Victory?" *Harvard Educational Review* 58(Feb.):54-84.

Kapel, D. E. and M. B. Kapel. 1982. *The Preparation of Teachers for the Urban Schools: The State of the Art of Pre- and In-Service Education.* New York: ERIC Clearinghouse on Urban Education.

Lee, V. E., A. S. Bryk, and J. B. Smith. 1993. "The Organization of Effective High Schools." *Review of Research in Education* 19:171-267.

Malone, T. W. and M. R. Lepper. 1987. "Making Learning Fun: A Taxonomy of Intrinsic Motivations for Learning." In *Aptitude, Learning, and Instruction. 3: Cognitive and Affective Process Analyses* ed. R. E. Snow and M. J. Farr, 223-54. Hillsdale, NJ: Lawrence Erlbaum.

Moore & Associates, Inc. 1994. *1992-1993 African-Centered Academies Evaluation: Final Report.* Detroit, MI: Moore & Associates. Inc.

Ogbu, J. 1985. "A Cultural Ecology of Competence among Inner-City Blacks." In *Beginnings: The Social and Affective Developments of Black Children,* ed. M. B. Spencer, G. D. Brookins, and W. R. Allen, 45-66. Hillsdale, NJ: Lawrence Erlbaum.

Orland, M. E. 1990. "Demographics of Disadvantage: Intensity of Childhood Poverty and Its Relation to Educational Achievement." In *Access to Knowledge: An Agenda for our Nation's Schools,* ed. J. Doodlad and P. Keating, 43-58. New York: College Entrance Examination Board.

Powell, A. G., E. Farrar, and D. K. Cohen. 1985. *The Shopping Mall High School: Winners and Losers in the Educational Marketplace.* Boston: Houghton Mifflin.

Rosenberg, M. 1979. *Conceiving the Self.* New York: Basic Books.

Steinburg, L. 1987. "Single Parents, Stepparents, and the Susceptibility of Adolescents to Antisocial Peer Pressure." *Child Development* 58:269-75.

Taylor, R. 1976. "Psychosocial Development among Black Children and Youth: A Reexamination." *American Journal of Orthopsychiatry* 46(2):4-19.

Watson, B. S. 1980. "The Realities of Urban Educators in the 1980s." In *Urban Education in the '80s: The Never Ending Challenge,* ed. National Association of Secondary School Principals, 1-15. Reston, VA: National Association of Secondary School Principals.

White, Joseph and James Johnson, Jr. 1991. "Awareness, Pride, and Identity: A Positive Educational Strategy for Black Youth." In *Black Psychology,* ed. Reginald L. Jones, 409-18. Berkeley, CA: Cobb & Henry.

PART

VII

Crime,
Unequal Law Enforcement,
and Punishment

RACE, REPRESENTATION,
AND THE DRUG POLICY AGENDA

RAE BANKS

◆◆◆

At the heart of the devastating impact of drugs on the African American community lies one of the paradoxes of U.S. drug policy: America's failed drug policy successfully reproduces African American oppression. By sheer force of circumstance, African Americans are among the nation's staunchest defenders of strict drug enforcement and strong advocates of drug treatment. But, in practice, seeking protection in enforcement and relief in treatment both reproduce structures of domination—a paradox rooted firmly in the history of American drug policy. From its inception in a policy of silence that shielded American merchants' opium trafficking in China in the nineteenth century (Downs 1968) to current laws devised exclusively for crack cocaine offenders, U.S. drug policy has been about racial domination first and drug control second (Banks 1991).

Yet in the extensive literature critiquing the nation's drug policy, the race factor seems to come and go with the prevailing political winds. Two decades ago, racism was identified as an inherent part of drug policy (Helmer 1975; Musto 1987). But in recent years, as race and racism become increasingly contested concepts, their roles in drug policy outcomes and policy formation have become more than a contentious issue. The normative framework used to contest the disproportionate racial effects of policy is no longer appropriate for identifying and understanding the critical role that race plays in American drug policy. More important, this framework reproduces rather than disrupts the social processes used to construct African Americans as targets of punitive drug policies.

My objective is to propose an alternative framework for understanding race and drug policy that is grounded in the conceptual cross-currents of agenda-setting research and the discursive analysis of racism. The primary advantage of a discursive approach is its compatibility with recent conceptualizations of race. But the secondary advantage is its potential to disrupt the deployment of race in setting the drug policy agenda. The current controversy over policies established in the late 1980s points to both the limitations of the present perspective and the advantages of a discursive alternative.

In the fall of 1995, both houses of Congress passed legislation overruling amendments to the mandatory minimum sentencing structure put into place in the Omnibus Drug Bill of 1986 and the Anti-Drug Abuse Act of 1988. These amendments, proposed by the U.S. Sentencing Commission (USSC) after an intensive study of policy outcomes, sought to overturn the 100-to-1 quantity ratio between sentences for trafficking in crack as opposed to powdered cocaine and the penalties for simple possession of crack. In specific terms, Congress upheld laws that selectively target crack offenders, a form of cocaine whose market is concentrated in but not exclusive to Black and Hispanic urban communities.

Implemented in 1987, the Omnibus bill imposes mandatory minimum sentences of five years for first offenders convicted of trafficking five or more grams of crack cocaine. To draw an equivalent sentence for trafficking in powdered cocaine requires 500 grams. In 1988, Congress created the first and only mandatory minimum sentences for simple possession (i.e., possession without the intent to sell). Conviction for possession of five grams of crack carries a minimum penalty of five years for a first offense. Only fractions of a gram in subsequent offenses means even stiffer sentences. Consequently, some crack abusers with multiple offenses, convicted of no more than being addicted to the drug, are forced to "bargain up." In other words, they plea bargain to be considered a trafficker in the hopes of getting a lighter sentence—a unique phenomenon that the USSC simply calls an "anomaly" (U.S. Sentencing Commission

1995). In contrast, conviction for possessing powdered cocaine or any other known illicit drug is a misdemeanor with a maximum penalty of one year's imprisonment (U.S. Sentencing Commission 1995).

These laws have a disproportionate effect on African Americans. In 1993, for example, the racial distribution of all convictions for drug trafficking in the federal courts was fairly even (whites, 30.8 percent; Blacks, 33.9 percent; Hispanics, 33.8 percent). But those convicted of crack offenses were overwhelmingly Black (88.3 percent) as opposed to white (4.1 percent) or Hispanic (7.1 percent). In 17 states and in many of the nation's largest cities, no whites have been prosecuted in federal courts for trafficking in crack cocaine. The U.S. Supreme Court has agreed to hear a Los Angeles case to determine whether the fact that since 1986, not one single European American has been convicted of a crack offense in the federal court district that serves Los Angeles and six surrounding counties is a matter of prosecutorial discretion or racism (U.S. Senate Committee on the Judiciary 1995). White offenders are prosecuted in California's state courts, where sentences are less severe. In all, over the past 10 years, 83 percent of those convicted of crack offenses in federal courts have been African Americans (U.S. Sentencing Commission 1995).

The vast majority of drug cases are tried in state and local jurisdictions. Because more than half of the states (32) enacted mandatory minimum sentences and many (14) make a distinction between crack and powder cocaine offenses, the overwhelming majority of those convicted of crack offenses at this level as well have been African Americans. Several studies confirm that current drug policy is a critical factor in the increasing racial disparity in convictions and sentencing (Blumstein 1993; U.S. Department of Justice 1993; U.S. Sentencing Commission 1995). The U.S. Department of Justice (USDJ) (1995) reports that in 1994, African Americans comprised 50.8 percent of the nation's prison population but only 12 percent of the total U.S. population.

Studies investigating discrimination are equivocal. Blumstein (1993) examined racial disproportionality in prisons but stopped short of concluding that the data meet the objective criteria for discrimination because African Americans comprised the vast majority of those convicted of serious crimes. Contrary to its earlier finding that race does matter in drug sentencing, the U.S. Department of Justice (1993) recommended upholding current law. And ironically, despite finding that racial minorities were adversely affected by the "exaggerated ratio" between crack and powdered cocaine offenses and recommending a change in policy, the USSC (1995) ruled that because there was no evidence that Congress acted with discriminatory intent, these laws are not discriminatory.

The debate on discrimination rests on the question of fair treatment and rigorous analysis of objective criteria. But it ignores the political and ideological foundations of the social construction of the drug problem and of the policy agenda. Definitions of what is and is not an illicit substance, the social construction of the drug abuser, the choice of moments when private drug use is transformed into a public problem, and the choice of policies to deal with it are all products of historically situated social processes. It is these social processes that allow "race neutral" policies to reproduce racial inequities (Myers 1993). In short, the construction of the drug problem itself is a very political and racialized process that problematizes the so-called objective basis of criteria for discrimination.

Because of their role in setting the policy agenda that framed this controversial legislation, both the print and the electronic media were criticized. Critics charged that the media overstated the prevalence of cocaine abuse (Goode 1990; Johnston 1989) and represented only the interests of powerful actors who, in turn, influenced both drug discourse and public opinion (Beckett 1994; Sharp 1992). The most common charge leveled at the media, however, was its inaccurate representation of racial minorities' drug use. Because government surveys in 1986 indicated that 80 percent of crack abusers were European American, the daily depictions of African Americans and Hispanics and the underrepresentation of European American traffickers and abusers in newspapers and on television were labeled racist (Beckett 1994; Lusane 1992).

Unlike those who examined the question of discrimination, critics of the media did question the objectivity of its representation. But their focus on accuracy is too narrow. Accuracy depends on correspondence, or whether or not cocaine abuse in the Black community is predominant enough to warrant a claim that it is a minority problem. But relying on a discrepancy between representation and "reality" distorts the conception of racism by reducing it to the simplistic notion of misrepresentation.

The crack cocaine episode has been the most intensively scrutinized in recent history. But the conceptual and analytic limitations of a normative framework, with its presumptive need for correspondence between claims of unfairness and objective criteria and the tendency to reduce a complex phenomenon such as racism to misrepresentation, does little or nothing to intervene in racist policy and practice. What this perpective leaves us with, from the standpoint of social justice and of effective policymaking, is an oppressive situation: racial inequities in policy implementation continue to mount; drug abuse and drug-related crime continue to plague the country in general and Black America in particular; and an inefficient, costly, and stubbornly punitive policy remains in place.

Alternatively, a discursive perspective is a more appropriate framework for dealing with the complexities of race and racism inherent in contemporary social theory (Omi and Winant 1994). In this analysis, I will first describe the discursive approach to racism. Second, to examine how race was deployed in drug discourse in the six months preceding the 1986 federal legislation, I will use a representative sample of articles from the *New York Times* (NYT) and the *Washington Post* (WP). These publications not only influence the electronic media (Danielman and Reese 1989), but their readers also shape public opinion and policy (Shoemaker, Wanta, and Leggett 1989). I conclude by discussing the advantages that a discursive approach has for identifying and disrupting the deployment of race in setting the drug policy agenda.

A Discursive Analysis of Racism

A discursive framework for the analysis of racism emerged out of the field of social psychology in the 1980s (see Edwards and Potter 1992 for an overview). From this perspective, notions of "objectivity" and "reality" are viewed as constructions that tend to serve the interests of power. The construction process is largely dependent on discourse—meanings, narratives, accounts, and explanations—but racism in discourse is not reducible to talk or any other singular practice (Wetherell and Potter 1992). Instead, a discursive approach conceives of racism as productive. In other words, its meaning is articulated and rearticulated in changing contexts, and social groups are recategorized accordingly. Discourse, then, is social action, or, put another way, social practice is realized in discourse (Edwards and Potter 1992).

Racism is not defined in terms of specific content or distinctive discursive features. Instead, discourse that justifies and legitimates the oppression of one group and the dominance of another group, regardless of its form or content, is racist (Wetherell and Potter 1992). In its broadest sense, the goal of a discursive analysis of racism is to understand how racist discourse is constructed and mobilized and what it accomplishes.

In specific terms, drug discourse is presumed to actively construct a version of drug abuse as a public problem that becomes a consensually validated reality. The focal point of an analysis will be to uncover the rhetorical techniques and social processes used to make this version real. In this analysis, then, I will examine three critical, intersecting dimensions of the public discourse on drugs: its sociopolitical context, claimsmaking (the actors and processes that identify and typify the problem), and social categorization. Within each dimension, the focal points for analysis are (1) the social interactional work that deploys race, (2) the inferences this work makes available, and (3) what these inferences accomplish.

Context

Critics of media coverage often associated the social and political climate surrounding the crack cocaine episode with the resulting policy (Beckett 1994; Lusane 1992; Reinarman and Levine 1990). But discourse analysis takes this association a step further when it argues that context actively constructs discourse. From this vantage point, context is constitutive. It feeds on the social landscape, intergroup relations, and their attendant material interests (Wetherell and Potter 1992). What emerges from their interpenetration is a discourse comprised of "situated and occasioned constructs whose precise nature makes sense . . . in terms of the social acts these descriptions accomplish" (Edwards and Potter 1992:2,3).

Of the several contextual features that contributed to the construction of the crack episode, three stand out. One pivotal factor was electoral politics. With no political opposition and rising public apprehension, the drug issue was characterized as a "politician's gravy" (McQueen 1986). But public mistrust of their motives in pushing antidrug legislation was also common (see Clymer 1986:A1 and Cannon 1986 for examples).

Another less frequent, but no less significant, contextual feature of this episode was the conflict between Congress and the White House over resources for military intervention in Central America. In June 1986, the *Washington Post* revealed that President Reagan had declared drugs a national security threat in a secret directive signed in April. Vice President Bush publicized the step to "make Americans understand the link between drugs and terrorism" (Richburg 1986:A28).

But the most prominent of these contextual factors was the intensifying intergroup conflict over race, rights, and access to increasingly scarce resources (see Edsall and Edsall 1992 for a comprehensive analysis of this conflict). Arguably, the combination of the national mood, heightened fears about terrorism, and election fever influenced the need to identify and exploit a common enemy in order to build election campaigns and a public consensus.

A number of drug analysts contend that the contemporary episode began with Ronald Reagan's declaration of a "war" on drugs in 1982—a time when there was some congressional interest but little public concern about drug abuse. Notably, it was a time when the expense of cocaine limited its accessibility to more affluent Americans.

Reagan claimed that drug abuse was growing because of a "new privileged class" of "repeat offenders" and a criminal subculture spawned by expensive social programs founded on "utopian assumptions about man as primarily a creature of his material environment" ("Text of President's Speech" 1982:A20). Reagan's unequivocal stance created a version of the problem that made putative links between race and drug abuse permissible and the distribution of public resources a politicized and contentious issue framing the policy agenda. From articles describing the "drain" on existing resources, such as hospitals, treatment facilities, and prisons (Kerr 1986a; " 'Godmothers' " 1986:B52; Kerr 1986c, 1986d) to partisan discussions of the saliency of tax increases, the notion of "the costs they impose on us" (H. Williams 1986) was a prevalent theme (see L. Williams 1986; "City Is Doubling" 1986 for examples).

Explicit references to African Americans within this theme were relatively few (Gately 1986; Gross 1986; Bruske 1986). Instead, Black America was evoked more frequently in references to the inner-city and publicly funded facilities (Kerr 1986a; L. Williams 1986; " 'Godmothers' " 1986; Walsh 1986c). But with the saliency of diminishing public resources and frequent references to Black America's role in the nation's economic woes, race was an undeniable subtext in this version of the problem. African Americans were constructed as undeserving. That characterization privileged punitive as opposed to nonpunitive sanctions.

As the congressional vote neared, politicians voiced the opinion that cocaine's threat to the nation was so great that money was no object. In September, a front-page article in the *New York Times* (Clymer 1986) carried the headline, "Public Found Fight." Using polls to demonstrate consensus, this article provided facts to warrant the claim that Americans were willing to support drug sentences up to and including the death penalty and prepared to bear the cost of tax increases to build more prisons.

The concept that context and discourse construct each other affords a view of the social actions that a particular version of the problem privileges. A racialized climate was exploited to position African Americans as undeserving of anything other than punitive policy—a discourse constructed to justify disciplining a "dark, evil enemy within" ("Text of President's Speech" 1982:A20).

Claimsmaking

In addition to the aforementioned charge of misrepresenting crack as a minority problem, media critics also focused on definitions of the problem. Problem definition is one of the most critical aspects of the agenda-setting process precisely because it helps to set the boundaries for policy initiatives. But the drug policy arena also has been described as a congested political space crowded with interest groups who have varying stakes in the policy process (Sharp 1994).

Claimsmakers are most often driven by their own interests and values. But with so little room to negotiate for ownership of an issue with virtually no opposition, claimsmaking was elevated to a dominant place in the discourse. Our task is to discover whether race was deployed in making claims, how they were warranted, and what they accomplished.

Claiming, often without benefit of evidence, that "the country is slipping away" (Courtney 1986:sec. 11, 5); graphic descriptions of an uncontrollable drug "contagion" (Kerr 1986a, 1986e; Schmidt 1986) and claims that drugs are the nation's "number 1 issue" ("O'Neill Vows" 1986; Schmidt 1986) inspired fear. Conflating cocaine abuse with family values (Raspberry 1986b), or the failures of the criminal justice system (Bruske 1986) brought the problem close to home for all citizens and promoted a "siege" mentality where there was "no room for neutrality" (H. Williams 1986:D5). Claims of this type were a regular feature of the discourse.

But even a cursory glance at claimsmaking activity in the sample reveals a "war of maneuver" (Wetherell and Potter 1992). The principle weapon used was undermining and discrediting competing claims. Politicians from federal to state and local levels, drug policy experts, practitioners, and law enforcement officials constantly undermined each others' claims as they negotiated for leadership in the policy process. Sometimes, undermining took the form of name calling or questioning another's integrity (Furnick 1986; Kerr 1986d; Eckholm 1986; Thornton 1986a; Raspberry 1986b). Partisan politics was the impetus for discrediting opponents of extremely punitive sanctions by calling them "the voices of permissiveness" (Walsh 1986c:A3) or for accusing opponents of looking for the "quick fix" rather than long-term solutions (McQueen 1986). But sometimes, there were more substantive reasons for discrediting another's position. The "war of words" surrounding proposals to impose the death penalty for drug offenses and to circumvent constitutionally protected laws against illegal search and seizures in drug cases is a case in point (Walsh 1986c).

Race was exploited most often in efforts to appear "tough." Again, undermining other views was the principle weapon (see Gross 1986, Bruske 1986, and Kilpatrick 1986 for examples). Arguably, the most blatant and exploitative deployment of race occurred in a congressional election campaign. The candidate called a press conference in a predominantly African American city and carefully positioned herself in front of an inner-city housing project known for its drug traffic. In a thinly veiled appeal to racist sentiment among potential voters, she proceeded to discredit her opponent for voting against the death penalty in drug cases. She offered no facts in support of the death penalty. She simply charged that her opponent "opposes putting teeth into federal drug enforcement" and was "out of step" with her constituents (McQueen 1986).

Claimsmaking was a potent site for racializing frequently unsubstantiated versions of a public problem that privileged punitive policy responses over alternative approaches. The potential for exploitation was so great that congressional criticism even came from within. The harshest and perhaps the most revealing indictment came from one congressman who described his colleagues' rush to pass antidrug legislation a "Congressional lynch mob" (Walsh 1986a:A10).

Social Categorization

As previously mentioned, the media's overrepresentation of African Americans was the linchpin of media criticism (Beckett 1994; Harris 1990; Lusane 1992; Reinarman and Levine 1990). Elsewhere in the expanding framework explaining the agenda-setting process, Schneider and Ingram (1993) argue that the rhetoric used to justify a particular policy and the choice of policy tools depend on the construction of targeted groups. But like the media critics mentioned above, their analysis was not concerned with identifying the social processes used to construct groups positively or negatively. Alternatively, a discursive approach takes us beyond the accuracy of representation and identifies the multiple ways that race is exploited to construct some groups as targets of policies that benefit and others as targets of policies that burden and coerce.

In the discourse prior to the 1986 legislation, the social categorization process placed a new group on the social landscape: the crack addict. The process involved not only the characterization of the group but also set the boundaries that differentiate it from other groups. Most important, the process made inferences available about causes and motivations for the group's behaviors.

Class descriptions of the crack addict are especially instructive. What is striking is that, at least in this sample of the discourse, there are just as many references to class that are explicitly racialized as there are references that include all classes and, by inference, all racial groups. But on closer examination, the way that race-exclusive versus race-inclusive references are mobilized is very different. Accounts mentioning that all classes were involved in cocaine abuse include reports of studies by experts (see Thornton 1986b for an example); pleas for treatment funds (Walsh 1986c) or the considered opinions of established columnists (see Raspberry 1986a, 1986b; Krauthammer 1986 for examples). In other words, they tend to be fact-based reports corroborated by evidence and expert opinion.

In contrast, accounts that refer specifically to or use class to make inferences about African Americans tend to be corroborated by law enforcement officials and crime statistics. These accounts graphically depict moral degeneracy (Kerr 1986b) and neighborhoods saturated with drugs (Gately 1986; Cannon 1986:B3; Gross 1986); describe failed law enforcement efforts (Bruske 1986); chart the spread of drugs from the inner city to other communities (Kerr

1986e) and sometimes advocate draconian measures such as "hanging a few [drug dealers] in a public place" (Kilpatrick 1986:A19).

Furthermore, the problem of crack abuse was strongly identified with "problem groups" (Rochefort and Cobb 1994) in an insidious and stereotypical fashion. African Americans who are young, poor, and unemployed were routinely constructed as contemporary versions of latter-day "dangerous classes" (Gordon 1994). Unemployed youth reportedly regarded drug dealing as "just a job" (Bruske 1986:A1). In an address to a historically Black college, Reagan spoke of an 8-year-old crack dealer (Walsh 1986b). In another graphic portrayal, a crack house in Harlem was likened to an opium den—an analogy that invites the reader to identify crack addicts with an early twentieth-century pariah that history has constructed as morally degenerate—the Chinese opium smoker (Kerr 1986b). These examples infer that at least one cause of the problem is an inherent moral degeneracy.

But as the categorization process identifies a new group, it also restructures the entire social framework. With the inclusion of the crack addict in an already racially divided social climate fueled by politicized and distorted claims, "problem groups" are foregrounded while a threatened citizenry formed a fearful, vulnerable backdrop. This emerging social landscape privileged disciplinary sanctions over treatment, for example.

The fullest sense of crack addicts as a new social group cannot be appreciated without understanding their emergence in a conflict-ridden, sociopolitical context. The particular ways in which race was mobilized in the social categorization process not only served to rearticulate the meaning of race and of African Americans, but they also helped to transform a group perceived as undeserving to a discredited and dishonored pariah in need of discipline. The combined effect of a racialized social climate, distorted claims, and the social construction of African Americans as an inherently immoral and dangerous group suggests that the public discourse on drugs actively positioned Black America as a fitting target for harshly punitive sanctions.

Conclusion

This abbreviated analysis suggests the multiple ways in which race can be deployed in discourse to shape a "constructed totality"

(Rochefort and Cobb 1994)—a framework for policy that privileges some options and rejects others. We have identified techniques that go beyond stereotypes, misrepresentations, and coded signifiers. Practices such as distorted claimsmaking, manipulation of racial fears, and conflation of structural changes in the economy with race and drug use effectively deploy race for racist ends but, at the same time, lend themselves to maximum deniability. Ultimately, these and other discursive practices resulted in shaping policy that selectively targeted African Americans for the harshest of the sanctions imposed by the 1986 and 1988 drug legislation.

A discursive approach to racism offers a number of advantages. Although it does not eliminate the need to protest the effects of policy, it suggests that efforts to counter racism can focus more profitably on the agenda-building process rather than on policy outcomes. But, as we have seen, it also goes beyond critiquing the policy-making process by identifying the techniques and practices that help to construct a racist policy agenda, policy tools, and specific social groups as policy targets.

Just as important, it opens up a link between the social construction of drug abuse as a public problem and its structural consequences. Put another way, the meanings assigned to the drug problem are determined by and have consequences for the social relations of power and, in turn, the social and economic fortunes of African Americans. It is notable that the crack episode was conflated with crucial decision making surrounding the distribution of public resources. But equally important, this approach expands on the notion that the drug problem is associated with low wages and a lack of jobs (see Myers 1992). It suggests that U.S. drug policy does the ideological work of connecting the meaning of drug abuse to the legitimation of a racially stratified job market. In short, the discursive approach to racism suggests that American drug policy is one of this nation's most effective and enduring racial projects (Omi and Winant (1994).

Opening up this critical link can provide Black America with a politicized perspective on drug abuse. It implies that contesting racist drug policy involves struggling at every level from its ideological foundations to its structural consequences. Given this perspective, nothing less than reconstructing America's social vision of the problem will disrupt the paradoxical effects of drugs and drug policy—one of the most destructive consequences of the layered and multiple paradox of being Black in America.

References

Banks, Rae. 1991. "Living the Legacy: Historical Perspectives on African American Drug Abuse." In *Drug Abuse Research Issues at Historically Black Colleges and Universities,* ed. Julius Debro and Catherine Bollek. Research Monograph. Tuskeegee, AL: Tuskeegee Press.

Beckett, Katherine. 1994. "Setting the Public Agenda: "Street Crime" and Drug Use in American Politics." *Social Problems* 41:425-47.

Blumstein, Alfred. 1993. "Racial Disproportionality of U.S. Prison Populations Revisited." *University of Colorado Law Review* 64:743-60.

Bruske, Ed. 1986. "A Law Meets Reality—and Loses: For D.C. Peddlers, Revolving-Door Justice Is Still the Rule." *Washington Post* May 11:A1.

Cannon, Lou. 1986. "Not Just a 'Motherhood Issue.' " *Washington Post* August 4:A2.

"City Is Doubling Anticrack Force." 1986. *New York Times* July 25:B2.

Clymer, Adam. 1986. "Public Found Ready to Sacrifice in Drug Fight." *New York Times* September 2:A1, D16.

Courtney, Marian. 1986. "Dark Side of Growth: Drugs." *New York Times* April 27:Sec. 11, 5.

Danielman, Lucig and Stephen Reese. 1989. "A Closer Look At Intermedia Influences on Agenda Setting: The Cocaine Issue of 1986." In *Communication Campaigns about Drugs: Government, Media and the Public,* ed. Pamela Shoemaker. Hillsdale, NJ: Lawrence Erlbaum.

Downs, Jacques. 1968. "American Merchants and the China Opium Trade, 1800-1840." *Business History Review* 42:418-42.

Eckholm, Erik. 1986. "Ending the Cocaine Habit: Experts Differ on Methods." *New York Times* September 8:B1.

Edsall, Thomas and Mary Edsall. 1992. *Chain Reaction: The Impact of Race, Rights, and Taxes on American Politics.* New York: Norton.

Edwards, Derek and Jonathan Potter. 1992. *Discursive Psychology.* London: Sage.

Furnick, Joyce. 1986. "Officials Join Koch to Press New Attack on Drug Abuse." *New York Times* July 31:B3.

Gately, Gary. 1986. "On City Street Corners, Night of Antidrug Vigils." *New York Times* July 22:B1.

" 'Godmothers' Cuddle Ailing Infants." 1986. *New York Times* May 31:B52.

Goldman, Ari. 1986. "Clergy Expands Its Role in Fight Against Crack." *New York Times* August 4:B3.

Goode, Erich. 1990. "The American Drug Panic of the 1980s: Social Construction or Objective Threat?" *International Journal of the Addictions* 25:1083-98.

Gordon, Diana. 1994. *The Return of the Dangerous Classes: Drug Prohibition and Policy Politics.* New York: Norton.

Gross, Jane. 1986. "Drugs and Parents' Fear Taint Washington Hts." *New York Times* August 10:A28.

Harris, Ron. 1990. "Blacks Take Brunt of War on Drugs." *Los Angeles Times* April 22:A1.

Helmer, John. 1975. *Drugs and Minority Oppression.* New York: Seabury Press.

Johnston, Lloyd. 1989. "America's Drug Problem in the Media: Is It Real or Is It Memorex?" In *Communication Campaigns About Drugs: Government, Media and the Public,* ed. Pamela Shoemaker. Hillsdale, NJ: Lawrence Erlbaum.

Kerr, Peter. 1986a. "Drug Treatment in City Is Strained By Crack, a Potent New Cocaine." *New York Times* May 16:A1.

———. 1986b. "Opium Dens for the Crack Era." *New York Times* May 18:A1.

———. 1986c. "Overcrowded City Drug Programs to Be Told to Treat More Addicts." *New York Times* August 2:A1.

———. 1986d. "City Criticized in Report on Drug-Abuse Policies." *New York Times* August 7:B2.

———. 1986e. "Use of Crack: The Future." *New York Times* September 1:B25.

Kilpatrick, James. 1986. "Hang a Few Drug Dealers." *Washington Post* June 18:A19.

Krauthammer, Charles. 1986. "Crazy About Crack." *Washington Post* August 22:A19.

Lusane, Clarence. 1992. *Pipe Dream Blues: Racism & the War on Drugs.* Boston: South End Press.

McQueen, Michel. 1986. "Chavez Raps Mikulski for Stand on Drug Bill: Democrat Voted Against 2 Amendments." *Washington Post* September 16:B3.

Musto, David. 1987. *The American Disease: Origins of Narcotic Control.* New York: Oxford University Press.

Myers, Samuel. 1992. "Crime, Entrepreneurship, and Labor Force Withdrawal." *Contemporary Policy Issues* 10:84-97.

———. 1993. "Racial Disparities in Sentencing: Can Sentencing Reforms Reduce Discrimination in Punishment?" *University of Colorado Law Review* 64:781-808.

Omi, Michael and Howard Winant. 1994. *Racial Formation in the United States: From the 1960s to the 1990s.* 2d ed. New York: Routledge.

"O'Neill Vows House Will Wage War on Drugs." 1986. *Washington Post* July 24:A8.

Raspberry, William. 1986a. "And So, Onward to Bolivia." *Washington Post* July 23:A21.

———. 1986b. "Bennett's Drug Counsel." *Washington Post* July 14:A11.

Reinarman, Craig and Harry Levine. 1990. "Crack in Context: Politics and Media in the Making of a Drug Scare." *Contemporary Drug Problems* (Winter):535-77.

Richburg, Keith. 1986. "Reagan Order Defines Drug Trade as Security Threat, Widens Military Role." *Washington Post* June 8:A28.

Rochefort, David and Roger Cobb. Eds. 1994. *The Politics of Problem Definition: Shaping the Policy Agenda.* Lawrence: University Press of Kansas.

Schmaltz, Jefrey. 1986. "Cuomo to Establish 20-Member Panel on Narcotic Abuses." *New York Times* August 7:B2.

Schmidt, William. 1986. "Police Say Use of Crack Is Moving to Small Towns and Rural Areas." *New York Times* September 10:A1.

Schneider, Anne and Helen Ingram. 1993. "Social Construction of Target Populations: Implications for Politics and Policy." *American Political Science Review* 87:334-47.

Sharp, Elaine. 1992. "Agenda-Setting and Policy Results: Lessons From Three Drug Policy Episodes." *Policy Studies Journal* 20:538-51.

———. 1994. "Paradoxes of National Antidrug Policymaking." In *The Politics of Problem Definition: Shaping the Policy Agenda,* ed. David Rochefort and Roger Cobb. Lawrence: University Press of Kansas.

Shoemaker, Pamela, Wayne Wanta, and Dawn Leggett. 1989. "Drug Coverage and Public Opinion, 1972-1986." In *Communication Campaigns About Drugs: Government, Media and the Public,* ed. Pamela Shoemaker. Hillsdale, NJ: Lawrence Erlbaum.

"Text of President's Speech on Drive Against Crime." 1982. *New York Times* October 15:A20.

Thornton, Mary. 1986a. "Drug Tests Legal, Meese Says." *Washington Post* March 5:A3.

———. 1986b. "Heroin and Cocaine Use Rising, Panel Reports: Overdoses and Middle Class Consumption Up." *Washington Post* March 5:A3.

U.S. Department of Justice, Office of Justice Programs, Bureau of Justice Statistics. 1993. *Sentencing in the Federal Courts: Does Race Matter?* Washington, DC: Government Printing Office.

————. 1995. *Prisoners in 1994.* Washington, DC: Government Printing Office.

U.S. Senate Committee on the Judiciary. 1995. *The U.S. Sentencing Commission and Cocaine Sentencing Policy.* Hearing, 104th Congress, First Session. Washington, DC: Government Printing Office.

U.S. Sentencing Commission. 1995. *Cocaine and Federal Sentencing Policy.* Washington, DC: Government Printing Office.

Walsh, Edward. 1986a. "GOP Senators Propose Antidrug Compromise: House Measure Deemed Too Severe." *Washington Post* September 26:A10.

————. 1986b. "Senate Republicans Unveil Antidrug Plan." *Washington Post* September 20:A12.

————. 1986c. "Senate Starts Debate on Drug Bill Amid Go-Slow Warnings." *Washington Post* September 27:A3.

Walsh, Edward and Helen Dewar. 1986. "Congress Gives Drug Plans Top Priority." *Washington Post* September 10:A1.

"The War of Words Over the Drug Bill." *Washington Post* September 16:A13.

Wetherell, Margaret and Jonathan Potter. 1992. *Mapping the Language of Racism: Discourse and the Legitimation of Exploitation.* New York: Columbia University Press.

Williams, Hubert. 1986. "Drug Users are Bums: And We Need More Than Cops and Money to Stop Them." *Washington Post* September 14:D5.

Williams, Lena. 1986. "U.S. Drive on Drugs Urged." *New York Times* June 26:B9.

RACE, GENDER, AND
THE TIMING OF JUSTICE

Age at First Arrest and Incarceration
for African American Women

VERNA M. KEITH
GARRY L. ROLISON

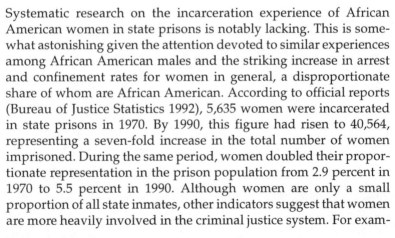

Systematic research on the incarceration experience of African American women in state prisons is notably lacking. This is somewhat astonishing given the attention devoted to similar experiences among African American males and the striking increase in arrest and confinement rates for women in general, a disproportionate share of whom are African American. According to official reports (Bureau of Justice Statistics 1992), 5,635 women were incarcerated in state prisons in 1970. By 1990, this figure had risen to 40,564, representing a seven-fold increase in the total number of women imprisoned. During the same period, women doubled their proportionate representation in the prison population from 2.9 percent in 1970 to 5.5 percent in 1990. Although women are only a small proportion of all state inmates, other indicators suggest that women are more heavily involved in the criminal justice system. For example, in 1990, women represented 18.7 percent of all those arrested, 15 percent of those on probation, and 9.3 percent of the jail population (Bureau of Justice Statistics 1992). Compared to their male counterparts, women inmates are more likely to be arrested and incarcerated for more traditional female crimes, such as larceny, and less likely to be incarcerated for more traditional male crimes, such as violent offenses (Bureau of Justice Statistics 1992, 1994). However, this pattern may be changing. The proportion of women serving time for property offenses, including larceny and fraud, has declined, whereas the proportion serving time for drug-related offenses increased in recent years (Bureau of Justice Statistics 1994). Indeed, by the mid-1980s, women were more likely than males to be incarcerated for drug offenses (Owen and Bloom 1995).

African American women are overrepresented among incarcerated women. In 1991, 46 percent of all female prisoners were African American, whereas 36.2 percent were white and 14.2 percent were Hispanic. This pattern may be more pronounced in large cities. For example, Chilton and Datesman's (1987) study of arrests in five urban areas found that minority women accounted for much more than three-fourths of the increase in larceny rates between 1960 and 1980. Not only were these female inmates disproportionately African American, they were also disproportionately young and economically disadvantaged, and a substantial number of them were recidivists. Among all women prisoners, the median age at first arrest was 17 years in 1990 (Fletcher, Rolison, and Moon 1993), and the median age of those serving time in 1991 was 31 (Owen and Bloom 1995). Just under 72 percent had served time prior to their current conviction. Among the latter, 20 percent served time as a juvenile. Labor force data indicate that in 1991, slightly more than 53 percent had not been employed at the time of arrest (Bureau of Justice Statistics 1994). Minority female inmates are also overrepresented among those reared in mother-only households, a family arrangement that is highly predictive of poverty (Wilson 1987). In 1991, the proportion of African American, Hispanic, and white female inmates reared in female-headed families was 46 percent, 41 percent, and 29 percent, respectively. Taken together, these social and economic characteristics indicate that involvement in the criminal justice system at an early age may play a key role in perpetuating poverty among African American women. As noted by Gibbs (1988), early arrests place limitations on educational and occupational opportunities. This often results in a vicious cycle characterized by incarceration, recidivism, and chronic criminal careers.

Using the 1986 Survey of Inmates compiled by the Bureau of Justice Statistics, this chapter investigates factors contributing to age at first arrest and age at first incarceration among African American women who are currently serving sentences in state prisons. White women are included for purposes of comparison because of the possibility that explanatory factors may vary by ethnicity. For example, Hill and Crawford (1990), using self-reported data from the National Longitudinal Survey Youth Cohort, found that structural variables such as the gap between educational aspirations and achievement were more predictive of Black female crime than for others. Three perspectives on criminogenesis guide our work: differential association, social control, and victimization perspectives. Although a comprehensive discussion or empirical evaluation of these perspectives is not attempted, they are used to ground our selection of explanatory variables.

Perspectives on Crime

Differential association and social control theory are used as the guiding framework for numerous studies of criminal involvement (e.g., Agnew 1985, 1991; Hepburn 1976; Jensen 1972; Matsueda 1982, 1989; Matsueda and Heimer 1987). Both were developed to explain crime and delinquency among males, but they may also be useful for understanding crime and delinquency among women. Differential association, initially developed by Edwin Sutherland (1947), suggests that criminal behavior results from excess exposure to definitions favorable to violations of legal codes over definitions that are unfavorable to violations of legal codes (Sutherland and Cressey 1978:81). These conflicting definitions are learned through social interaction within intimate social groups. Exposure to favorable and unfavorable definitions vary in frequency, duration, priority, and intensity such that persons have a higher probability of engaging in criminal activity if they are (1) exposed to definitions favorable to law breaking over those unfavorable to law breaking, with greater frequency, (2) if exposure is initiated at an early age, and (3) if sources of these unfavorable definitions are highly respected (Sutherland and Cressey 1978:81-82; Matsueda 1982). The differential association perspectives may be especially salient for

African American women. For example, Miller (1986), in her study of a deviant street network in Milwaukee, found that poor African American women often were involved in shifting households composed of kin, nonkin, and pseudokin, which made it especially difficult for parents to control their daughters' exposure to crimes. In contrast, white females living in poverty had less extensive networks and, therefore, less exposure to those holding favorable criminal norms. In short, we expect that because Black women may be exposed at an early age to people regularly engaged in the violation of criminal norms, they will experience arrest and incarceration at a younger age.

In contrast to differential association, Hirschi's (1969) social control theory addresses the issue of why people do not pursue criminal activity (Matseuda 1982, 1989). According to Hirschi, individuals refrain from committing criminal acts because they are bonded to society and to conventional behavior. This bond consist of four elements that are conceptually distinct but closely associated— attachment (perhaps the most important), commitment, involvement, and beliefs. In Hirschi's conceptualization, people do not engage in criminal behavior when they are strongly attached to family, school, and other institutions that support conventional behavior; when they are strongly committed to conventional activities that would be disrupted or lost as a result of criminal behavior; when involvement in conventional activities reduces the time and opportunity to engage in deviant behavior; and when they have strong moral beliefs against criminal acts. Conversely, criminal behavior results when these bonds are broken. Indeed, as noted by Smith and Paternoster (1987), lack of attachment to family is one of the leading explanations of female delinquency. In short, lack of attachment to conventional institutions and relationships may contribute to early arrest and imprisonment.

The victimization perspective, developed explicitly to address crime and delinquency among women, argues that women's involvement in criminal activity often stems from violence and sexual abuse experienced in the home. Noting that many women offenders are victims of abuse, Chesney-Lind (1978) and others (e.g., Arnold 1991; Gilfus 1992) suggest that girls often cope with abuse by running away from home. After leaving home, these girls often survive by stealing money, food, and clothing and by using their sexuality. As noted by Arnold (1991), these activities quickly get these girls labeled as status offenders who are later institutionalized in girls' homes and eventually imprisoned as their criminal offenses esca-late. Extending the victimization perspective, Rolison (1993) argues that these girls, who as women are further exposed to violence and abuse through their involvement with lovers and spouses, are placed at additional risk for arrest and incarceration. Involvement with such men, the perspective suggests, is likely to produce low self-esteem and a diminished sense of control and mastery. This may result in alcohol and drug abuse among these women (Rolison 1993). Given that women became more likely to be incarcerated for drug crimes in the 1980s, this perspective may offer a good expla-nation of arrest and incarceration among women. Lake's (1993) research supports this contention in her study of self-reported inci-dents of sexual and physical assault among women inmates in a Washington state correctional facility.

Empirical studies have found support for each of the three per-spectives, although which is most influential is still debated. Nu-merous articles, for example, have evaluated the relative importance of differential association and social control theory (e.g., Agnew 1985, 1991; Hepburn 1976; Hirschi 1969; Jensen 1972; Matsueda 1982; Matsueda and Heimer 1987), whereas Chesney-Lind (1978, 1989) contends that traditional theories of crime and delinquency are inappropriate for understanding women's criminality because they are primarily male based. It is our contention that each of the perspectives may increase our understanding of the incarceration experience of African American women.

Method

Data

The data for this study come from the Survey of Inmates of State Correctional Institutions in the United States conducted by the Bureau of the Census under the jurisdiction of the Bureau of Justice Statistics in 1986 (Bureau of Justice Statistics 1988). The survey is a two-stage stratified probability sample of inmates throughout the United States that contains more than 14,000 cases. Special care was taken to oversample female inmates. This resulted in a female sample size of more than 3,000 cases. This large sample size, along with the fact that the database represents the only nationwide sample of state correctional inmates, makes it invaluable for this study of African American female inmates in the United States.

Model Specification

Age at first arrest and age at first incarceration measures are used as our major variables. In particular, we use one block of sociodemographic variables and three blocks of theoretically derived variables to test their associative pattern with age of first arrest and incarceration among African American and white female inmates.

The basic sociodemographic measures are age, level of preincarceration income, level of preincarceration education, and whether a respondent is Black or white.

From the social control perspective, we look at the association between whether the respondent was married, held a job, or was self-employed before incarceration and whether she was a parent at first arrest and at first incarceration.

Finally, to measure what could be called "victimization" factors, we measure some of the variables that Chesney-Lind found to be predictive of female criminality and look at their association with age at first arrest and age at first incarceration. These include whether the respondent was a victim of early sexual abuse, whether she was alcohol dependent, and whether she was drug dependent before incarceration.

Next, we draw on the differential association perspective of Sutherland, which suggests that individuals involved in a criminal subculture are more likely to commit crimes and become involved in the criminal justice system. We look at the association between whether the respondent has had an incarcerated family member and whether she had received illegal income prior to incarceration by age at first arrest and age at first incarceration.

Results

Tabular Results: Racial Differences

From the descriptive results, it is apparent that Black women are arrested and incarcerated at earlier ages than are other women. Indeed, the average Black female inmate was first arrested at age 21,

TABLE 13.1 Comparison of African American and White State Prison Female Inmates by Mean Age of First Arrest, Mean Age of First Confinement, and Current Mean Age with Associated Standard Deviations

	African American	White	t test
Mean age at first arrest	21.9	24.0	6.33 ($p < .000$)
Standard deviation	7.6	9.8	
Mean age at first confinement	24.6	26.3	5.29 ($p < .000$)
Standard deviation	9.8	9.7	
Mean current age	30.5	31.3	2.52 ($p = .012$)
Standard deviation	7.7	9.1	

first confined at age 24, and is now 30 years of age. These numbers compare to age at first arrest for white female inmates of 24 years, first confinement of 26 years, and average current age of 31 years (see Table 13.1).

Table 13.2 displays the racial differences within our population among the variables of interest. We collapsed age at first arrest into two categories, those arrested prior to their 21st birthday versus those arrested at an older age (almost one-half of the total sample was first arrested before age 21 and one-half after). Similarly, our measure of age at first confinement is collapsed into whether someone was first confined before the age of 25 or not (40% of the sample report first being confined before age 25). Level of preincarceration income is dichotomized between those who received less than $5,000 in the year before their current confinement and those who received more (almost one-half of the total sample reports income before incarceration of less than $5,000 and one-half reports more). Finally, the level of preincarceration education is dichotomized between those completing their high school education before their current confinement and those not doing so.

The results show that significant differences are present among Black and white female inmates with respect to each of our variables except whether or not an inmate had received illegal income before her current confinement. It is worth noting, however, that the victimization variables seem better suited to describing the incidence of early arrest among the white subsample, whereas socioeconomic

TABLE 13.2 Comparison of African American and White State Prison Female Inmates by First Arrest before Age 21, First Confinement before Age 25, Demographic, Social Control, Victimization, and Differential Association Factors (in percentages)

	African American	White	Chi-square
Age of first arrest			
Before age 21	52.1	45.8	11.01**
Age of first confinement			
Before age 25	59.6	51.0	20.87**
Preincarceration income			
$5000 <	54.4	40.9	39.95**
Preincarceration education			
High school <	58.4	48.6	26.83**
Juvenile sexual abuse			
Yes	6.2	8.9	6.90*
Drug dependency			
Yes	43.2	56.5	35.68**
Alcohol dependency			
Yes	12.2	22.2	35.50**
Unemployed			
Yes	57.0	48.9	18.27**
Received illegal income			
Yes	20.4	21.3	0.28†
Family member do jail time			
Yes	46.9	34.8	41.81**
Have children			
Yes	79.7	72.9	18.10**

Chi-square significance levels reported for 1 degree of freedom.
$†p > .05$; $*p < .01$; $**p < .001$.

factors seem better suited to describing the incidence of early age of arrest for the African American subsample. More to the point, white female inmates who are arrested at a younger age report greater sexual abuse and drug and alcohol dependency than do young arrested African American females inmates. In contrast, young arrested African American female inmates were more likely to be unemployed and to have less income and less education than were their white counterparts.

TABLE 13.3 The Association of First Arrest before Age 21 by Demographic, Social Control, Victimization, and Differential Association Factors among African American State Prison Female Inmates (in percentages)

	Arrested before age 21	*Arrested after*	*Chi-Square*
Preincarceration income $5000 <	55.9	53.2	0.76†
Preincarceration education High school <	64.7	51.3	25.19***
Juvenile sexual abuse Yes	7.8	4.7	5.80*
Drug dependency Yes	47.5	37.3	9.86**
Alcohol dependency Yes	13.9	10.2	2.94†
Unemployed Yes	61.6	51.5	14.13***
Received illegal income Yes	26.0	14.5	23.83***
Family member do jail time Yes	52.3	41.5	15.57***
Have children Yes	74.8	84.9	21.74***

Chi-square significance levels reported for 1 degree of freedom.
†$p > .05$; *$p < .05$; **$p < .01$; ***$p < .001$.

Early Arrest Among African American Women Inmates

Table 13.3 contains the results of analyses of youthful arrest within the African American female inmate subsample. The results show that those African American women who were arrested before age 21 were more likely to be drug dependent and unemployed, to have received illegal income in the year prior to their current incarceration, and to have had an intimate family member who had done jail time. They were less likely to have been a parent and to have completed a high school education or its equivalent. However, they were not any more or less likely to report having less preincarceration income or a higher alcohol dependency rate.

TABLE 13.4 The Association of First Confinement before Age 25 by First Arrest before Age 21, Demographic, Social Control, Victimization, and Differential Association Factors among African American State Prison Female Inmates (in percentages)

	Confined before age 25	*Confined after*	*Chi-square*
Early arrest			
First arrest before age 21	75.2	17.5	435.26***
Preincarceration income			
$5000 <	57.7	50.2	5.76*
Preincarceration education			
High school <	60.9	54.6	5.29*
Juvenile sexual abuse			
Yes	7.6	4.4	5.62*
Drug dependency			
Yes	45.5	38.8	3.96*
Alcohol dependency			
Yes	13.3	10.6	1.61†
Unemployed			
Yes	59.6	52.5	6.82**
Received illegal income	24.5	14.8	16.06***
Family member do jail time			
Yes	49.2	44.2	3.26†
Have children			
Yes	75.1	86.9	28.02***

Chi-square significance levels reported for 1 degree of freedom.
†$p > .05$; *$p < .05$; **$p < .01$; ***$p < .001$.

Table 13.4 contains the results of analyses of early confinement within the African American female inmate subsample. From the table, we see that being arrested before age 21, having low income and a low educational attainment level, being sexually abused as a juvenile, being drug dependent, being a parent, and receiving illegal income all serve to differentiate between those first confined before age 25 and those who were confined at an older age. Together with the results regarding early arrest for this subsample presented in Table 13.3, there is strong evidence for the utility of the perspectives that we employed in this chapter. In short, there is evidence that our socioeconomic, social control, differential association, and victimization factors are all associated with the youthful immersion of African American women into the criminal justice system.

As a rough guide, one might think that a percentage difference of about 5 to 10 percent would be substantive. However, one should keep in mind that it is easier to move 10 percentage points between 25 percent to 75 percent than it is to move 10 percentage points at either end of distribution. Give this caution, we return to the results presented in Tables 13.3 and 13.4 to discuss their substantive importance.

Reexamining Table 13.3, we see that the substantively most important factors associated with early arrest among African American inmates appear to be the level of preincarceration education, the receipt of illegal income, and being a parent. These factors are followed in substantive importance by whether one has had a family member who has done jail time; whether one was unemployed before her current confinement; and whether, at one time, one reported being drug dependent. A reexamination of Table 13.4 shows that the overwhelming factor accounting for early confinement among African American women in our subsample is arrest at young age. Additionally, being a parent and receiving illegal income also appear to be substantively important factors. Given the rather strong association between youthful age at first arrest and youthful age at first confinement among our African American subsample, it is reasonable to assume that those factors associated with youthful first arrest also are substantively important in describing youthful first confinement in this subsample. Hence, in the discussion that follows, we focus primarily on these factors.

Discussion and Policy Suggestions

Three factors stand out with respect to African American women coming to the attention of the criminal justice system at a young age. Those factors are whether a woman has completed high school, whether she has been involved in an environment in which she could receive illegal income, and whether she is a parent. In sum, a high school education and the responsibilities of parenthood appear to retard youthful entry into the criminal justice system for African American women, whereas environments that make it possible to receive illegal income promote that involvement.

Receipt of illegal income is worthy of further discussion because of three of the remaining four substantively important factors noted with respect to youthful contact of African American women with the criminal justice system. In particular, being unemployed, having had an intimate family member who has done jail time, and having been drug dependent are probably each related to the receipt of illegal income. Specifically, it is reasonable to assume that much of the illegal money that these young women receive is tied directly or indirectly to the drug trade and its culture, which may, in turn, be promoted by conditions of unemployment.

The above fits quite well with the social trends of female incarceration with which we began this chapter—the increase in the 1980s of incarceration of women for drug-related crimes and the disproportionately high numbers of African American women in state prisons. Our research supplements this general picture by pointing to the unemployment of young African American women as being part and parcel of this process, and it raises further the specter that a drug culture in which it may be normative to have an intimate family member jailed might make it easier for these young women to get involved in the drug trade.

We believe that such a position is supported further by a reexamination of the data we presented earlier in Table 13.2 regarding racial differences between African American and white female inmates. As we mentioned earlier, African American women inmates are affected more severely by socioeconomic disadvantage than are white women inmates. In particular, there is, on average, a 10 to 11 percentage point difference between African American and white women inmates with respect to low preincarceration income, low educational attainment, being unemployed, and having had an intimate family member in jail. Clearly, this suggests that African American inmates come from more economically disadvantaged positions than do their white counterparts. This relative disadvantage is associated with their incarceration.

The pattern of African American socioeconomic disadvantage has as its obverse the greater impact of victimization factors such as substance abuse for white female inmates. Indeed, the percentage difference between white and African American female inmates with respect to drug and alcohol dependency is about 10 percent to 13 percent. However, what is most fascinating is the factor on which the two groups do not differ. That factor is the receipt of illegal income before current incarceration.

The Black-white similarities in the receipt of illegal income, combined with the higher incidence of drug dependency (56.5 percent to 43.2 percent), would seem to suggest that white women comprise a larger proportion of state prison inmates than do African American women given the rising female incarceration rates that are primarily due to drug-related offenses. One can only surmise that the reason this is not the case is because of bias in the criminal justice system that punishes African American women more harshly for drug-related offenses.

Given that African American women are about half of all female inmates and comprise a slightly larger proportion of female inmates in state prisons than African American men comprise of male inmates, it is important to understand the factors that give rise to this disproportionality and to design public policy to address it. From our research, using a nationally representative sample of female state prison inmates, we have identified educational and economic disadvantage as being strongly associated with the early arrest and confinement of African American women. This calls for intervention at the high school level to provide African American girls more incentives to stay in school. In addition, it also may be important to develop job training and income-enhancing programs for young African American women who are not in school. Indeed, one could combine these strategies via job training programs targeted specifically to poor African American female dropouts.

Finally, it has become somewhat fashionable in the mid-1990s to talk of the War on Drugs as being a War on African American Men. However, we hope that we have also indicated that the drug war is also a War on African American Women and that African American women have lost disproportionately more. It is our hope that future research on African American women and the criminal justice system will continue to search for the reasons that this has occurred and is occurring. More to the point, we hope that as we move to the next century, drug interdiction policies will have as a key component more equitable adjudication with respect to race and gender.

References

Agnew, Robert. 1991. "A Longitudinal Test of Social Control Theory and Delinquency." *Journal of Research in Crime and Delinquency* 28:126-56.

———. 1985. "Social Control Theory and Deliquency: A Longitudinal Test." *Criminology* 23:47-61.

Arnold, Regina A. 1991. "Processes of Victimization and Criminalization of Black Women." *Social Justice* 17(3):153-66.

Bureau of Justice Statistics. 1992. *Sourcebook of Criminal Justice Statistics*. Washington, DC: Bureau of Justice Statistics.

Bureau of Justice Statistics. 1994. *Special Report: Women in Prison*. Washington, DC: Bureau of Justice Statistics.

Chesney-Lind, Meda. 1978. "Young Women in the Arms of the Law." In *Women, Crime and the Criminal Justice System,* ed. Lee H. Bowker, 171-223. Boston: Lexington Books.

———. 1989. "Girls' Crime and Woman's Place: Toward a Feminist Model of Female Delinquency." *Crime & Delinquency* 35:5-29.

Chilton, Roland and Susan K. Datesman. 1987. "Gender, Race, and Crime: An Analysis of Urban Arrest Trends, 1960-1980." *Gender & Society* 1:152-71.

Fletcher, Beverly R., Garry L. Rolison, and Dreama Moon. 1993. "The Woman Prisoner." In *Women Prisoners: A Forgotten Population,* ed. Beverly R. Fletcher, Linda Dixon Shaver, and Dreama G. Moon, 15-24. Westport, CT: Praeger.

Gibbs, Jewell Taylor. 1988. "Young Black Males in America: Endangered, Embittered, and Embattled." In *Young, Black and Male in America: An Endangered Species,* ed. Jewell Taylor Gibbs, 258-293. Westport, CT: Auburn House.

Gilfus, Mary. 1992. "From Victims to Survivors to Offenders: Women's Routes of Entry and Immersion into Street Crime." *Women & Criminal Justice* 4(1):63-90.

Hepburn, John R. 1976. "Testing Alternative Models of Delinquency Causation." *Journal of Criminal Law and Criminology* 67:450-60.

Hill, Gary D. and Elizabeth M. Crawford. 1990. "Women, Race, and Crime." *Criminology* 28:601-26.

Hirschi, Travis. 1969. *Causes of Delinquency.* Berkeley: University of California Press.

Jensen, Gary F. 1972. "Parents, Peers ad Deliquent Action: A Test of the Different Association Perspective." *American Journal of Sociology* 78:63-72.

Lake, Elise S. 1993. "An Exploration of the Violent Victim Experiences of Female Offenders." *Violence and Victims* 9(1):41-51.

Matsueda, Ross L. 1982. "Testing Control Theory and Differential Association: A Causal Modeling Approach." *American Sociological Review* 47:489-504.

———. 1989. "The Dynamics of Moral Beliefs and Minor Deviance." *Social Forces* 68:428-57.

Matsueda, Ross L. and Karen Heimer. 1987. "Race, Family Structure, and Delinquency: A Test of Differential Association and Social Control Theories." *American Journal of Sociology* 52:826-40.

Miller, Eleanor M. 1986. *Street Woman.* Philadelphia: Temple University Press.

Owen, Barbara and Barbara Bloom. 1995. "Profiling Women Prisoners: Findings from National Surveys and a California Sample." *The Prison Journal* 75:165-85.

Rolison, Garry L. 1993. "Toward an Integrated Theory of Female Criminality and Incarceration." In *Women Prisoners: A Forgotten Population,* ed. Beverly Fletcher, Linda Dixon Shaver, and Dreama G. Moon, 135-146. Westport, CT: Praeger.

Smith, Douglas A. and Raymond Paternoster. 1987. "The Gender Gap in Theories of Deviance: Issues and Evidence." *Journal of Research in Crime and Delinquency* 24:140-72.

Sutherland, Edwin H. 1947. *Principles of Criminology.* 4th ed. Philadelphia: Lippincott.

Sutherland, Edwin H. and Donald R. Cressey. 1978. *Criminology.* 10th ed. Philadelphia: Lippincott.

Wilson, William Julius. 1987. *The Truly Disadvantaged: The Inner City, the Underclass, and Public Policy.* Chicago: University of Chicago Press.

WHICH WAY TOWARD EQUALITY?

*Dilemmas and Paradoxes
in Public Policies Affecting
Crime and Punishment*

Darnell F. Hawkins

Racial and ethnic comparisons are a ubiquitous and widely accepted aspect of public discourse and social scientific research in the United States. Such comparisons often appear to reflect a kind of empirical nihilism. For example, there is a tendency in modern social science simply to add race and ethnicity to multivariate analyses of assorted social phenomena without any theoretical basis for doing so. Theory aside, however, ethnic, racial, and, increasingly, gender comparisons in American society are almost always rooted in implicit or explicit considerations of social policy. It is this grounding of ethnic/racial contrasts in social policy that is the focus of discussion in this chapter.

During the past half century, interracial comparisons in the United States have been influenced greatly by American civil rights law and have embodied notions of racial equity or parity. Whereas extant legal doctrines typically mandate equality of treatment rather

than outcomes, extremely disproportionate outcomes often are assumed to provide at least prima facie evidence of unequal treatment.
Thus, in both law and social science, proof of racially disproportionate outcomes has served as a starting point for more intensive
scrutiny and investigation of the source of racial differences. Cross-
racial comparisons are used to make an assessment of the extent to
which the nation has lived up to the ideals embodied in the prohi-
bitions and injunctions found in the 14th Amendment or the Civil
Rights Act of 1964. American social scientists before and after Myrdal
(1944) have used the study of racial differences as a way to monitor
the nation's adherence to core values and principles that are said to
go beyond mere legal edicts.

Inherent in the logic of racial comparisons has been the obvious
necessity of establishing normative guideposts. This has led to the
practice of using the condition or status of Whites as an "optimal"
standard to which the plight of Blacks and other racial minorities is
compared. Modern social scientists have been quick to note that in
the past, this practice has sometimes led to ethnocentric and racist
depictions of racial minorities as pathological, substandard, or deficient subgroups. But most analysts acknowledge the utility of such
contrasts where basic, materialist concerns and contrasts are involved. For example, if median household income figures show
Blacks trailing Whites by a substantial margin, this gap is said to be
unacceptable, and the contrast itself constitutes an appeal for an
increase in Black income levels as a policy goal. Similarly, the greater
incidence of disease, interpersonal violence, drug abuse, and other
antisocial conduct among minorities is deemed unacceptable and is
said to call for policies aimed at reducing such undesirable conditions to levels closer to those found among Whites.

In contrast to the presumptions and examples just described, this
chapter examines several concerns for which the public policy implications and the nature of the social goals thought to be derived
from racial comparisons are much less straightforward and much
more contestable. Specifically, I discuss three areas of documented
racial inequity in the study of crime and justice: (1) Black-White
disparities in the imposition of the death penalty in the United
States, particularly differences that are due to greater punishment
for those who kill Whites; (2) the "race effects" of federal and state
laws and sentencing guidelines that provide different levels of
punishment for "crack" versus powdered cocaine; and (3) race-of-
victim effects in newspaper coverage of homicide in Chicago. Racial

comparisons in each of these areas have led to considerable debate regarding whether the treatment accorded whites or that accorded nonwhites should be used as the public policy "standard."

Race and the Death Penalty

The voluminous social scientific and legal literature on the use of the death penalty in the United States has reached several major conclusions: (1) In comparison to their numbers in the general population, Blacks are disproportionately represented among those who receive the death penalty and are subsequently executed by the state (Jaynes and Williams 1989:488); (2) the greater involvement of Blacks in serious criminal activity explains much, but not all, of the racial difference; and (3) among those who commit murder, the race of the victim is a more significant predictor of the odds of being legally executed than is the race of the offender—the odds of receiving the death penalty are much greater if the victim is white than if the victim is nonwhite. Most of the variance in the treatment of white versus Black victim homicides appears to stem more from the actions of prosecuting attorneys than those of judges or juries (Johnson 1941; Wolfgang and Riedel 1973; Radelet 1981; Zeisel 1981; Baldus, Pulaski, and Woodworth 1983; Paternoster 1984; Smith 1987; Keil and Vito 1989; Aguirre and Baker 1990).

Recently, much of the defendant's appeal request in the U.S. Supreme Court case *McCleskey v. Kemp* (1987) was based on social scientific evidence showing race-of-victim effects in the decision to impose the death penalty in several American jurisdictions. In that case, the court upheld the death penalty imposed on McCleskey despite its acknowledgment of the persuasiveness of social scientific evidence that showed that the race of the victim was statistically associated with the decision to seek and impose the death penalty in several states. Most legal scholars acknowledge that, absent additional evidence, which proves that the race-of-victim effects seen in the imposition of the death penalty are the result of overtly expressed, racist, discriminatory intent and actions on the part of decision makers, the Court is unlikely to declare such effects to be in violation of the Constitution. Even then, as *McCleskey* held, evidence must be presented to show that such bias was evident in the case brought to the court on appeal. It is not sufficient to show bias in other similar cases or to provide statistical proof of patterns of bias.

Apart from the Constitutional questions that this case and others have raised, an important, much broader, public policy-related debate has also emerged—one also based on notions of racial equity. As media accounts of this practice have shown, many minority and majority group commentators find race-of-victim effects in the imposition of the death penalty to be objectionable, whether or not they reach the level of Constitutional impropriety. Given such opposition, several questions are warranted:

1. What is the basis for arguments that individual defendants and American society would benefit from the elimination of race-of-victim disparities in the imposition of the death penalty?

2. Assuming acceptance of the need for reforms, what should be the precise nature of those reforms? What changes in social policy are needed to attempt to correct the observed racial disparities in the imposition of the death penalty?

3. Should death penalty standards reflect the "experiences" of Black victims or those of white victims?

These are not purely academic queries. Responses to them in the form of either formal or informal policy within the criminal justice system may have significant implications for the fates of individuals charged with capital murder. Furthermore, given the racial patterning of homicide victim-offender dyads in the United States, such change may profoundly affect the future magnitude of legal executions in the United States and may have the potential to further widen extant levels of racial disparity.

For instance, in response to recent increases in gang-related and youth violence in their communities, Black Americans have begun to move in the direction of greater support for the moral and public policy acceptability of the death penalty. A part of this movement appears to be an insistence that Black-on-Black killings be punished more severely than they customarily have. The seeming leniency accorded to those who kill Blacks in comparison to those who kill Whites has long been cited by African Americans as a significant factor contributing to their distrust of the American legal system (Hawkins 1983).

Arguably, important legal and social objectives could be achieved by treating Black-on-Black or White-on-Black homicides in a manner more consistent with the treatment of Black-on-White or White-on-White murders. Such parity would be in keeping with 14th Amendment requirements of "equal protection under the law" and the legal doctrines that are said to underlie basic American values. It might also counter perceptions of the "cheapness" of the life of African Americans in comparison to those of European ancestry (e.g., see Hawkins 1983, 1987b). But, as the title of this chapter suggests, constitutionally acceptable parity may be achieved either by raising the standard for the imposition of all death penalty cases to the treatment currently accorded White victims or, alternatively, by lowering it to that currently accorded victims who are non-White.

Let us suppose that in the spirit of reform, legal rules are enacted that use past capital murder cases involving White homicide victims as the standard for the future imposition of the death penalty for all offenders. Given the "law and order" and "get tough on crime" stances now commonly seen as acceptable by both Whites and non-Whites in the United States, the seemingly more punitive standard represented by those cases would probably receive more public support than would the more lenient standard said to be used for the adjudication of Black victim cases. This hypothetical but foreseeable change would, of course, not completely alter the landscape of death penalty sentencing. The typical death penalty case would remain one characterized by premeditated murder involving victims who were strangers to or nonintimates of their offenders. It would also typically be an act committed during the commission of another felony and would typically be a murder that is more heinous than other felony-murder homicides. Currently, the death penalty is much less likely to be imposed on those who kill intimates, regardless of the race of the victim.

Yet the acceptance of a "White victim" standard for the imposition of all death penalty cases could conceivably have major repercussions in other ways. This arguably more consistently punitive standard, if applied to the large number of felony-murder cases committed against Black victims, would likely mean a significant increase in the overall number of bona fide death penalty cases. Furthermore, because cases involving White victims, most of whom are killed by other Whites, presumably already are evaluated by this more stringent standard, the expected increase in the size of the nation's death row would come from those defendants involved in the large number of Black-on-Black homicides that are committed each year. Many gang- and drug-related killings and most felony-murders within the Black community likely meet all of the criteria used to impose the death penalty in the incidents involving White victims. If evaluated in a manner consistent with typical White victim cases, many Black-on-Black killings would be "upgraded" from sentences involving prison terms to capital punishment.

Supporters of these plausible and increasingly widely advocated changes in death penalty sentencing practice can point to several potential benefits. Among them is the possibility that such change may lead the public to view death sentencing practices as more just and procedurally fair. Furthermore, to the extent that harsher punishment is believed to deter offending, its deterrent effect on the very high rates of Black-on-Black homicide found in the United States may be seen as a benefit by some. At the same time, however, it is obvious that these changes would also have the effect of contributing further to the existing racial gap in the actual imposition of the death penalty. Between 1930 and 1962, Blacks were 54 percent of all prisoners executed in the United States. In more recent years, they have made up between 40 percent and 45 percent of prisoners under the sentence of death (Jaynes and Wiliams 1989:488). This disparity undoubtedly would increase with greater punitiveness toward those involved in Black-on-Black homicide.

Race and the War on Drugs: Crack versus Powder Cocaine

Whereas many of the public policy implications of the death penalty debate remain somewhat amorphous and futuristic, a similar but more tangible public policy dilemma can be seen in the current debate over contrasting penalties for crack and the powdered form of cocaine. "Crack" is the term used for a smokable derivative of powdered cocaine. It first came to the notice of law enforcement officials in Los Angeles in 1984 and in New York and Miami in 1985. Before the advent of crack, cocaine users were aware of the enhanced high that came from smoking rather than snorting cocaine. This practice was known earlier as "freebasing." Given the market price of cocaine in the 1970s and before, the quantity of cocaine necessary for freebasing was beyond the means of the average cocaine user. Thus, freebasing was generally reserved for middle- and upper-income cocaine users (Fagan 1995). The widely publicized, nearly fatal incident involving freebasing by comedian

Richard Pryor during the 1970s exposed many Americans to the practice for the first time. Fagan (1995) notes:

> With the price break in cocaine in the mid-1980s, the raw material for smoking cocaine became widely available as a mass consumer product. Crack simply was a "poor man's freebase." It was an ingenious product, easy to make on a stovetop from a small and now inexpensive amount of cocaine. It was marketed in small doses ($10-$20 per vial), so low-income users could afford purchases. It was highly portable compared to the elaborate and volatile process of freebasing. . . . The high lasted less than 20 minutes per rock, and users typically made several purchases in order to sustain their high. (p. 3)

Fagan further notes that crack represented new opportunities for drug selling in a context of declining work opportunities. Because the most severe of these declining opportunities were likely to be found in the nation's inner cities (Wilson 1987), trafficking in and use of the drug were initially associated with the nation's minority communities. For those reasons, it appears that crack came to be perceived by law enforcement officials as the drug of choice among Blacks and Latinos, whereas the powder from which it was derived continued to be associated with White, affluent populations. A kind of media hysteria about the perils and uniqueness of this "new" drug epidemic was also evident in the mid to late 1980s. Recent research has shown the inaccuracy of the view that crack use and the problems associated with it are limited to minorities or to inner cities (Lockwood, Pottieger, and Inciardi 1995).

One not unexpected consequence of these initial perceptions was the specification of crack in criminal legislation as a different form of cocaine worthy of more severe punishment than powder. Fagan (1995:4) reports that in the state of New York, legislators reduced the threshold for a felony cocaine possession from one-eighth ounce (3.5 grams) to approximately one gram of powder, or six vials of crack. Fagan notes that one-eighth ounce of powder HCL cocaine typically converts to 40 to 55 vials of crack depending on the size of the rocks and the contents of each vial. These changes in the law were said to be due to the reasoning of legislators that possession of six or more vials of crack indicated intent to sell rather than personal use of the drug. Similar changes in the law were made in other states and at the federal level. *Significantly, the rash of legislative innovation during the mid-1980s did not result in a stiffening of penalties for the possession or sale of powdered cocaine.* This is rather ironic because those who manufacture crack must rely upon suppliers of cocaine powder for needed raw materials.

It is now quite evident that increases in the severity of mandatory sentences for the crack variety of cocaine coupled with the lack of change for powder has produced a two-tiered punishment regimen. As recent media accounts have shown, critics of this regimen have used the lack of change in the penalties for cocaine powder as evidence of racial, ethnic, and class bias in the nation's War on Drugs. They note the extent to which crack arrests and prosecutions account for much of the recent increase in the racial disproportionality of the nation's prison population (Fagan 1995; Mauer 1990). Supporters of the more punitive stance toward crack have argued that it represents a more addictive form of cocaine that increases harm to users and also leads to escalating rates of violence among those who sell and distribute it. Much of the recent increase in youth violence has been said to result from involvement in the trafficking of crack.

In the death penalty debate, racial bias in the administration of justice (prosecutors, juries, etc.) is believed to produce the racial differences observed. However, the race-based criticisms of cocaine sentencing guidelines are grounded largely in an attack on the legislative process and what might be termed "indirect de jure" bias. The de jure bias of the past typically involved laws that criminalized the behaviors of Blacks while failing to sanction similar behaviors among Whites or, alternatively, punished Blacks more severely than Whites for the same illegal behaviors. Critics charge that, like legislators of the past, modern legislators who reacted to the appearance of crack sought to differentially target and punish Black offenders. Such results are achieved through their knowledge that most offenders charged with the possession or sale of crack are likely to be Black while those charged with violations of cocaine powder laws are typically White (Fagan 1995:8-9). Indeed, recent crime data show that whereas more than 80 percent of all arrests for crack involve Blacks, a similar proportion of all arrests for cocaine powder involve Whites.

It is beyond the scope of this chapter to explore fully the merits of these competing perspectives. Increasingly, however, much of the logic upon which recent legislative and public policy initiatives are based has come into question. Especially vulnerable to attack is the argument of some lawmakers during the 1980s rush to criminalize

crack that there are significant pharmacological distinctions between crack and powdered cocaine. Also questionable are assertions
that there are major differences in rates of violence attributable to
crack as compared to powder cocaine or other drugs. Fagan (1995:5-
8), echoing the sentiments of many criminologists who have studied
patterns of drug use in the United States, concluded that there is no
social science evidence to support any of the assumptions that led
to the creation of a vast sentencing disparity for crack offenses
compared to other cocaine offenses. The federal government's own
sentencing commission reached similar conclusions in its 1995 report and called for an end to such gross differences in criminal
penalties at the federal level.

To date, federal officials have not heeded these recommendations.
However, as the themes explored in this chapter suggest, if they
were to do so, an important question remains unanswered: Should
extant penalties for cocaine powder be increased or should those for
crack be lowered? As in the instance of the imposition of the death
penalty, purely Constitutional or equal treatment objectives can be
achieved by moves in either direction. And, as expected, proponents
can be found for either legislative solution. Those who advocate
tough stances toward drug use and trafficking, including many low-
and middle-income minority citizens, would not be satisfied with
the message that might be sent by a reduction in current penalties
for crack. At the same time, many avowed critics of the War on Drugs
and the perceived overimprisonment of minorities would see little
to be applauded in the establishment of law or policy that attempts
to achieve racial equality by presumably exposing larger numbers
of middle- and upper-income whites to the increased risk of imprisonment.

As in the death penalty debate, these competing views of the
optimal public policy toward cocaine also can be found in the Black
community. Jesse Jackson has argued that the crack versus powder
cocaine disparity has contributed to the growth of the Prison-Industrial
Complex and the overincarceration of Black males. Some Black law
enforcement officials and community leaders have insisted that
violence and other problems in their neighborhoods may be exacerbated by any move toward more lenient treatment of crack dealers
and users.

The dilemma and paradox inherent in the interaction between
current cocaine law and racial equality/inequality is quite obvious.
Tough, mandatory sentencing of crack users and sellers coupled

with law enforcement tactics that target lower-income, Black communities will have the inevitable effect of widening the racial gap in rates of exposure to the criminal justice system. In a widely publicized report published in 1990, Marc Mauer reported that largely because of the effects of the War on Drugs, 23 percent of Black men in the United States between the ages of 20 and 29 were in prison, jail, or on probation or parole on any given day (p. 3). In a follow-up report published in 1995, that figure had increased to nearly one-third (Mauer and Huling 1995).

Any efforts aimed at reducing such inequality through simply equalizing statutory law and sentencing guidelines may be more illusory than real. Even if penalties for powder are raised to levels equivalent to those of equal amounts of crack, the "victory" for advocates of racial equity will be largely symbolic. The kind of law enforcement protocols and patterns of drug consumption and distribution found in middle- to upper-income White communities make it unlikely that the number of arrests for cocaine will rise dramatically. Middle-class people involved in drugs generally purchase and sell them in private rather than public places. Furthermore, drug detection sweeps such as those commonly used in lower-income, minority neighborhoods will not be tolerated in more affluent, White communities. And if arrested, even with mandatory sentencing, more affluent defendants will have the economic and social capital needed to mitigate their offenses and reduce the likelihood of long prison terms.

Race and Newspaper Coverage of Homicide

The final example of public policy paradoxes involves racial differences in the reporting of homicide incidents in major daily newspapers in the city of Chicago. In two earlier studies on this subject (Johnstone, Hawkins, and Michener 1994; Hawkins, Johnstone, and Michener 1995), we reported that the race, ethnicity, and social class of 684 victims of homicide in Chicago during 1987 affected the likelihood that their deaths would be reported in the city's two major daily newspapers, the *Tribune* and the *Sun-Times*.

Logistic regression models confirmed, as expected, that many nonrace-related factors affected the newsworthiness of incidents. For example, cases involving multiple victims or offenders, child or female victims, or those involving unusual methods of killing had an increased likelihood of being reported. However, we also observed that after controlling for these attributes, Black and Hispanic victims and those incidents occurring in low-income census tracts of the city were significantly less likely to be reported than were incidents involving White victims or those living in middle- to high-income tracts. Somewhat surprisingly, we did not find that, once reported, White victims received significantly more prominent or extensive coverage than nonWhite victims. There was, however, a trend in the direction of more "banner" coverage for Whites, and we suspected that the lack of significance may be partly attributable to our small sample size for reported cases.

The study is now being replicated to determine if the patterns of selective coverage observed in 1987 can be found in 1990 and 1993. There is also some question of whether our findings are applicable to reporting in other large urban centers. See our earlier studies for more caveats regarding a conclusion that the racially differential reporting we observed results from conscious, racial bias. Nevertheless, we suggest that our initial findings raise many of the same policy-related questions seen in our discussion of the death penalty and the crack/cocaine sentencing debate. In this instance, there is an issue of whether equality of coverage should be the policy goal for the reporting of victims or offenders of homicide and other crime by the media. For example, all things being equal (aspects of newsworthiness), should Black and Hispanic victims of homicide in Chicago be reported at the same rate as Whites?

As in the previous debates, arguments both in favor and against purely statistical equality of treatment can be made. As we noted in our earlier studies, the underreporting of minority homicide victims may simply be another reflection of the devalued status of minorities in the United States (see also Hawkins 1983, 1987b). Thus, a policy that leads to greater reporting of minority victims might be advocated on the basis of its positive effects on the self-esteem and feelings of self-worth of the nonWhite population. It may also be argued that increased coverage may bring more public attention to the tragic loss of life due to homicide that occurs daily in many lower-income, minority communities. Indeed, many of the violence prevention efforts of the federal Centers for Disease Control and Prevention were aimed initially at raising public awareness of the level of violence that is found in American society. Even within minority communities, grass-roots violence prevention advocates have found that they have had to raise the level of awareness among citizens of the high levels of violence found within their communities, such as domestic violence and other more commonplace acts of aggression less subject to media glare.

Similarly, however, the sheer magnitude of violent acts found within many minority communities also argues against a simplistic, statistical equality approach to homicide or other crime reporting. One of the perennial complaints of the minority community, and one confirmed by media analysts, is the tendency of the media to over-report "bad," pathological, antisocial conduct among minorities while downplaying more positive, prosocial conduct. This penchant for "bad news" does characterize all media reporting efforts, but an even greater imbalance than usual is said to be apparent in the reporting of Blacks, Latinos, and other nonWhite minority groups. To raise the reporting of Black homicides to the level currently seen for White victims may simply exacerbate this media tendency.

Some evidence of this potential can be seen in a homicide reporting innovation introduced by the Chicago *Tribune* during the 1993 calendar year. During that year, the newspaper published extensive media accounts of all 62 children (under 14 years of age) killed in the Chicago area. Going beyond the frequent one- or two-paragraph accounts given to such victims, most of the accounts became front-page stories. They often included photographs of and interviews with grieving family members. The series, titled "Killing Our Children," was also published as a special year-end supplement (January 25, 1994). Because most of these children were Black or Latino, the series graphically depicted the tragic loss of life in these communities. Toward the end of the series, the newspaper was accused of a kind of journalistic "overkill," with some readers writing to complain about the "blood and gore" nature of the reporting. And, although the series writers struggled to explain the causes of the tragic deaths reported, some of the reporting lapsed at times into repeated accounts of missing fathers, abusive parents, the pitfalls of Aid to Families with Dependent Children, the dangers of gangs, and the like. Despite our "do everything" expectations of the media, their effort in this series raises important questions about the desirability of simplistic, statistical equity in the reporting of homicide or the possibility of the media serving as an objective, balanced, truly informative tool for education or social reform.

Summary and Conclusion

Although the conflicting public policy-related perspectives described in this chapter may be described as dilemmas or paradoxes, they are not anomalies in the sense that they represent completely unexpected observations. Instead, these conflicts are evident in many other policy debates in the arena of race, ethnic, and other forms of intergroup relations in the United States and other societies. Within American social science, especially during the past half century, America's purported norm of racial and ethnic equality has been discussed and analyzed largely as a legal mandate rather than a social construct. This has meant that social scientists have often spoken of equality and policies designed to promote it in terms more comprehensible to experts in American constitutional law than to critical analysts of social thought and public discourse or those who analyze the philosophical and ideological bases of social policy. To a greater extent than often acknowledged by social scientists, their approaches to the study of racial inequality have been affected by the growing influence of the law on social science theory and reasoning (e.g., see Hawkins 1991).

The intent of my discussion in this chapter has been to move the discussion of racial inequality beyond the public policy objectives inherent in a purely legalistic approach. Similar observations to the ones made in this chapter can be found in Daly's (1994) excellent discussion of how social scientists have interpreted gender disparities in the administration of criminal punishment. As in the study of racial and ethnic differences, Daly notes the frequently expressed, but sometimes unstated, belief that the social control and punishment of women should be equal to that of men. This position is usually taken in response to empirical research showing that generally women tend to receive less severe sentences than men. In contrast to this position, Daly begins by asking whether defendants should be punished equally for the same offense and what criteria should be used in deciding if decisions are just (p. 117). In an earlier discussion, I concluded that racially motivated sentencing of Black and White criminal defendants need not always result in greater punishment for Black than White defendants (Hawkins 1987a).

The present discussion approaches this set of issues from a slightly different angle. I assume racial and ethnic equality (of both treatment and outcome) to be a valued American ideal. Given such goals, I explore the expected and unexpected consequences of attempting to achieve those goals. Clearly, each one of the examples discussed above illustrates the salience of the query: Which way toward equality? Like Daly (1994), I have argued that a purely statistical approach to achieving racial, ethnic, or gender equality may produce outcomes that are substantively unjust for those very groups that American civil rights law refers to as "protected classes." It may also produce social problems for the larger society as significant as those targeted for "correction." But perhaps the larger lesson to be learned from this discussion is not one of choosing up-down policy directions. It may be that limited and bounded strides toward equal treatment and outcome in a society characterized by deeply rooted and widespread racial, ethnic, and class inequality will inevitably produce policy paradoxes.

References

Aguirre, Adalberto and David V. Baker. 1990. "Racial Discrimination in the Imposition of the Death Penalty." *Criminal Justice Abstracts* 22(1):135-53.

Baldus, David C., Charles Pulaski, and George Woodworth. 1983. "Comparative Review of Death Sentences." *Journal of Criminal Law and Criminology* 4:661-753.

Chicago Tribune. 1994. *Killing Our Children.* Series reprint, January 25.

Daly, Kathleen. 1994. "Gender and Punishment Disparity." In *Inequality, Crime, and Social Control,* ed. G. S. Bridges and M. A. Myers, 117-33. Boulder, CO: Westview.

Fagan, Jeffrey. 1995. "Cocaine and Federal Sentencing Policy." Testimony before the Subcommittee on Crime of the House Judiciary Committee, U. S. House of Representatives, June 29.

Hawkins, Darnell F. 1983. "Black-White Homicide Differentials: Alternatives to an Inadequate Theory." *Criminal Justice and Behavior* 10:407-40.

————. 1987a. "Beyond Anomalies: Rethinking the Conflict Perspective on Race and Criminal Punishment." *Social Forces* 65:719-45.

————. 1987b. "Devalued Lives and Racial Stereotypes: Ideological Barriers to the Prevention of Family Violence among Blacks." In *Violence in the Black Family: Correlates and Consequences,* ed. Robert L. Hampton, 189-205. Lexington, MA: Lexington Books.

————. 1991. "The 'Discovery' of Institutional Racism: An Example of the Interaction between Law and Social Science." In *Research in Race and Ethnic Relations,* Vol. 6, ed. R. M. Dennis, 167-82. Greenwich, CT: JAI.

Hawkins, Darnell F., John W. C. Johnstone, and Arthur Michener. 1995. "Race, Social Class, and Newspaper Coverage of Homicide." *National Journal of Sociology* 9(1):113-40.

Jaynes, Gerald D. and Robin M. Williams, Jr. Eds. 1989. *A Common Destiny: Blacks and American Society.* Washington, DC: National Academy Press.

Johnson, Guy B. 1941. "The Negro and Crime." *Annals of the American Academy of Political and Social Science* 217:93-104.

Johnstone, John W. C., Darnell F. Hawkins, and Arthur Michener. 1994. "Homicide Reporting in Chicago Dailies." *Journalism Quarterly* 71:860-72.

Keil, Thomas J. and Gennaro F. Vito. 1989. "Race, Homicide Severity, and Application of the Death Penalty: A Consideration of the Barnett Scale." *Criminology* 27:511-35.

Lockwood, Dorothy, Anne E. Pottieger, and James A. Inciardi. 1995. "Crack Use, Crime by Crack Users, and Ethnicity." In *Ethnicity, Race, and Crime: Perspectives across Time and Place,* ed. D. F. Hawkins, 212-34. Albany: State University of New York Press.

Mauer, Marc. 1990. *Young Black Men and the Criminal Justice System: A Growing National Problem.* Washington, DC: The Sentencing Project.

Mauer, Marc and Tracy Huling. 1995. *Young Black Americans and the Criminal Justice System: Five Years Later.* Washington, DC: The Sentencing Project.

McCleskey v. Kemp, Supreme Court of the United States, 1987. 481 U.S. 279, 107 S. CT. 1756, 95 L. Ed. 2d 262.

Myrdal, Gunnar. 1944. *An American Dilemma.* New York: Harper Brothers.

Paternoster, Raymond. 1984. "Prosecutorial Discretion in Requesting the Death Penalty: A Case of Victim-Based Racial Discrimination." *Law and Society Review* 18:437-78.

Radelet, Michael L. 1981. "Racial Characteristics and the Imposition of the Death Penalty." *American Sociological Review* 46:918-27.

Smith, M. Dwayne. 1978. "Patterns of Discrimination in Assessments of the Death Penalty." *Journal of Criminal Justice* 15(4): 279-286.

Wilson, William J. 1987. *The Truly Disadvantaged: The Inner City, the Underclass, and Public Policy.* Chicago: University of Chicago Press.

Wolfgang, Marvin E. and Marc Riedel. 1973. "Race, Judicial Discretion, and the Death Penalty." *Annals of the American Academy of Political and Social Science* 407:119-33.

Zeisel, Hans. 1981. "Race Bias in the Administration of the Death Penalty: The Florida Experience." *Harvard Law Review* 95:456-68.

BALANCED OPPORTUNITY

REVEREND JESSE L. JACKSON

A New Freedom Movement

We need a Freedom movement to expand the political landscape and our own options.

The current White House political strategy is to box Republicans in—but without a new Freedom movement, it will also lock us out. We must expand our options by creating a new climate in America.

Our options in 1996 are

1. Not to support the president, which helps Gingrich and Dole and the extremists on the right
2. To support Clinton quietly, as if we accepted the premises on which he will campaign and govern
3. To support him while focusing on the Moral Center and moving to expand our options outside the political tent.

Right now, option 3 makes sense to me. I prefer Clinton to Dole. Clinton's speech presented a kinder and gentler conservative; Dole is meaner and harsher.

But just as Gingrich needed a right-wing movement to create the political place for his speakership, President Clinton needs the help of a Freedom movement to allow him to follow his soul more than his pollsters, to allow him to move to *the Moral Center*.

The Tent

The president's State of the Union speech was more hopeful than Dole's, who looked like an embalmed undertaker, spouting themes discredited during the Nixon era. But the priorities enunciated in the State of the Union address and in the Republican response do not address the biggest issues that affect the young, the locked out. Neither party's political tent provided coverage for the locked out, for the least of these—for those Americans living in fear and economic crisis.

- ◆ For workers displaced by corporate mergers and downsizing and NAFTA, no place under the tent
- ◆ For abandoned urban dwellers, whose lives grow harder every day, no place under the tent
- ◆ For our youth, especially young black men now being jailed in record numbers that exceed those of South Africa under apartheid, no place under the tent

Why, in more than an hour of speeches, was there no space under the tent for the young, caught in the Jail-Industrial Complex?

- — Jails, the number one growth industry in urban America
- — Jails, making up one-half the public housing built in our nation in the past decade

What is the state of our Union?

- — In most major cities, there's a new jail and a new stadium, the hallmarks of America's urban downtowns—two mountains and a dark urban canyon in between.
- — 200,000 more African Americans are in jail than in 4-year colleges.

— There is a new prison labor force, creating $9 billion in products next year and displacing 400,000 private jobs, and certainly not unionized.

— Our Attorney General proudly displays a plaque in her office that reads "Furniture Made by Prisoners."

Why, in this State of the Union address, was there no mention of unions, the only serious hope for improving the wages and incomes of American families now working harder for less, with growing insecurity, at the mercy of merging, purging corporations seeking overseas profits?

Why no recognition on prime-time national television for the president's strong allies, the backbone of a new Labor movement, the new leadership of the AFL-CIO, Sweeney and Trumka and Chavez?

Why no space for our children?

Hillary Clinton is an ardent advocate for children, with a recent book on just this subject, eloquently discussing the plight of America's children.

Elizabeth Dole led the Red Cross and worked for years directly with children in dire, emergency need.

But neither of their spouses spoke of the fact that one out of every four of our children lives in poverty or that one out of every two Black children is in poverty in this, the wealthiest nation in the history of the world.

Why no room under the tent to reverse America's rising income and wealth inequality, the worst in the industrialized world?

A Coca Cola-Shaped Economy

We have a Coca Cola-shaped economy, with a few at the top sharing great wealth and so many at the bottom, abandoned to lives of poverty and despair. The bottle looks shapely, neat, and perfectly trimmed, yet so many are left out of the bottle, abandoned and locked out.

Our political democracy is threatened by big money, by corrupt special interest campaign contributions, by lobbyists for the rich and powerful.

Our economic system is threatened by a growing economic monopoly over the vital organs of communication and capital.

Wealth is flowing upward, jobs outward and overseas. The middle class is falling downward, government and corporations are downsizing, and the base of poverty is expanding.

The average American family has seen its standard of living *decline* in the past generation. Most Americans feel *insecure*, threatened by downsizing, and worried that their children's lives will be even less safe and secure.

Our economy is in crisis. Over the past two decades, 90 percent of the increase in income has gone to the top 20 percent of the income pyramid. This is wrong.

Just today, the news announced a new merger and downsizing. Wells Fargo beat out Interstate in a bidding contest to see who could downsize the most workers to increase shareholder profits. Now Interstate is no more than a branch bank working for Wells Fargo with fewer workers, restricted service, and increased concentration of wealth and power.

Yet there is *no* political response.

No political response to Chemical merging with Chase.

No political response when Westinghouse/CBS and Disney/ABC take over more and more of our communications network.

No effective political response to a magazine millionaire who wants to install a flat tax that would remove the income tax for dividends and capital gains.

On all these issues, the real tough issues that face our people, the two parties share one tent.

— Two parties, one assumption
— One party, two names

My fear is not that African Americans, workers, city voters will choose Dole over Clinton. My fear is that they will abandon the system and simply stay home in despair and rejection, just as they did in 1994.

Balanced Opportunity

Balancing the budget in seven years will not *balance opportunity* in seven years. Today, both parties are more interested in balancing the budget than they are in balancing opportunity for our people.

We are facing cuts in public investments, no matter who wins. Cuts in education, job retraining, day care. Cuts in FDR's and Dr. King's safety net.

We cannot accept the idea that government has no role in securing a safety net for our people to offset capital greed.

We are opposed to rising crime and irresponsible parenting, but we also recognize a direct causal relationship between a lack of investment, a lack of jobs, a lack of education—and crime.

When politicians attack AFDC, Aid to Families with Dependent Children, they get applause.

— $17 billion cost
— 14 million people, 9 million children covered

But when it comes to AFDC, Aid for Dependent Corporations, there is only silence.

Corporate welfare serves only a few but costs us all $236 billion in tax and spending subsidies. It is protected by business lobbyists in our capitol, on behalf of capital, even to the point where these lobbyists are *writing* the new laws and the new regulations for Gingrich.

This corruption must stop. But when the president called for campaign finance reform—even a weak, bipartisan version that would leave the power of the wealthy lobbyists largely intact—Newt sat frozen on his Go-PAC icepack of frozen legal corruption.

To clean up the muddy water, we must first get the hogs—the special interest lobbyists—out of the creek.

Affirmative Action

When President Clinton made his affirmative action decision last summer—and he did the right thing—he concluded that we needed to "mend it, not end it."

His own studies proved that continuing racism, sexism, and inequality of opportunity obligated him to continue to support a government-enforced plan for opportunity—affirmative action.

We recognize that affirmative action is a key to a balanced budget as well as balanced opportunity.

Without affirmative action, there will be no trained workforce of the majority population for the next century—Blacks, Hispanics, women.

Without affirmative action, the Olympics would not have come to Atlanta.

Without affirmative action, the Super Bowl would not look the same. Think of our sports—no Deion, no Emmitt, no Scottie, no Michael.

None of this growth in America could happen without the expanded tent that affirmative action provides.

Reconstruction

But the same old order that sought to keep the tent narrow in the 1960s is on the move today. There is a frightening parallel between the period 1863 to 1896, when the first Reconstruction ended, and the period 1963 to 1996, as we fight to save the second Reconstruction. This reactionary movement is too real to ignore.

The end of the first Reconstruction met with too little resistance. We must not make the same mistake.

We cannot depend solely on either *the courts* or *the political order* now. They have remarried, just as they did a century ago, and they are working together to take away our balanced opportunity.

Redistricting

The biggest symbol right now—redistricting. Consider Congressman Cleo Field's district in Louisiana. Last year, he represented a district that was 65 percent Black; today, after the courts got through with it, that same district is only 27 percent Black.

Who might benefit the most from this new "legality"—rules set up by the high courts and applauded by the politicians? David Duke.

Coalition

The political tent is too small. We must depend on our own movement.

But no small movement for change can take us to the promised land.

No nationalistic, conservative, exclusive effort can change this reactionary course.

We must have *coalition* in our Freedom movement.

We need a revival of massive, disciplined, direct action.

We cannot merely settle for a choice between Bill Clinton and Bob Dole. That's not structural change; that's just tinkering around the edges, marginal distinctions, cosmetic.

A War on Poverty

Everyone knows we need a real war on poverty.

Is the answer to our social crisis three strikes and you're out, or four balls and you're on?

Prenatal care and Headstart—Ball One. An adequately funded education—Ball Two. A marketable skill or a college education—Ball Three. And a job—Ball Four.

We need a serious War on Poverty.

We need to understand who the poor in America really are.

Most poor people are *not on* welfare; they work every day.

Most poor people are *not Black*; they are White and female.

Two-thirds *are* children.

Ronald Reagan put a false Black mask on the face of the White poor to blunt the edge of his meanness and to cover up the depth of our crisis. He did the American people a disservice. We need a War on Poverty.

A War on Drugs

We also need a real War on Drugs.

There is nothing more destructive to our families, our young people, than the drug culture, but the president appointed a general without an army.

We need at least five battalions to fight the war on drugs:

1. Interdiction and intervention
2. Treatment

3. Education

4. Jobs

5. Punishment

I support the peace effort in Bosnia. When President Clinton sends our young troops abroad, they are well-equipped, trained, provided with proper intelligence, assisted by strong allies, and given good equipment. The troops for a proper war on drugs have not been mobilized. They have no such preparation and commitment.

Outside the Tent

The immediate answer, as a practical matter, is that we must choose kinder and gentler over meaner and harsher.

Historically, however, the answers for change have come from outside the system, not inside it.

In recent years, as many of us have succeeded in climbing inside the tent, we have developed too much confidence in the system. This is a mistake.

Those inside the system also need outside forces to change the environment—outside movements to hold them accountable and to open up new options. (a) Montgomery, (b) Birmingham, (c) Atlantic City, (d) Selma. Outside action opened up the political option.

Martin Luther King, Sr. was a Republican.

Martin Luther King, Jr. was a Democrat.

Both had to go to the back of the bus without help from either party.

The political parties of the time were hip-locked, with one set of assumptions about race, and our people were left unprotected, outside the tent.

This did not make Dr. King cynical, but instead committed.

He understood the limits of the political system and set about on a course of determined action to create a new landscape, to expand the tent.

Dr. King chose JFK over Nixon, but neither one ran on the right of public accommodations.

The movement in Birmingham, outside two-party politics, changed Kennedy's options and gave him the chance to follow his heart and choose the right side of history.

Dr. King supported and campaigned for LBJ over Goldwater.

But neither had room for Fannie Lou Hamer under the tent.

It was the movement in Selma and Montgomery that won the right to vote.

I remember Dr. King, upon his return from Oslo, Norway, where he won the Nobel Peace Prize.

Dr. King was given a White House reception by President Johnson.

Martin said, "Thanks, but my people need the right to vote."

LBJ said, "I like you and I respect you, but I can't grant that, and anyway, the Congress won't go along."

Again, two parties hip-locked on one assumption.

It was the Freedom movement between Selma and Montgomery that expanded LBJ's political horizons and options and opened up the tent to all of us.

The Margin of Hope

This year, we may finally choose Clinton, but the margin of our enthusiasm, our hope, over our people's despair will be critical. This was just demonstrated conclusively in 1994, when so many of our allies just stayed home.

Target '96

The National Rainbow Coalition, our civil rights organizations, the women's movement, our labor unions, our church networks— all of us must work together in coalition to target 75 house districts, to reverse the right-wing offensive.

In those key districts, we need

1. Targeted voter registration
2. Direct action, street heat
3. Exciting candidates
4. Multiracial coalitions based on need and a quest for justice

We can be supportive and critical of the White House, not detached and detrimental.

If we spread cynicism, our people's "nonvote" becomes a vote for the extremists, and we will lose Dr. King's victories.

We, the People

We must reassess the new kinship between Republicans and Democrats, and between Congress and the courts, and find solace in the real source of our freedoms—We, the People.

We must never forget that *all our great movements*—the abolitionists, the labor struggles, the civil rights movement, women's suffrage, antiwar, and the environmental movement—all took place *outside the system*, outside the tent.

These movements *changed the political and social landscape* and expanded our options.

We, the People, created these movements.

Economic Opportunity

We must remember that the private sector economic opportunities we now enjoy were stimulated by boycotts and negotiations outside the tent.

Our soft drink and fast food franchises, auto dealerships, the shift of bank dollars—all resulted from boycotts and pickets. We must reopen that front again. We can challenge the mergers and ask *compelling interest* questions. For example, we met with United Airlines. Twelve white board members.

The current cutbacks of minorities on Wall Street and cutbacks in promotion and procurement by major corporations is alarming.

Ham and Egg Justice

If the president jumps on the government downsizing bandwagon, and all our major corporations are busy downsizing their workers, where do the people go?

If welfare reform requires people to get a job, where will they go?

We need to fight for a government that secures our people's futures in an era of insecurity and turmoil.

The balanced budget as we know it is "ham and egg" justice.

It sounds equal, the aroma blends nicely.

But the chicken—the wealthy—only drops an egg and moves on to enjoy the flat tax.

The hog—working America—drops a leg and is forced to sacrifice a limb or a life.

I should also point out that those most vocal in support of downsizing government are also those most insistent on sending the Pentagon more money than it asked for, even with the cold war over. These right wingers are not for smaller government; they are only for a smaller social safety net.

An Action Plan

My concerns go beyond poll watching and run in conflict with the current balanced budget preoccupations of popular politicians.

What are the long-term needs of this country?

How do we organize to meet those needs?

I offer the following five-part action plan to expand the tent:

1. *Urban Development Banks*

I'm handing out some copies of the rules that established the Polish American Development Bank.

When the United States decided to support the solidarity movement, we knew that the Polish people were our allies, but they had been redlined and disadvantaged.

We did not offer them a plan for behavior modification but rather a plan for development and economic growth.

Forty-year loans, three-fourths of 1 percent, first payment in 10 years, concessionary bank loans.

We need the same concept for urban America. We should seek to have hearings around this nation with mayors, legislators, and the people to develop such a plan.

2. *Pension Funds*

There are $6 trillion in private and public pension funds.

We should take 10 percent of this money, government secured, to enable us to build a series of development banks around the country.

This would generate revenue without new taxes. It would expand the taxpayer base and the number of productive citizens.

We must take this case to the working people of America and demonstrate on Wall Street to bring this idea to life.

3. *Target '96*

The National Rainbow Coalition held a major conference in Chicago on Thursday, February 29th, Friday, March 1st, and Saturday, March 2nd.

I wish that you would join us to help us build a coalition to regain the Congress.

We need to target 75 house districts for

— Targeted voter registration
— Direct action, street heat, on issues that affect our people
— Good candidate recruitment
— Multiracial coalition building among our organizational allies to blunt the right-wing offensive

Together, we can win. We must plan for victory.

4. *Economic Direct Action*

At the Rainbow conference, we also reviewed some corporate targets for negotiation.

Thirty years ago, we would shut down a highway or boycott a company or picket a corporate headquarters to expand balanced opportunity.

This new, hip-locked government is using shutdown as a form of legal civil disobedience to reverse our gains and reduce opportunity.

We must fight back to expand both the public tent and the private tents.

5. *Reclaim Our Youth*

We must take the initiative and responsibility to reclaim our youth.

We must challenge this generation to lift morals, character, and a sense of duty to a level higher than the cultural norms.

This generation must be transformers, not conformers.

Our Reclaim Our Youth Program consists of 20,000 parents in each of 50 cities—for a total of 1 million parents—who will take a six-point pledge in a joint venture with their children's teachers to promise to

1. Take a child to school.
2. Meet your child's teacher.
3. Exchange home telephone numbers.
4. Turn off the television set three hours each night.
5. Pick up a report card every nine weeks.
6. Initial report cards.

Our Reclaim Our Youth Program also involves 100 ministers in each of 50 cities, to reclaim 20 youth per church from the criminal justice system.

This means 100,000 youth reclaimed by our churches rather than claimed as victims by our jails.

With this commitment to action and balanced opportunity, we balance families and offset despair with hope to help create a new balance in so many lives that have been warped and broken by the system.

Is It Right?

Dr. King would always say:

— Vanity asks, Is it popular?
— Politics asks, Will it work?
— But Conscience and Morality ask, Is it right?

We must keep asking, Is it right?

A New Freedom Movement

This new marriage between the politicians and the right-wing Reagan courts; between the Democrats and the Republicans; this new, hip-locked arrangement must be broken by disciplined, direct political and economic action.

We must struggle to expand the tent, to be big enough for all the American people.

Let us sing again the hymns of our freedom struggle.

— Ain't Goin' to Let Nobody Turn Me 'Round

— We Shall Overcome

Dr. King's Dream

Let us again embrace Dr. King's dream.

Not a passive dream, not a dream that leads to quietness, passive reflection, and absence of noise, but an activist dream, a dream whose content is justice.

Let us become, once again, drum majors for justice.

We need love, power, justice.

We must dream beyond circumstances, like Joseph in the face of hate, jealousy, threats, and the fear of death. A minority with a majority dream, he stood firm.

Joseph saw a new economic order in Egypt—seven years of plenty for all. Not a balanced budget so much as balanced opportunity.

Like Dr. King, he protested that Egypt, a wealthy and powerful nation, was abandoning its people.

Dr. King did not just dream.

He reminded us that the wealthiest nation in the history of the world was bouncing its checks to its people.

America was failing to honor the promissory notes it had written to its workers, those who built this nation, its veterans, and the time was right to honor those promises.

Let us embrace Dr. King's dream, and, like John, banished to the remote island of Patmos, see a new earth of hope and healing emerge as the old one of hate and hostility disappears.

Keep Hope Alive.

AUTHOR INDEX

267

SUBJECT INDEX

ABOUT THE AUTHORS

Rae Banks is Visiting Associate Professor of African American Studies at Syracuse University. She received her Ph.D. in social psychology from the City University of New York (1979) and has completed postdoctoral fellowships at Cornell University, the Hubert H. Humphrey Institute of Public Affairs at the University of Minnesota, and the Narcotic and Drug Research Institute in New York City. She has had teaching appointments at Brooklyn College and the University of the Virgin Islands. She is currently working on a book titled *A Matter of Justice: The Politics of Drugs in the African American Community.*

Juan J. Battle (Ph.D. in sociology, University of Michigan, 1994) is Assistant Professor at Hunter College and the Graduate Center of the City University of New York. His fields of interest include race and ethnicity, survey research, social problems, and the family. With a particular emphasis on families of color, his research examines the effects of family structure on children's educational outcomes.

Michael D. Bennett (Ph.D. in English, University of Virginia, 1994) is Assistant Professor of English at Long Island University, Brooklyn. He was a Research Associate of the Carter G. Woodson Institute for African and Afro-American Studies at the University of Virginia, and is now a member of the Institute for Research in African-American Studies at Columbia University. His current research is focused on the abolition

283

movement and antebellum American culture, ecological criticism from an urban perspective, and representations of the African-American female body in the nineteenth- and twentieth-century American culture.

Michael I. J. Bennett (Ph.D., University of Chicago) is Assistant Professor at the Jane Addams School of Social Work and in the Center for Urban Economic Development at the University of Illinois at Chicago. Prior to joining the UIC faculty, Dr. Bennett served as Vice President of Shorebank Corporation and its affiliate, the Arkansas Enterprise Group. He has research interests in social and economic development. He is currently a co-principal investigator on the National Empowerment Zone Action Research Project.

Sharon M. Collins received her Ph.D. in sociology from Northwestern University and is currently Associate Professor at the University of Illinois at Chicago. She studies racial segmentation in labor markets, with a focus on the aspects of Black economic mobility that are politically mediated. Her research on Black managers looks at the relationship between new job opportunities for middle-class Blacks and post-1965 civil rights policies and pressures. She is the author of a forthcoming book titled *Black Corporate Executives: The Making and Breaking of a Black Middle Class.*

Douglas Gills (Ph.D., Northwestern University) is Assistant Professor in the College of Urban Planning and Public Affairs and in the Center for Urban Economic Development at the University of Illinois at Chicago. He specializes in community planning, politics, and development policy, and he has amassed a wealth of experience on community organization processes and community-based coalition politics. He co-authored *Harold Washington and the Crisis of Black Power.*

Darnell F. Hawkins is Professor of African American Studies and Sociology at the University of Illinois at Chicago, where he is also a faculty affiliate of the Department of Criminal Justice. His research interests include race and ethnic relations, criminology, and the sociology of law. He is editor of *Homicide Among Black Americans* (1986) and *Ethnicity, Race, and Crime: Perspectives across Time and Place* (1995).

Cedric Herring (Ph.D., University of Michigan, 1985) is Professor in the Department of Sociology at the University of Illinois at Chicago and in the Institute of Government and Public Affairs at the University of Illinois. He is also a Fellow in the Great Cities Institute at the University of Illinois at Chicago and Faculty Associate at the Irving B. Harris Graduate School of Public Policy Studies at the University of Chicago. He has published extensively in social policy, political sociology, labor force issues and policies, stratification and inequality, and the sociology of Black Americans. He is the author of *Splitting the Middle: Political Alienation, Acquiescence, and Activism* and co-author of *Empowerment in Chicago: Grassroots Participation in Economic Development and Poverty Alleviation.* He served as President of the Association of Black Sociologists in 1994-1995.

Reverend Jesse L. Jackson is the founder and Executive Director of Operation PUSH and of the National Rainbow Coalition.

Charles Jarmon is Professor of Sociology and Associate Dean of the College of Arts and Sciences at Howard University, where he has taught in the areas of urbanization, urban policy, and social stratification. He is the author or co-author of several books, monographs, and articles about issues in the African American community, and in nation-building, urbanization, and development in sub-Saharan Africa. He has served in editorial positions for the *Journal of Asian and African Studies* and the *Canadian Review of Studies in Nationalism.* He has served as a consultant for the African Development Foundation.

Verna M. Keith is Associate Professor of Sociology at Arizona State University. She received her Ph.D. from the University of Kentucky. Her work examines the interrelationship between race, class, gender, and emotional and physical well-being.

Katrina Bell McDonald (Ph.D., University of California, Davis) is Assistant Professor of Sociology at Johns Hopkins University, where she specializes in race, gender and the family, Black maternal health, psychosocial stress, and maternal support systems. Her dissertation, titled "Sister-Friends: Re-Creating Maternal Support in the African-American Community" (1995), is a study of social class relations among Black women and of Black activist mothering. Her recent article, "Kin Support and Family Stress: Two Sides of Early Childbearing and Support Networks," coauthored by James Cramer, has been published in *Human Organization.*

Kerry Rockquemore is a Thomas and Elvira McGuire Fellow at the University of Notre Dame. Her research interests include Afrocentric education, the politics of school reform, and the biracial experience in the United States.

Garry L. Rolison is Assistant Professor of Sociology at Arizona State University. He received his Ph.D. from the University of California, Santa Cruz. His work concerns the nexus of race, gender, and class in the United States.

Steven J. Rosenthal received his Ph.D. from Brandeis University, taught in Boston during the 1970s, and has been in the Department of Sociology at Hampton University since 1981. His recent publications include "The Pioneer Fund: Financier of Fascist Research," *American Behavioral Scientist* (1995) and "The Global Danger of Fascist Resurgence," *East-West Review* (1994). He is an active member of the Association of Black Sociologists, the Society for the Study of Social Problems, the Southern Sociological Society, and the Race and Ethnic Minorities and Marxist Sections of the American Sociological Association.

Yvonne Scruggs is the Executive Director, Black Leadership Forum, Inc., a 19-year-old confederation of the nation's 20 oldest and largest civil rights and service organizations that is headquartered in Washington, DC. She formerly directed the Urban Policy Institute and the National Policy Institute of the Washington-based Joint Center for Political and Economic Studies. She has held professorships at various institutions, including the University of Pennsylvania and Howard University, where she also was departmental chairperson. Dr. Scruggs was Deputy Mayor of Philadelphia, New York State's Housing Commissioner, and Deputy Assistant Secretary of the U.S. Department of Housing and Urban Development (HUD). A former Fulbright Fellow to Germany, she also served as Executive Director of President Carter's Urban and Regional Policy Group, which prepared the first formal national urban policy. Dr. Scruggs holds a Ph.D. in city and regional planning from the University of Pennsylvania.

Gail E. Thomas is Professor of Sociology and Director of the Race and Ethnic Studies Institute at Texas A&M University. She earned her Ph.D. in sociology from the University of North Carolina at Chapel Hill. Her main research interests and areas of concentration are the educational and occupational attainment and achievement of underrepresented racial minorities and women, and racial and social stratification and inequality. She has published extensively in national and international journals in the social sciences and higher education. She is also the editor of *U.S. Race Relations in the 1980s and 1990s* (1990) and *Race and Ethnicity in America: Meeting the Challenge in the 21st Century.*

Assata Zerai is Assistant Professor of Sociology at Syracuse University. She received her Ph.D. in sociology from the University of Chicago (1993) and completed postdoctoral study at the Carolina Population Center at the University of North Carolina at Chapel Hill (1993-1994). Her research interests include multilevel analyses that reveal social determinants and consequences of various indicators of maternal and infant health among people of African descent.